I0079204

THE
MISSING
LINK

YOUR JOURNEY WITH PETER FROM
SELF POWER TO HOLY SPIRIT POWER

SAM HUNTER

HIGH BRIDGE BOOKS

HOUSTON

The Missing Link
by Sam Hunter

Copyright © 2019 by Sam Hunter.
All rights reserved.

Printed in the United States of America
ISBN (Paperback): 978-1-946615-43-5

All rights reserved. Except in the case of brief quotations embodied in critical articles and reviews, no portion of this book may be reproduced, stored in a retrieval system, or transmitted in any form or by any means—electronic, mechanical, photocopy, recording, scanning, or other—without the prior written permission from the author.

High Bridge Books titles may be purchased in bulk for educational, business, fundraising, or sales promotional use. For information please contact High Bridge Books via www.HighBridgeBooks.com/contact.

Scripture passages taken from the Holy Bible, NEW INTERNA-TIONAL VERSION®. Copyright © 1973, 1978, 1984 by Biblica, Inc. All rights reserved worldwide. Used by permission. NEW INTERNA-TIONAL VERSION® and NIV® are registered trademarks of Biblica, Inc.

Published in Houston, Texas by High Bridge Books.

CONTENTS

This book would not be possible
if not for two influences:

Larry Huntsperger and *The Fisherman*

The continuing support and encouragement
of my dear wife, Dina, without whom I
might have given up many times

INTRODUCTION:
MY FIRST CHRISTIANS

I WAS THINKING THE OTHER DAY ABOUT THIS SCENARIO: what if you had never met any Christians and had never attended a Christian church? Let's say you are Chinese and all you have is a tattered copy of the Bible.

You get to the New Testament, and at John's Gospel, especially chapters 14 and 16, you read Jesus' promise to send a different aspect of God—a God who lives in you, a God within you who gives you new power. Jesus says this new "power" will never leave you. You continue reading through Acts, watching as this promise of Holy Spirit power manifests itself in the apostles' lives.

"Wow!" you think to yourself, "this world would be wondrous."

As you read the book of Acts, you see Peter and the disciples preaching boldly in the face of death and even speaking foreign languages they've never known before. Even the earth responds—buildings rumble and jails crumble. The apostles heal the sick and perform other miracles. Ananias and Sapphira drop dead because they "lied to the Holy Spirit."

You cannot help but think, "I don't really understand this Holy Spirit, God, but this power must be something to behold!"

After a time, as a born and bred Chinese national, eager to see for yourself this new power in action, you visit America. For the first time, you meet these Christians about whom you've been reading. "What will they be like?" you think to yourself. "Will they be superhumans? Spiritual giants? Will they stand out in every crowd, shining like the sun?"

That's the promise right there in Acts. You've been reading about this incredible transformation throughout the New Testament. Jesus promised it and guaranteed it. You may not know a lot about the Bible overall, but one thing you do know—if Jesus promised it, it must be true. This incredible power afforded through salvation happened to everyone—everyone who places their saving trust in Jesus.

"This is going to be great!" you exclaim. You have lived among ordinary people all your life. You've witnessed firsthand their mediocre lives. You've seen most of your friends just getting through the day, coping with their ups and downs as best they can manage. They have no Holy Spirit, so they have no power.

Surely, they know something is missing. They just don't know what the missing link is. But now, after reading about this Holy Spirit, you do. Or at least you think you do.

You plan your trip to arrive in the American South because you have been told it is the buckle of the Bible Belt. As you arrive, you are bursting with excitement to see these Holy Spirit-powered Christians. What will their Christian church services be like? Surely, they will be filled with joy and thanksgiving, practically overflowing with enthusiasm and gratitude. Will the roof rumble off the church building as it did in Acts?

No doubt, these Christians will radiate love, joy, peace, and patience. Their unity and community will be profound and heartfelt. They will have compassion, kindness, and humility. As Jesus said, they will be like fountains of living water overflowing into the lives of everyone, with energy, clarity, and creativity.

No mediocre lives for them, that's for sure.

Obviously, they would not be like everyone else, caught up in a rat-race of busyness and distraction. They will not carry grudges; they will not harbor resentment. How refreshing it would be to witness lives lived with the certainty that the world around them is God-powered and God-saturated.

MEDIOCRE CHRISTIANS

The big day comes, and as you walk down Main Street, you eagerly look around for the Christians. But where are they? Besides some racial differences, no one seems any different from anyone else. As your desperation grows, you seek out the churches in the area. "This is where I'll see these spiritual giants," you assure yourself.

But after attending a few church services around the community, you are left wondering, "What was that all about? Nothing happened. Where are these Christians who are filled with this wondrous Holy Spirit power?"

Eventually, you sit down and speak with someone who says, "Listen, I've been a Christian all my life, and that Holy Spirit stuff you're looking for, well, that only happens with those weird people out in the country in those crazy churches. Normal people don't act like that. Being a Christian is about doing good, being good, and being a good member of the community. Nobody expects that kind of unpredictable power. I doubt anyone even wants it. Things might get out of hand."

"But what about Jesus' promise, 'You will receive power when the Holy Spirit comes on you?'" you stammer, dazed and confused.

"Oh that," he stiffens, "that was for back then. Nowadays, we just do the best we can. Nobody expects to see miracles, child. No need to get all worked up. Just stay with us a while and you'll settle down and get used to the real world of religion. It's comfortable. It's practical. You'll get used to it."

As we begin this journey together to better understand the Holy Spirit, my question to you is… have you gotten used to it?

PROLOGUE

MY NAME IS SIMON PETER, AND I HAVE A STORY TO TELL.
This story involves me but is not about me. Nor is it about
my fellow disciples and apostles—John, James, Andrew,
Barnabas, Silas, or even Paul. It is about the Holy Spirit and
how he came to live with us, in us, and all around us.

One afternoon, John and I were going up to the temple
at the time of prayer—it was about three in the afternoon.
The sun was shining, and it was hot, very hot. But the heat
was only a distraction because we were talking about Jesus,
as we typically did these days, and his recent return to
heaven. We could hardly stop thinking and talking about
the coming of the Holy Spirit on Pentecost a few days ago,
just as Jesus had promised. We had each experienced the
Spirit's astounding arrival on that disquieting morning of
the Pentecost feast. Oh, what an arrival it was.

Since then, we were becoming increasingly and more
acutely aware of the presence and the expanding power of
the Holy Spirit. Now everything was different. And yet today seemed like any other day—except that after the Holy
Spirit starts to fill you, any day might be filled with … well,
just hear my story.

AT THE GATE CALLED BEAUTIFUL

At the temple was a man lame from birth, who sat every day begging for money. He was pitiful. His legs were wasting away. His face was drawn and wearied, wrinkled with the pain and sadness of a thousand disappointments.

He sat at the temple gate called Beautiful. I have walked this way so many times I rarely even notice the incredible craftsmanship of the expensive Corinthian bronze, glistening in the sun. Sadly, the same would be true of this beggar. I'm sure I was one among many who failed to notice this lame man, and I am equally sure he lived every day with our callous rejection, knowing he was invisible to those walking by, lost in our busy world.

But for some reason today, as John talked, I was noticing the craftsmanship and beauty of the bronze and studying the incredible detailing. Yet instead of being in awe, I was thinking about how this kind of raw display of wealth and power once dazzled me. I wanted more luxury in my life. I wanted more money. I wanted more power. I wanted my version of this Corinthian bronze gate—that is, before Jesus redefined the desires of my heart.

As I reflected on how much Jesus had changed me, and how little allure money and power now held for me, I happened to notice the lame man gesturing to John and me as we were about to enter the temple; he asked us for money. I looked straight at him, as did John. Then, for some reason, I said, "Look at us!" The man gave me his undivided attention, expecting to get money, or at least something, from us.

Oh, yes, he was about to get something from us; only neither of us expected what would happen next.

THE HOLY SPIRIT'S MOVEMENT

At that moment, I felt the Holy Spirit moving in me. I cannot adequately describe the feeling, and even if I could, you might not be able to understand it. Something was happening and power was surging through me. I didn't know what to expect next, but I knew the unexpected was coming.

Without hesitation or any forethought at all, I said, "Silver or gold I do not have, but what I do have, I give you. In the name of Jesus Christ of Nazareth, walk." I then reached down and took him by the right hand and helped him stand up. Instantly, the man's feet and ankles became strong. He jumped to his feet and began to walk around.

He was as surprised as I was. I was shocked, actually. Stunned. Later, John told me I looked like I had seen Judas Iscariot himself rise from the grave. This lame man was healed by my touch. My touch? What kind of power surged through my veins in that moment? I had healed before, but that had been when Jesus was with us. Back then, I had just assumed we could heal because Jesus was with us.

But now he was in heaven. It was just us. Just me. Or so I thought. How can I explain it so you can understand? I simply cannot. But I can say it was indeed the power of the Spirit moving through me. It was a spontaneous experience that I did not plan or anticipate. As the years have gone by, I have come to expect the unexpected—these Spirit-driven surges of divine power running through me. But I rarely see them coming in advance and certainly do not plan them.

THE LAME MAN'S CELEBRATION

Now the lame man was hopping around and exclaiming, "I can walk, I can walk! Look, everyone, a miracle has happened! I can walk. Look at my legs. Watch how high I can jump!" He grabbed me, and the next thing I knew, we were in a dance. There we were—me, Peter, a big, gruff, weathered fisherman—dancing around in circles with this scrawny little man. John was buckling over with laughter. What a sight I must have been.

As the man grabbed and hugged both John and me, all the people around the temple came running toward us— astonished. I can still hear them saying, "These men were with Jesus, the miracle worker. They are ordinary men like us. This man was lame all these years, and they healed him? Are they now to be prophets and miracle workers?"

Thankfully, most of the attention was on the lame man as he jumped around crying out praise and laughing, grabbing whoever he could for a dance. John and I quietly slipped away through the crowd into the temple.

But word spread quickly about this amazing miracle. As a result, over the next few days and weeks, people brought the sick into the streets and laid them on beds and mats, hoping that even my shadow might fall on some of them. Crowds gathered from the towns around Jerusalem, bringing their sick and those tormented by impure spirits, and we healed all of them.

I've seen Doctor Luke's notes on our days with Jesus— some are calling it the Gospel of Luke. But now he tells me he has composed a second letter to his friend and sponsor, Theophilus—a follow-up letter to explain what happened to us after Jesus returned to heaven and the Holy Spirit arrived.

But I do not need his notes; I remember it all so well. I remember those days that followed, the days of "Peter's shadow." Those were amazing days, filled with surprises and adventures—and a few dangerous encounters with the Sanhedrin.

NOT BY MY POWER

Are you impressed by this story of healing? Do you think, as so many now do, that I am a great apostle? I guess you do. You probably think that, having been filled with this kind of healing power, I would spend the rest of my days "soaring like eagles with wings." "The great Apostle Peter," some say. "He was the *first* apostle! He was the one Jesus singled out to carry the keys of the kingdom."

But those who think I am some type of superhuman are wrong. If you think of me this way, you are missing the point. I am just a man. I have no more ability on my own to perform the supernatural than do you. But our Lord's commitment to us all is that the Holy Spirit can and will indwell us and equip us with all we need for the work and the life he has prepared for each of us. You could do this very same healing. Yes, you—or I should say the Holy Spirit could do this same thing through you.

Do you believe this?

If you think highly of me because of this miracle, and the many others that followed, then I say to you, as I did to my fellow Israelites after that lame man stood up and walked for the first time, "Why does this surprise you? Why do you stare at us as if by our own power or godliness we had made this man walk? It is not our power; it is by the Holy Spirit's power."

I then raised my voice with a new inner sense of confidence and exclaimed boldly, "By trust in the name of Jesus, this man whom you see and know was made strong."

That evening after the healing of the lame man, John and I sat down together over our supper of bread and stew. I was silent and musing, still recovering from the surge of power I had experienced (and maybe a little from my public dancing display). As we reflected on the healing miracle, John winked at me and said, "I tell you the truth, whoever trusts in me will do the works I have been doing, and they will do even greater things than these because I am going to the Father."

Those were Jesus' exact words to us over dinner on our last night together, before his crucifixion. They made no sense then, but now his words were starting to coalesce into a new clarity.

MAKING JESUS WELL-KNOWN

That healing incident was 30 years ago. I am older now, and death cannot be far away. When one sees his end approaching, one cannot help but reflect on one's journey through life. My journey took me to a new life, a life renewed by the Holy Spirit. And what a journey it has been—a journey of learning to live without Jesus physically with me but with his Holy Spirit in me.

No longer with me, but even more so, in me.

Christ in me, in you—the hope, the confident expectation of glory—this is why I am writing to you today. I once wanted to be well-known, but now I just want Jesus to be known. I once wanted to be praised, but now I just want Jesus to be praised. I want you to know Jesus.

The more you know him, the more you will like him. Yes, you will adore him and worship him. But you will actually *like* him because you will realize he likes you too. And, in this process, he will change your life.

My end is near. The Master has made this clear to me. In my remaining time, I feel a growing urgency to share my experiences with you, but not just my experiences. I want you to see what was happening within me and within the other apostles. I want you to see the inner life of salvation behind the outer life of the day-to-day world. This transformation culminates in the spiritual understanding that the Holy Spirit changes everything and that the Holy Spirit has changed the world.

After Jesus, my friend and my Lord, returned to the Father that fateful day 30 years ago, none of us could have imagined what would follow. Those early days, as we stumbled through our efforts to represent Jesus to the world, remain so vivid in my memory. What dolts we were at times! What a dolt I was at times—so many times. And yet he used us in such mighty ways.

THE ONLY GOD LEFT ON EARTH

Our dear brother and friend, Doctor Luke, has recorded an excellent account of these last 30 or so years. Perhaps you have read parts of it or, more likely, have heard it read in your meetings. Some have taken to calling it "The Acts of the Apostles." Personally, I find it unnecessary to name it anything, but if Luke's written history needs a name, it should be "The Acts of the Holy Spirit."

We apostles were only the Holy Spirit's conduits. We were only minor characters; he was the star. He was, and he still is, the main event. He did everything. He changed everything. We did only our part as he worked through us.

I know Luke's account tends to make me look like some super apostle, or a super *Christian*, as those of us who follow Jesus are now being called. I would laugh at this idea if it were not so dangerously inaccurate. I'm no super anything, and that is why I want to put my experiences in writing. I want to set the record straight. I have even heard some whisperings that the great Peter is to be God's bishop.

I regret this because it is misguided to lift me up as anything special but also because I am so unworthy. No, Luke's account is not the Acts of the stumbling, bumbling apostles but, instead, the Acts of the Holy Spirit. He is the super Christian. He is the super apostle. The Holy Spirit is the first Bishop and the first of anything and everything — first, that is, after our dear Lord Jesus returned to be with the Father.

He is, in fact, the only God left on earth.[1]

I am only an echo; he is the Voice. I am only a mirror; he is the true Light.

LEARNING TO LIVE WITH THE POWER OF THE HOLY SPIRIT

Please indulge me and allow this old man to describe how the Holy Spirit worked inside me, and inside all of us. He was both in us and all around us, setting the world on fire with the good news Jesus came to bring. Luke has done an excellent job in his second letter to Theophilus, keeping the Holy Spirit front and center. He accurately depicts how everything that happened was directed and empowered by the Spirit.

We could have accomplished nothing, not one thing, in our own power. That should be obvious from Mark's, Matthew's, and Luke's accounts of our three years with Jesus. It had to be the Holy Spirit. If you knew what we now know, you would certainly understand this. To correct my earlier statement, it's really not my journey—it is our journey, yours and mine, as we learn to live with and in the power of this incredible Holy Spirit.

Instead of only teaching you principles, I'm going to tell you our story. My story, our story, is one that helps us learn to live with the power of the Holy Spirit.

Learning to live with the Holy Spirit is a process. I will teach you some of the truths we learned but also tell you our stories about life with the Holy Spirit so you can see how these truths played out in our day-to-day lives.

Teaching truths and telling stories—after all, that is precisely how the Master did it.

THE MISSING LINK

I hope you will allow me to show you how we grew from our former days of such ignorance and self-absorption to living with the incredible power of the Holy Spirit. I fear this power that is available to all of us, available to *you*, is already being overlooked and ignored, and therefore missed completely.

The Holy Spirit is, in fact, the missing link. He is what you are missing. No, actually, he is *who* you are missing. Please do not miss this—the link between God the Father, Jesus the Son, and you is the Holy Spirit.

But is he your missing link?

If this ignorance of the Holy Spirit continues, I can only imagine one day a whole world of Christians who know nothing of the power within them. They will know nothing of the love, the joy, the peace, the patience, and the confidence Jesus lived with himself and gifted to us through his Spirit.

This simply cannot be allowed to happen. It would be tragic.

Jesus told us one day, "I have come so you may have life, and have it to the full." Listen closely as I share with you my journey, our journey, *your* journey. I went from having no understanding at all what Jesus meant by "life to the full" to living this new full life, powered by the Holy Spirit.

Perhaps you will learn to live the same.

---

[1] Statement attributed to Jack Taylor.

PART ONE

A NEW POWER

1

SELF

I AM SIMON PETER, A SERVANT AND APOSTLE OF JESUS
Christ. I am writing to those of you who, through the righteousness of our God and Savior Jesus Christ, have received
a faith as precious as ours.

Grace and peace be yours in abundance through the
knowledge of God and of Jesus our Lord.

Yes, I am Simon Peter, the apostle, but I am just a
man—an ordinary man like you. If we differ, it is only in
that I have learned to live with the power of the Holy Spirit.
However, this does not mean I am better than others or that
I am spiritually superior to anyone. It just means I am living
with a power they… you … likely are not.

I understand why you have missed this power. It took
me years to learn to appropriate this new power within me.
But please hear me—there is so much more to this life with
the Spirit than you are currently experiencing. Too many
Christians are missing this and are blind to the riches of the
kingdom so readily available to them.

They are missing the Holy Spirit's energy, clarity, and
creativity.

Are you?

LIFE TO THE FULL

I am still flawed and still fragile at times, but not nearly as much as I once was. Self, my old nemesis, is still trying to regain control, but now that I am living with the power of the Holy Spirit, Self has faded from a master to a mere nuisance.

I am still a sinner. Yes, I am merely a human just like you. But if I acquiesce to the idea that we are all sinners and will never be perfect, I will live in defeat, denying my Lord's grace and power. I have a divine power within me to destroy strongholds, and I have learned to live with and through this divine power.

And I want you to as well.

I remember that day Jesus said, "I have come so you may have life, and have it to the full." I was sitting near him, and after the crowd dispersed, I said, "Lord, you make it sound as though the chief reason you came was to give us a different life—a life to the full, whatever that means?"

Jesus sat quietly, not responding, so I continued: "I thought you have come to defeat the Romans. I thought you have come to kick the religious frauds out. I thought you have come to defeat Satan. I thought you have come to defeat death. You make it sound like you came to give us a better life."

Jesus looked at me, as he had so many times before, not with condemnation, nor with any sense of disappointment, but with understanding, compassion, and love. As time has passed, I now understand that, yes, he came to destroy sin and Satan. But as he gave us this life, *his* life to the full, powered by the Holy Spirit, we did indeed do all those things as well. And do you know why, and how? I will give you

Jesus' simple answer: "Because greater is he who will be in you than he who is in the world."

POWER

At the time, I was baffled by Jesus saying, "He who will be in you." Will be *in* me? That made no sense and, quite frankly, was just illogical. I remember thinking, "You, Jesus are the ultimate power, not some spirit to come." I said to him, with a slight tone of annoyance, "What is this talk about us having your power? Why would you not just do it all yourself?"

He just smiled and said, "My friend, you will see."

This is why you hear me say so often, "His divine power has given us everything we need for a godly life through our knowledge of him who called us by his own glory and goodness. Through these, he has given us his very great and precious promises, so that, through them, you may participate in the divine nature, having escaped the corruption in the world caused by evil desires."

"Participate in *his* divine nature—*his* divine power." This is what we came to see. My friend and fellow apostle, Paul, echoes this in one of his favorite prayers:

"I pray that out of his glorious riches, he may strengthen you with power through his Spirit in your inner being, so that Christ may dwell in your hearts through faith, through trust. And I pray that you, being rooted and established in love, may have power, together with all the saints, to grasp how wide and long and high and deep is the love of Christ, and to know this love that surpasses knowledge—that you may be filled to the measure of all the fullness of God."

Do you see what the Spirit is saying through Paul? He is praying that you will live your life strengthened with the power of the Spirit. He wants you to be so rooted in Jesus' perfect love that you will sense his presence always, and through this awareness of his presence in you, you will live with his power—a power to change the world, your community, your church, the world, a power to change … to *transform* you.

My purpose in writing down my thoughts today is so you will live this better life—this life to the full. I want you to know my best friend, Jesus, personally. I want you to know there is so much more and that you are missing it. I want to paint a picture of what this "so much more" looks like so that, as Paul writes, "You may be filled to the measure of all the fullness of God."

I want you to experience the riches of life in the kingdom. I now do, and so can you.

JESUS-PLUS?

But I am getting ahead of myself, as I am wont to do. I did not always have this power. Before I met Jesus, I did not have any power at all. I thought I was full of power—the power of Peter! But it was all about me. "Self" was in charge, and I was as blind as a man could be. Oh, I thought my life was good, even great at times. But looking back, I can see just how lost I was, and how much I was missing it. You see, back then, I did not know what I did not know. That is how blind I was.

After I met Jesus, and during my almost four years with him, some of that changed, but not nearly enough. Does this surprise you? Surely you have heard about how Jesus sent us out on two different trips without him. We went out two by two and he gave us the power to perform miracles, healing the lame and the sick.

Yet I was *still* blind, even after experiencing this healing power myself. We were all still blind. Sadly, it was still all about me—Self. Self was still in charge, and I was still viewing Jesus through the lens of what he could do for me—because I did not yet have the Spirit living in me.

I knew he was the Son of God, and I knew only he could guide me to a better life. But I still thought it was "Jesus-plus" that would make life great. I thought it was Jesus plus my fishing career; Jesus plus my income; Jesus plus my success; Jesus plus my wife and children; Jesus plus my efforts; Jesus plus my religious performance.

You see, I knew it was Jesus, but Jesus plus Peter.

Oh my.

WHAT I DID NOT KNOW

Then came our last night together—the night he was arrested and crucified. We had dinner together, just Jesus and the 12 of us. No big crowds, no feeding of the thousands. Just us.

We all loved those quiet times together—no crowds, no Pharisees, though Jesus loved them too. Yes, it is true—the Son of God, the Savior of the world, so loved just sharing a meal with his friends. During our many times together, Jesus was engaging, full of life, and even funny. He had such a great sense of humor.

But that night he was reserved, reflective, and even a bit sad.

He told us yet again that he was going to be arrested, tried, and killed. You have perhaps heard about my typical blustery performance. How I blurted out, "Lord, I am ready to go with you to prison and to death?" Ha. I still did not know what I did not know.

You see, I did not even know myself, and I still did not know Jesus—not fully. As he said that night to Philip, "Don't you know me, Philip, even after I have been among you such a long time?" No, Philip did not know him yet and neither did I—not even after those years together. I knew about him, but I did not know *him*. How could I? I was still living in my own kingdom. The kingdom of Self.

Are you?

I could not truly know him because I did not yet have the Holy Spirit.

SELF-SIFTED

That same night during our last supper together, Jesus said to me, "Simon, Simon, Satan has asked to sift you as wheat. But I have prayed for you, Simon, that your faith may not fail. And when you have turned back, strengthen your brothers."

I did not know what sifting meant, but I soon found out. You know the story: Jesus was arrested, tried in a mock trial by our Jewish leaders, taken to Pilate for another mock trial, beaten, and then crucified. And all the while, most of us hid. I even denied knowing Jesus, swearing oaths of scathing denial. Simon Peter: Super Apostle! The Rock! The Bishop! Before I met Jesus, I was operating in my own power, sitting atop the throne of the kingdom of Peter.

Even after those years with Jesus, I was still atop my throne—until I was toppled off.

Back then, Self was my master. Self was always in control. Since then, I have come to see Self—what many call the flesh—as my number-one enemy. I know my true enemy is Satan, but when Satan dominates Self, he has you right where he wants you. You are defeated and you do not even know it.

But you see, I did not know what I did not know. I did not know the Holy Spirit, and I certainly knew nothing of Holy Spirit power. I was still operating in my own power. My kingdom was threatened that night, and I panicked. Even though this was a very public failure on my part, it had played itself out many times before, in the less public details of my life.

Then came that surreal morning, three days after the crucifixion. Jesus was alive! I saw him. He spoke to me, to all of us. We had seen him dead and even buried, but now we saw him alive.

This changed everything for us, right? Anyone would be profoundly changed to see a dead man now walking and talking, would they not? John had watched as a Roman centurion thrust a sword into Jesus' heart, his blood spilling out. John personally witnessed him breathe his last breath on that hideous cross.

He was dead. He was buried. But then we saw him again, alive, very much alive.

I know you are certain you would be a completely transformed person after witnessing this, right? But I was not, and you likely would not be either without the Holy Spirit indwelling you. I even went back to my old way of life a few weeks later. Can you imagine that? I went back to my fishing business. The kingdom of Peter back in business!

Do you see the theme here? Can I help open your eyes to the reality of my life, even after the resurrection? And to yours? No Holy Spirit, no transformation. With the Holy Spirit yet to come, Self was still in charge.

I think it was that time between his resurrection and the feast of Pentecost that most disappoints me about myself — about all of us. We had seen Jesus alive several times, and yet I was still so blind. I am not surprised at my blindness before knowing Jesus, and I can even try to rationalize my ignorance after I had spent so much time with him. But to have seen him dead, then alive, and to still be so blind?

HOLY SPIRIT IS EVERYTHING

I can guess you are ready for me to move on, to get to the Holy Spirit's magnificent arrival on Pentecost. Well, I will not be hurried. I must help you see the stark difference between knowledge, and even experience, and the gift of the Spirit's presence inside you. Without him, you are blind. Without him, you are lost. Without him, you can do nothing.

Not one thing.

Without the Spirit's indwelling, you cannot know what you just do not know, and we surely did not.

Knowledge will only get us so far. Knowledge, without the Spirit, will not, cannot, take us very far, and it will often take us in the wrong direction. The person without the Spirit does not accept the things that come from the Spirit of God but considers them foolishness, and cannot understand them, because they are discerned only through the Spirit.

Even experience will leave us blind because experience fades, or perhaps just leaves us with feelings. Our own experience over those years with Jesus did change us, a little, but it was only with and through the Holy Spirit that we were transformed. Only the Holy Spirit could enable us to defeat Self.

How can I convey to you the Jesus I knew? How can I convey that he was my best friend? Yes, he was my Savior and, yes, he is the Son of God, but in the end, he was my best friend. I could turn to Jesus for guidance but also comfort and companionship. This may surprise you, but I could also turn to Jesus for laughter and fun. I want you to be able to as well.

But the true purpose of this story is to convey to you how the Holy Spirit became all of these to me! After Jesus bodily left this earth, I missed him terribly. I could hardly bear losing him, losing his constant presence. I would have never believed this back then, but the Spirit has filled that void. He has become my constant companion. He has filled me to the full measure of God.

I still talk with my best friend Jesus often, but now I feel his presence in a deeper, richer way than I did even when he was sitting beside me around a fire, cooking fish. You can have this too, and I know your heart longs for it.

2

KING PETER

I WOULD LIKE TO SHARE WITH YOU THAT FATEFUL DAY that started my personal journey toward surrender. I was, as always, fishing, just running my business. The water was beautiful, and the air was crisp. I was doing what I absolutely loved doing. It was just an ordinary day in the kingdom of Peter. But Jesus was already on the scene, and when he approached me that particular day, well, it would be the beginning of my journey toward surrender, and the death of Self.

You see, I had been aware of this Jesus. My little brother Andrew was enamored with this new prophet, so, naturally, I had already been introduced to him and had even spent some time with him. I had even seen him perform miracles—healing miracles. He had even healed my mother-in-law when she was deathly ill. However, up until that day, I knew about this Jesus, but I did not know *him*. If you had asked if I knew Jesus, I would have answered something like, "Yes, but not well."

I'm sure you know what it is like to know about someone, to even know them casually, but not truly know them. Jesus and I certainly had no prior history together—no shared intimacy, which I have since realized is essential to really knowing someone. Perhaps you can relate to my casual awareness of Jesus. Perhaps you know a lot about Jesus yet do not really know *him*.

Until that day, I had yet to begin following Jesus. I simply could not because I was still following Peter. I was a devoted disciple of me. Yes, I was attending the synagogue regularly, but only as a matter of duty. It was the right thing to do in our culture.

Everyone went to the synagogue at least once a week, but there was no energy there for me, and certainly no insight or meaning. It was flat and meaningless—it just did not apply to the real world as far as I could tell. I did not know what I was missing back then because I did not yet know what I did not know.

MY FATEFUL DAY WITH JESUS

This Jesus was a great speaker and a wonderful teacher, and he was friendly and personable, even charismatic. But he was just a preacher. Okay, I could see if I followed his teaching my life would be better—anyone could see that. But to follow *him*? Out of the question.

Jesus knew then what I would soon learn, and would have to repeatedly learn over my lifetime—until I saw him for who he was, I could never see me for who I am. And until I could see me for who I am—a lost and blind sinner in desperate need of Jesus—why would I put anything, or anyone, ahead of me?

Luke talks about my fateful day with Jesus in his first letter to Theophilus: the Gospel of Luke. You should read it because I am only going to give you the highlights. It began with me having already fished all night and caught nothing. I was tired and grumpy, which meant everyone else was tired and grumpy too. If Peter is not happy, no one can be happy. Along comes preacher Jesus, and, after teaching, he commandeered my boat and said, "Put out into deep water and let down the nets for a catch."

"Let the nets down *for a catch*," mind you, not, "Let down your nets and see what happens." No, he assertively said, "for a catch." Who does he think he is? I am the fisherman. He is the preacher. This is my area of expertise. Yes, I can probably learn some good life lessons from this man, but in the details of my life—the work details? Please, do not be ridiculous.

Abandon the Outcome to God

I learned that day that fishing is just like any other profession: I do not control the outcome. This is obvious for us fishermen—there is skill involved, but the fish are either there or not. But it is just as real for you, no matter your profession. It is true even in your personal life, even in your family. None of us, no matter how hard we work, controls the outcome.

But he does.

Let me repeat that: you do not control the outcome—any outcome. You never have and you never will. If you think you do, you are delusional. If you think you do, I can only imagine that everyone around you is miserable. Just ask my wife, Ruth, what it was like when King Peter took charge and tried to control the outcome.

I listened to Jesus, and you know the story. Our nets filled to almost bursting and the boat was so filled with fish, we almost sank. Until that day, I thought I was in control. I thought I had been a success because I was me—King Peter.

Until that day, I was not about to follow Jesus because I was busy running the kingdom of Peter. He was a great speaker and a wonderful teacher, but he was just a rabbi. He could improve my spiritual life—that is, if I would listen to him—but not my business life. I lived in the real world.

I could not see the Lord because all I could see was Self. My security was in my status, my accomplishments. Maybe yours is too? Or maybe your security is in something or someone else. The details matter little—as long as you find your security in anything other than the Lord, you will have no true security at all. None. I do not care how much you accomplish or how much everyone admires you. There is no true security in anyone or anything other than the Lord.

It is not Jesus-plus. It is only Jesus.

PROPPED UP

Perhaps if you examined your life, you would see that your security is based on your accomplishments, or is propped up by your job, someone you love, or even someone else's accomplishments—your parent's, your spouse's, your children's?

My wife Ruth will tell you that before Jesus, she found her security in me. Ruth says many women tend to seek their security in their husbands and sometimes even their children. She says a woman's family can become her foundation for security. That is a shaky security at best, isn't it?

I was certainly no one in whom Ruth should base her security, but no human ever is. Ruth has since learned she can only find true security in the love of the Father. And now that she has learned this, our relationship is so much better. She is no longer looking to me for her security, so her frustration and disappointment with me is far less.

Back then, I found my security in my work because there I was in control. My pride and identity were in my work. The fact that I was earning my way on my own was propping me up and making me feel secure, in me.

I was doing all right at the time, or so I thought.

My fishing business was humming along just fine. I had no need for the Lord, so Jesus had to knock my props out in another way—by showing me how little control I had over anything and, please do not miss this, showing me how much control he had over everything—even fish!

Once he knocked those false props—my sense of control—out from under me, I could finally start to see my true self—a lost, blind, and ignorant little king sitting atop my make-believe throne, strutting around like a little moron. Only then could I finally start to see my desperate need for a Savior. Jesus' words ring true for all of us: "For whoever wants to save his life will lose it, but whoever loses his life for me will find it."

You, too, my friend, must see that you are in desperate need of a Savior. Until you do, you will not surrender. Why would you? At some point—the point of surrender—we all have to stop trying to "save" whatever is propping us up before we can hope to "find" the life Jesus promises.

You, too, must see your props and surrender them, because you do indeed have them. You are leaning on them, and they will fail you. Oh, yes, they will.

But Jesus never will.

NAAMAN, ANOTHER KING OF SELF

One of my favorite stories from our holy Scriptures is one where I see myself so vividly in the primary character—Naaman, the army commander of Aram.

Naaman is a perfect example of this theme of desperate surrender. His is the story of a very prideful man (is there any other kind?) who had to be humbled in order to see the Lord for who he is. Before the events of this story unfolded, he, like me, could not see the Lord because all he could see was Self.

By the end of the story, he learned that until he could see himself for who he was —a man in desperate need of a Savior—he would never see the Lord for who he is. Allow me to share his story with you. Perhaps you will, like me, see yourself somewhere in this story.

LARGE AND IN CHARGE

Naaman was a successful warrior general and the right-hand man to the king of Aram. Everybody loved and respected him because of all he had accomplished. This is where he was basing his security; this is how he defined himself. He was large and in charge, sitting high atop the throne of his life. Like me, he was in control of everything and everyone around him—or so he thought.

But Naaman developed a skin issue, likely leprosy. He had hidden it from everyone because, well, someone like Naaman does not show weakness. Period. But as his skin condition worsened, his Hebrew servant girl told him about this famous prophet in Israel who could cure him. Naaman was likely skeptical about the power of any common Hebrew prophet, but since he could not control his skin problem, and he had always been in control, he decided to set out for Israel.

He arrived in style at the pitiful hovel of a house in which the prophet Elisha lived. Naaman had to humble himself to even seek this prophet's help, but you better believe he arrived in style—chariots, horsemen, silver, and gold. He intended to impress this little prophet, and he was going to pay him well for his services.

HUMBLING INSTRUCTIONS

Someone like Naaman does not accept free help from anyone. Grace was for weaklings. He had earned his way all his life, and he would earn his way with this prophet. He arrived in style, but this little pipsqueak prophet did not even come out to greet him. No doubt, Naaman expected Elisha to come out and bow down to him with all the flourish and fanfare he deserved. Instead, Elisha sent a servant out to tell him to go dip in the Jordan River seven times. A servant telling the great Naaman what to do? Elisha did not even come out himself. Did he understand who Naaman was?

Naaman turned around abruptly and left in a rage. As he was leaving, he growled to his servant, "I thought he would surely come out to me and stand and call on the name of the Lord his God, wave his hand over my skin, and cure me of my leprosy."

Naaman wanted a grand ceremony befitting his stature. He expected to be treated with respect, even awe. The great Naaman! Instead, Elisha sent his lowly servant out to instruct him to dip seven times in that muddy Jordan River

... in front of his servants, mind you. Seven times—in front of his servants, in front of the entire entourage. After grumbling and throwing his little tantrum, his chief servant pointed out his true stumbling block: "My father, if the prophet had told you to do some great thing, would you not have done it?"

There it was—his pride. Just like me, he could not see the LORD because all he could see was Self. His security was in his status, his accomplishments. Maybe yours is too? Or maybe your security is in something or someone else. The details matter little; as long as you find your security in anything other than the Lord, you will have no true security at all. None. I do not care how much you accomplish or how much everyone admires you. There is no true security in anyone or anything other than the Lord.

DIP SEVEN TIMES

Naaman had to humble himself; he had to yield to a lowly Hebrew prophet and dip seven times. With each dip into those muddy waters—one, two, three, four ... seven inglorious times—grace was growing, and his insecure security was flowing away with the river.

Naaman's pride had to surrender to grace. He could not control this problem, and he could not earn his way out of this. His security, his trust, had to be transferred from Self to God. A transfer of trust is the key that unlocks the gate into eternal life. Are you clinging to some false god for your security? Perhaps if you examined your life, you would see your security is based on your accomplishments, your job, someone you love, or even someone else's accomplishments—your parent's, your spouse's, your children's?

Will you humbly dip seven times to be free? Will you dip seven times to find the only true security there is?

Naaman was such an important man, and so very successful. No doubt, all his success was blocking him from knowing the LORD. He had been in control all his life—or so he thought. But leprosy showed him he was not in control of anything. It also showed him he was basing his security on his many accomplishments. Everyone's respect was propping him up, making him feel happy and secure.

I can relate because I had the same props as well. Oh, they were different from Naaman's, but only on the surface. I was finding my security in my work because that is where I was in control. My pride in my work, and the fact that I was earning my way, was propping me up and making me feel secure in me.

DESPERATION AND SURRENDER

Please keep these two words at the forefront of your mind: desperation and surrender. Until you realize you are in desperate need of a Savior, you will never surrender. And surrender you must.

Looking back on that day on the beach, I can easily see why I did not yet know Jesus—I did not even know me. How could I see the awesome, incredible power and majesty of this Savior of the world when I had no need for a Savior? I was doing fine, thank you.

But when he became real, in the very details of my life, even my work details, suddenly my eyes were opened and I could see him for who he was, and I could finally see me for who and what I was—that silly little pretend king strutting around in my silly little kingdom. Suddenly I cried out, "Go away from me, Lord; I am a sinful man!"

But he would not go away, and for that, I am eternally grateful.

He is calling you too, you know. Will you "drop your nets," your busy activities and myopic ambitions, surrender your silly little throne, and follow him?

This was the start of my personal relationship with Jesus, which has now fully flourished through the presence of the Spirit. The journey began that day, and it continues as I experience times of shared intimacy with my best friend, my Savior, in the details of my life—in my work details as well as in my family.

Where are you in your journey? Are you still stuck in an average religious life? Perhaps you have started to follow Jesus, but now you have plateaued? Take a close look at yourself today and see yourself for who you are.

Yes, you are loved and adored by Jesus, but are you lost, blind, and missing it? Are you propped up by something or someone other than Jesus? Or perhaps you have arrived at the point where you know there must be more, but you just do not know where to look.

See you; see him. And let the journey begin!

3

STEP BY STEP

AS WE BEGIN THIS JOURNEY OF EXPLORING HOW TO LIVE
with the Holy Spirit day by day, in the details of our lives,
I want to share with you the very simple process by which
we learn to live with this power: step by step. I am reminded of the prophet Isaiah's words:

> Do you not know?
> Have you not heard?
> The Lord is the everlasting God,
> the Creator of the ends of the earth.
> He will not grow tired or weary,
> and his understanding no one can fathom.
> He gives strength to the weary
> and increases the power of the weak.
> Even youths grow tired and weary,
> and young men stumble and fall;
> but those who hope in the LORD
> will renew their strength.
> They will soar on wings like eagles;
> they will run and not grow weary,
> they will walk and not be faint.

Many times, I am so full of emotion and feel I can soar on wings like eagles. Many times, I am so excited about Jesus I feel like I can run all day and not grow weary. Those are wonderful times when I can feel the power of the Spirit pressing me on.

But those are the exception, not the rule. Most days, I need the Spirit to empower me to *walk* and not grow faint. I have found that much more ministry is done walking than running. High vibrating energy is great; I've felt it and I've climbed mountains with it. But it is when I am walking with the Holy Spirit, step by step, that I have seen mountains moved.

He moves the mountains; I just walk along with him. Our journey is a process, not a goal. Jesus showed us this many times as we walked with him. I think the Father is perhaps more pleased when I can remain focused and faithful while walking than when I am running. It will take time for you to learn to walk by the Spirit. It will take experiencing his presence and then his power.

None of this will happen overnight, so please do not become discouraged. The Holy Spirit is here to provide you with the power to live with his power. Does this sound odd, perplexing? It should because it is, because the Spirit moves in ways in which we are not yet accustomed.

Spiritual formation is more about changing the source of behavior than behavior modification. When the source is changed from you ... from your Self ... to him, the behavior begins to take care of itself.[1]

LITTLE BY LITTLE, DAY BY DAY

You may think it was easy and natural for us to learn to walk with the Spirit, having walked with the Master, but that was not the case. I once thought God's purpose was the end goal—living with Spirit-filled power!—and yes, this is his desire for us. Yet I also sense his pleasure and his purpose in the process. It is in the process wherein we grow, step by step.

The process is all about progress, little by little, not perfection.

Whatever you may think the Father's purpose for you is in the long run, his real desire is for you to learn to depend on him now, to learn to depend on the Holy Spirit today, in the little things, in the details, now.

God's purpose is to enable me to see that he can walk with me day by day, especially in the storms of life. If I have a further goal in mind, I am not paying enough attention to the present time. However, if you and I can realize that, moment by moment, step by step, walking with the Spirit is the goal, then his precious power begins to pervade our being.

As we walk with him, we learn that, in him, we live and breathe and have our being.

WALKING ON WATER

I had my first experience walking by faith in the storms of life that night years ago when we saw Jesus. Notice he was walking on the water, not running. I don't recall Jesus ever being in a hurry. He had a calm, relaxed pace about him, not fast and frenetic.

ATTEMPTING TO GET AWAY

That day, we had just received the news that John the Baptizer had been beheaded by Herod. And for such a heinous reason: the wish of his wife's daughter. This news really shook the Master. He was quiet and withdrawn for some time. I could tell he was struggling with this injustice. John was his cousin and one of his favorite people.

To be honest, John the Baptizer intimidated me. He had a look—how to say it—he had fire in his eyes. His eyes blazed with passion and energy. The few times I was around him, I sensed he could see straight into my soul, and that made me very uneasy. When John would say, "He must increase and I must decrease," I thought, *Why can we not both increase?* King Peter, my, oh my.

But Jesus loved John, and he was hurt deeply by the news of his untimely death. Later that morning, I was sitting near Jesus and he nudged me and looked toward my boat. I knew he wanted to be alone, to get away to a solitary place, so I announced to the disciples we were going across the lake to Bethsaida, Philip's home.

They all looked at me in a funny way, but then Andrew jumped up and started preparing the boat, and everyone followed. It was a few miles across the Sea of Galilee, and when we arrived, we pulled our boat up in a solitary area. Jesus walked right out of the boat and off into the surrounding hills to be alone.

We knew he was weary, so we just set up camp and sent Philip into town to pick up some provisions. That was my idea, and it turned out to have been a mistake. When Philip returned, an enormous crowd followed him. As the day went on, more and more arrived until there were at least 5,000 men, plus women and children. You know the story. Jesus fed the entire crowd with just five loaves of bread and two fish.

KEEP MY EYES ON JESUS

Immediately after everyone was fed, Jesus quietly told us to get in our boat and go ahead of him. He said he would catch up with us, whatever that meant. But we could all see he was deeply disturbed and didn't want to challenge him, so we got into the boat and headed back home to Capernaum.

The wind was terrible that night, and we were struggling mightily to make any headway. I was sweating and my muscles ached, but no one was going to out-work me — not back then, anyway. We had rowed about three miles, and everyone was miserable. I was inwardly blaming Philip for having attracted so many people to our getaway and, thus, putting us all in this tenuous position.

Shortly before dawn, just about the time I felt I could row no longer, Jesus came out to us, walking on the lake. When we saw this strange figure walking on the water, we were terrified. "It's a ghost," several of us cried out, with fear rising in our hearts.

But Jesus immediately said to us, "Take courage! It is I. Do not be afraid."

When I realized it was the Master, I blurted out without thinking, as I am wont to do, "Lord, if it is you, tell me to come to you on the water."

"Come," was all Jesus said. This was the way of the Master — just "Come."

I stretched my legs over the bow of the boat and hesitated, but with everyone watching, my pride was suddenly on the line. I began to walk on the water toward Jesus. I was shocked the water held me up, but when I saw the wind and the waves, I became terrified and tried to run to Jesus. Suddenly, I began to sink and cried out, "Lord, save me!"

Immediately, Jesus reached out his hand and caught me. "You of little faith," he said, "why did you doubt?"

I doubted because I took my eyes off Jesus. I tried to run instead of walk to him because that is my default — when things are difficult, uncertain, or even scary, my tendency is to go faster. Walking with a calm, relaxed pace was not an option for the old Peter.

Moving quickly, going faster, even if I am unsure of the right direction feels better than walking. "If it is to be, it's up to me" was my personal mantra. But this is not the way of the Spirit. To learn to live with his power, we must learn to walk with him, step by step, letting him lead the way.

STEPS TO BEING CARRIED BY THE SPIRIT

Recently, I wrote a second letter to all our church families. In it, I said, "For prophecy never had its origin in the human will, but prophets, though human, spoke from God as they were carried along by the Holy Spirit."

Brother Paul says it like this: "Since we live by the Spirit, let us keep in step with the Spirit. I say walk by the Spirit, and you will not gratify the desires of the flesh."

Here is how my journey of learning to live with the power of the Spirit has progressed. First, I started walking with the Spirit. I started reminding myself he was with me, indwelling me, all around me. It was not natural at first, but as I learned to think about the Spirit's presence, it seemed he was walking with me.

The next step was to "be led by the Spirit." To be led by anyone requires we slow down and let them take the lead. Notice we have to slow down, not something I was particularly accustomed to. But as I slowed down, as I learned to wait on the Spirit to lead me and guide me, just as Jesus said the Spirit would do, his power began to pervade my walking.

After learning to let the Spirit take the lead, eventually, I found myself walking in step with the Spirit. His will became my will. His choices became my choices. I still sometimes tried to take the lead, but this new experience of keeping in step with the Spirit was so refreshing and empowering.

The next step in my process was just as I wrote in my second letter, "So they were carried along by the Holy Spirit." Now, as I conform my will to the Father's will, I feel I am literally carried along by the power of the Holy Spirit. As the prophet Isaiah said, "They will soar on wings like eagles; they will run and not grow weary, they will walk and not be faint."

WALK, DON'T RUN

When Brother Paul says, "Walk by the Spirit, and you will not gratify the desires of the flesh," just think Self. This is precisely what he means. Notice he says we are to "keep in step with the Spirit." Keep in step, not run ahead. This requires patience, yes, but it requires a sense of confidence in the Spirit as well.

I like to run ahead. I like motion. I like action—fast, quick action. I feel in control when I am moving, or at least I have the illusion of control. But the flesh—Self—desires what is contrary to the Spirit, and the Spirit what is contrary to Self. They conflict with each other. But as Paul says, "If you are led by the Spirit, you are not under the control of the flesh, of the Self."

The Holy Spirit leads us step by step. This is his way.

We are led by the Spirit like a shepherd leads his sheep. I never liked shepherding because it's too slow for me. Shepherding a bunch of nitwit sheep is not my style. (I guess this says a lot about me.) But it is a perfect picture of this principle. The shepherd leads the sheep. He walks ahead of them, step by step, with a calm, relaxed pace.

He leads them, just as the Spirit leads us. He doesn't harass them, threaten them, or force them with harsh words and demonstrative histrionics. That type of behavior would frighten the sheep. I have witnessed hired hands treating the sheep this way. They do not have the patience to lead or love, so they instead hurry and harass the sheep. But this is not the way of the Master.

WITHIN OUR ACTIONS, BEYOND OUR POWERS

Jesus propels us rather than pushes us. He leads, and we follow. Jesus called himself a shepherd. This was his way for the three-plus years we walked with Jesus, step by step, day in and day out, learning his quiet, calm, but steady and purposeful pace.

The Holy Spirit works within our actions but beyond our powers.[2] He seems to mix his power with our efforts. You do know, do you not, that the Father is not opposed to effort? He is not opposed to effort, but he is opposed to earning.[3] The Father is opposed to you trying to earn his affection or his love, or even some extra credit above and beyond others, but he is not opposed to your effort.

For this very reason, make every effort to add to your faith goodness; and to goodness, knowledge; and to knowledge, self-control. But the Spirit moves within and through your efforts, beyond what we could accomplish on our own—within our actions, but beyond our powers.

Recently, I read Paul's letter to the family of believers in Colossae. Near the beginning of his letter, he wrote, "To this end I labor, struggling with all his energy, which Christ so powerfully works in me."

Do you see what the Spirit is saying through Paul? Paul is laboring, he is struggling, he is making every effort, yet he understands he is doing so with the energy that so powerfully works through him by the Holy Spirit—within his actions, beyond his powers.

Step by step, we are laid hold of by a movement, a power, a Spirit greater than ourselves, who expands our energies and our efforts beyond our own power. We know it, and it is a beautiful thing to experience.

Holy Spirit Power: Energy, Clarity, and Creativity

It is like this when we are out fishing. We set the sails, but it is the wind that carries us along. Jesus likened the Spirit to the wind. It blows and we see the results, but we do not see the Spirit—at least not with the eyes in our head. We see the movement of the Spirit with the eyes of our heart.

If we do not set the sails, there will be no movement. We do our part, but the wind of the Spirit powers us—no effort on our part, often no movement by the Spirit, within our actions, beyond our powers.

However, sometimes the Holy Spirit moves entirely on his own. I have experienced both, and both are immensely joyous. In both situations, it is obviously him who is moving. If we think it is us, the Spirit will likely not move. He knows our hearts. He is not eager to interfere with Self's plans. If we want to be the mover, if we want to get the credit, he will let us. Good luck with that. But if we want him to be the true movement, if we want to be moved by him, then we will see his power pervade.

Step by step, led by the Spirit. Think about the patriarchs and heroes of our Hebrew Scriptures—Abraham, Isaac, Jacob, Moses, Joseph, King David, and our prophets. We see only the major shifts in their lives. Can you imagine the day-in-and-day-out struggles? Their doubts, their stumbles? I can! This is exactly what it looked like for us, and it will for you as well.

As Isaiah writes,

> But you will not leave in haste or go in flight; for the LORD will go before you, the God of Israel will be your rear guard.

Step by step. The Holy Spirit is a lamp to guide your feet and a light for your path.

If you are willing to be led by the Spirit, then, step by step, you will more and more see him leading you. With each step, you will grow more confident in his presence and his power. I wish I could give you a shortcut, but there are no shortcuts with the Holy Spirit.

---

[1] Statement attributed to Dallas Willard.

[2] Statement attributed to Dallas Willard

[3] Statement attributed to Dallas Willard.

4

THE ASCENSION

ONE DAY, ABOUT 40 DAYS AFTER THE RESURRECTION, John and I awoke earlier than the others and went up on the roof, enjoying the cool breeze and the rising sun over Jerusalem. We watched as the various craftsman set up their tents in the marketplace. The noisy merchants jabbering back and forth, arms waving and heads bobbing, so typical of our Hebrew culture, was an amusing distraction.

We had just returned to Jerusalem after my ill-fated attempt to revive my fishing business up in Capernaum in Galilee. After a long and fruitless night of fishing, Jesus met us on the beach that morning and cooked us fish for breakfast.

That was the morning I am sure you have heard about—the one where he took me off to the side and made sure I understood two things: he loved me and I was still of great worth to him. He did this by pressing me with three separate but similar questions—more like challenges—asking me if I loved him.

After that, we had packed our bags and made the long walk back to Jerusalem. We had not seen Jesus since. This particular morning, John and I decided to leave the roof and spend some time on the Mount of Olives. Since that day on the beach in Galilee, we were both missing him badly. John was trying to smile as he said, "Peter, do you think often about that last night with Jesus, when after dinner he led us out to the Mount of Olives, humming the hymn we had just sung with him in the upper room?"

I, too, tried to smile, but I was not fooling anyone. The memory is still so bittersweet to this day. "Yes, dear friend, I think about our last night during Passover, perhaps too much. It was such a sweet time, walking out together to one of Jesus' favorite places. Do you remember how often he would sit out there on the side of that little mountain at night, looking back on the lights of Jerusalem? He always felt such peace there."

John replied, "Oh, yes, I do remember, and that is where Nicodemus came out to see Jesus. Do you remember that, Simon? I made a few notes after their conversation. Something told me a visit from such a powerful Pharisee like Nicodemus would turn out to be important."

Thinking about how Jesus spoke so frankly to Nicodemus brought back a flood of memories for me. "John, that was the night Jesus cut the powerful Nicodemus off in midsentence, and said, 'You must be born again, Nicodemus.' Nicodemus was so bewildered, and so was I. I still am. Do you have a better feel for what 'born again' means, my Brother?"

"No," John answered, holding his hands up, "unless it has something to do with the Holy Spirit Jesus kept talking about over dinner that last night. But I was so befuddled by what being born again meant, I never asked Jesus about it after the Pharisee left. Whatever it means, it must be important because Jesus told Nicodemus in no uncertain terms, 'No one can see the kingdom of God unless they are born again.'"

EXPOSED

May I pause and reflect for a moment? I am an old man and can too easily forget important points if I do not address them while I am thinking about them.

Jesus' encounter with Nicodemus still rings true for you today. Just come to him. Just spend time with him. You will be encouraged, you will feel welcomed, and you will likely be surprised. One thing is for sure: you will not be bored. No one emerged from an encounter with Jesus the same as they were before.

Have you had this kind of encounter with Jesus? Can you remember in vivid detail the first time you really saw him for who he is—not just a passing glimpse in biblical stories, or perhaps being delivered out of trouble, but you saw *him*? This type of first encounter with Jesus always becomes a defining moment, the first of many, as we get to know the real Jesus.

Over our years with Jesus, it became clear he wanted us to know that when the Father peers into our soul, he sees every thought, every past hurt, every present longing, every void, and, yes, even every fault and frailty. Yet he still says, "Look at my son; isn't he wonderful? Look at my precious daughter, so absolutely beautiful and alive; I just adore her. I am so proud of you."

This is what your soul is thirsting for, isn't it?

I remember my first encounter with Jesus—it felt like he had been waiting for me all my life. He looked right through my well-developed façade and into my heart and my soul. I could see in his eyes he knew everything about me—my heart's desires, my fears, my hopes and dreams, and my blind spots.

I remember feeling so exposed—yes, that is the best word: exposed.

SEEKING THE MORE

I bet the Pharisee Nicodemus had the same feeling that first night he encountered Jesus. Nicodemus was one of the elite. We all had heard about him, but lowly fishermen would never actually meet a man like that. He was rich, smart, and powerful. Nicodemus was *the* teacher of Israel, yet he risked it all for Jesus, coming to see this itinerant rabbi at night, seeking a truth that had evaded him.

He came with an open heart. Let us stop there for a moment. This is all Jesus asks of you: that you come with an open heart. Nicodemus' mind was, at first, still closed to anything beyond his fixed religious assumptions. But because he was sincerely seeking with an open heart, Jesus was able to penetrate beyond his entrenched positions and light up Nicodemus' mind to a new truth.

Why was Nicodemus compelled to risk his prominent standing by coming to see this man who was so disliked by his fellow Sanhedrin? Because he knew there was more. He had been immersed in religion all his life, but inside he knew—he just knew!—his religion could not be all there was. There had to be more.

One look at Jesus and he knew this Jesus was "the more" he was seeking, even if he did not yet know why.

He said, "Rabbi, we know you are a teacher who has come from God." A nice introduction, but it was obvious

Nicodemus was still off track. He knew there had to be more, so he pursued the cultural route of "Salvation by more knowledge." He came to see Jesus to find more knowledge.

He could not have been more surprised.

"YOU MUST..."

I could see by Jesus' reaction he would have none of this intellectual discussion. That is why he abruptly turned the conversation back toward Nicodemus with a blunt, "You must be born again."

It is so important to see what Jesus *did not* say to Nicodemus. He did not say, "Nicodemus, if you want to be part of my inner circle, you should consider being born again." Or, "It would be so helpful if you are born again." Or maybe even, "Nicodemus, you'll enjoy life more if you are born again, but I'm just suggesting it as a possible option. You could try being really good or getting really involved at church, or just be really sincere. Whatever feels best for you."

No. He did not say any of those lukewarm, flimsy things. Those options are exactly what he came to combat. Many of you have, no doubt, already tried those paths, which bring nothing more than a mediocre religious life. No, Jesus said, "You *must* be born again." He then added, and I am paraphrasing Jesus here, "Until you are, you won't have a clue about what living in my kingdom is like. You'll never even see it, much less live in it."

Jesus does not typically respond to those who approach him with "you *must*." He usually precedes his directives with an "If," as with the rich young ruler: "*If* you want to be perfect, go, sell your possessions." I now know Jesus insists, "You must be born again" because you *must*.

HEAD KNOWLEDGE AND HEART KNOWLEDGE

Jesus knew Nicodemus had the head knowledge, which is fine, but only when interwoven with heart knowledge. Jesus knew this was Nicodemus' blind spot and the idea of being born again his stumbling block. It might be yours too. It certainly was mine. Jesus brings Nicodemus to a crossroads—a crisis of faith. A defining moment.

When Jesus said, "You must be born again," he was saying to this man of ideas and knowledge, "You need a new heart, not new ideas; you need to let the Spirit invade you and then strip you all the way down to your core. It will feel like a new birth. It will be so radical, such a cosmic shift inside you, it will seem like you are being born all over again."

Jesus went on to say to Nicodemus, "Whoever believes in me shall not perish but have eternal life."

Again, I want you to understand what Jesus did not say. He did not say something like, "If you intellectually accept this information as true, if you affirm it as reliable in your head, you will be saved." No, in essence, he was saying, "If you surrender your whole being to this new light; if you cast your entire dependence on me; if you are so moved by this surrender that inside you know something has shifted and that you will never be the same again, then the direction of your life will shift too. You will know, beyond a shadow of a doubt, that you have entered my kingdom."

BELIEVING MEANS SURRENDERING

I have already seen this word *believe* taught in the weakest of ways. If misunderstood, it has the power to lead the masses straight down the path to hell. The Greek word is *pisteuo*. It means "to cast one's entire dependence upon; to put one's trust in, with an implication that an actionable response, based on this dependence and trust, will naturally follow." *Pisteuo* means to be committed to, to rely on, to surrender to, to believe *in* as opposed to believe *about*.

For Jesus to tell Nicodemus he just needs to accept with his mind this new information would not have changed his life one iota, nor will it yours. Jesus was saying, "You must surrender your life, Nicodemus, if you want to find salvation. It is all about surrender."

It is for you too. Have you surrendered? I plan to keep asking you this because surrender leads to being born again, which is salvation. There is no other way.

A WALK AMONG THE CLOUDS

While sitting with John on the roof in Jerusalem, I said to him, "Let's take a walk out to the Mount of Olives. All this talk is making me lonely for Jesus. Maybe spending time out there on the mountain will soothe my soul a bit."

I guess the others were feeling the same way, so we all walked out there together. It was only a short walk, and it seemed like just another ordinary day. The sky was clear, and a gentle breeze cooled the sweat on my face as we climbed the hill.

After we had settled into a little circle and built a small fire, Jesus was suddenly standing among us. "Peace be with you," he said, which is what he said each time we saw him after the resurrection. He must have known his appearance would startle us.

My heart leaped inside me. I was so overjoyed to see him, so I blurted out, "Master, how did you know we would be here?"

No sooner had the words left my mouth than I realized their silliness and shallowness.

But Jesus just smiled. He had bigger things on his mind that day. He turned to all of us and said, "From this point on, do not leave Jerusalem, but wait for the gift my Father promised. For John baptized with water, but in a few days, you will be baptized with the Holy Spirit."

There it was again, this Holy Spirit. What did "baptized with the Holy Spirit" mean?

Jesus had spoken of it … him? … this Spirit a few times, and especially over dinner during our last night together. But now there was an urgency in his voice. I had the sense he was not teaching but giving us instructions.

"Wait," he said. "Wait for the gift my Father promised."

Again, what did he mean by "the gift" and "in a few days?" We were all confused by this, and I know everyone wanted to ask him to explain what he meant. Yet again, I let my mouth go first and stammered out, "Lord, are you at this time going to restore the kingdom to Israel?"

The others all turned and just stared at me. Silence. They were as surprised as I was at my blundering big mouth. Thomas tried to suppress a snicker, I could tell, but the moment was too big to laugh.

Restore the kingdom? What? Where did that come from? Jesus is talking about a gift of the Holy Spirit coming in a few days, and I'm asking about kingdoms. Does that show you where my mind was still operating? kingdoms. As in my kingdom. Oh sure, I asked about the kingdom of Israel, but that was just a smokescreen. The only kingdom I still really cared about at that time was my own.

I did not know this was still so true about me then because I still did not know what I did not know. I did not know the Holy Spirit. The establishment of Jesus' kingdom meant the *reestablishment* of the kingdom of Peter alongside Jesus, at least in my thinking.

Jesus was a little more stern with me that day and responded while looking first at me, then the others: "It is not for you to know the times or dates the Father has set by his own authority. But you will receive power when the Holy Spirit comes on you, and you will be my witnesses in Jerusalem, and in all Judea and Samaria, and to the ends of the earth."

Before any of us had a chance to process what he meant, Jesus was taken up before our very eyes, and a cloud hid him from our sight.

I looked over at John, stunned, and he looked back at me, totally confused. The others were still looking up in the sky when, suddenly, two men dressed in white stood beside us. "Men of Galilee," they said, "why do you stand here looking into the sky? This same Jesus, who has been taken from you into heaven, will come back in the same way you have seen him go into heaven."

Then, suddenly, the angels disappeared, and there we stood, looking at each other, bewildered. It happened so suddenly. Jesus with us, then the clouds, then Jesus fading from our view, then the angels, and then just us. We just stood there, awed, befuddled, and dumbfounded.

GOOD AT DOING

I am reminded of another time on a mountain, a couple of years earlier, when Jesus took me, along with John and John's older brother James, early in the morning to be alone with him. We were in the area of Caesarea Philippi and had made our camp at the base of Mount Hermon. Perhaps you know the story?

The sun was just peeking out over the surrounding hills. Jesus was deep in prayer and I, as usual, was fighting off sleep. But as he was praying, the appearance of his face changed, and his clothes became as bright as a flash of lightning. His face shone like the sun, and his clothes became as white as the light. Two men, Moses and Elijah, appeared in the same kind of glorious splendor, talking with Jesus.

It was frightening, to say the least, to see Jesus transfigured like that. It was like getting a glimpse into a whole other world—the kingdom from which Jesus had come. James, John, and I were just standing there staring, not knowing what to do. Jesus took no note of us. He was in a different world.

As the men were leaving Jesus, I, yet again, let my mouth run where my mind should have just rested. "Master," I said, "it is good for us to be here. Let us put up three shelters—one for you, one for Moses and one for Elijah." I did not know what I was saying. But I was reverting to the one thing I was good at—doing ... doing something, anything, just to be *doing*.

While I was stammering, a cloud appeared and covered us. Seeing Moses and Elijah was incredible, and a bit unnerving, but this cloud was another thing altogether. We somehow knew it was God Almighty, and we were overwhelmed with fear. I think you would be too. The ground was shaking, and the air had a heaviness about it. I cannot describe it adequately, but it was scary and unsettling, to say the least.

Then a voice came from the cloud, saying, "This is my Son, whom I love; listen to him."

"Listen to him."

LISTEN

I'm not very good at listening, are you? I like to be doing. Even when I am listening, I am not really listening. I am hearing the words but not the heart behind the words. My focus is not what you are saying but, instead, what brilliant reply I can offer. In the kingdom of Self, this is how we all listen.

I had heard God's voice before. It is not the kind of voice you are likely to forget. Did you know that when Jesus was baptized by John in the Jordan River, God said the same thing: "This is my son, whom I love?" But notice that day on the mountain, he included a very distinct addition: "Listen to him."

He felt the need to give us this reminder because we don't listen. We like to *do*, not listen. It is easier to serve God than to know God.[1] It is far easier to be actively doing than to sit still and listen quietly for the Lord. We so often mistake motion for true movement. Over the years, the Holy Spirit has brought me back to that moment many times, often when I am reading my favorite Psalms:

"Be still and know that I am God."
"Be still before the LORD AND wait patiently for him."

I tend not to listen for the Lord, and I can assure you I do not like to be still. I prefer not to wait on the Lord either. Even when I read Scripture, my mind tends to wander off to my to-do list for the day. I have read whole passages without retaining anything. Ruth tells me I do not listen to her either. She says, "Peter, if you are not looking at me, I know you are not listening to me."

I would protest, but she is right, and we both know it.

Just before Jesus ascended into heaven for the last time that day on the Mount of Olives, he said, "Do not leave Jerusalem, but wait for the gift my Father promised, which you have heard me speak about. For John baptized with water, but in a few days, you will be baptized with the Holy Spirit."

The angels had disappeared, and there we were, standing alone, looking around, looking at each other. It all happened so suddenly. But as there was nothing else to do and I like to be doing something, I said, "Well, friends, Jesus told us to go back to Jerusalem, so let's go."

But he had actually said, "Go back and *wait*." Did I listen to him?

---

[1] Statement attributed to Cubby Culbertson.

5

THE WEIGHT OF WAIT

AS WE RETURNED TO JERUSALEM, WE WENT UPSTAIRS TO the room where we had been gathering since the resurrection. It was Mary's house, Mark's mother. You know Mark, my faithful companion, friend, and sometimes secretary. He was just a young man then. In fact, he was with us the night Jesus was arrested. None of us can joke about that night in any way, but it is a fact that as Mark ran away, his clothes were pulled off by one of the guards, and he ran away naked as the day he was born.

Mark has been constantly taking notes over all these years as I preach, or even just from our conversations. He loves to hear me talk about my time with Jesus. He has gathered all his notes together and written a summary of our time with Jesus.

I know my old friend and fellow disciple Matthew has done the same. His heart is for his fellow Jews, so he crafted his gospel toward them, with an eye to Jesus' fulfillment of our Hebrew Scriptures. Doctor Luke has traveled around interviewing all the eyewitnesses to Jesus' life. He even sat down with Jesus' mother, Mary, for an extensive session. Luke told me that several times she would close her eyes as if she was shifting to another world altogether, and she would say, "I have treasured all these things and pondered them in my heart." I have no doubt Luke's, as well as Matthew's and Mark's accounts, will add much to the understanding of Jesus. John has hinted he will one day do the same. For that, I can hardly wait.

GATHERING IN THE UPPER ROOM

I am an old man and I have wandered again. Back on that day in Jerusalem after Jesus ascended to heaven, we were gathered in the big upper room. Those present were John, James, and my little brother Andrew; Philip and Thomas; Bartholomew and Matthew; James son of Alphaeus and Simon the Zealot; Judas son of James; and me. Also gathered with us were some women who had followed Jesus as well as Jesus' mother and, surprisingly, his brothers.

His brothers had been skeptics during Jesus' earthly ministry. They even teased him about claiming to be the Messiah. I say teased, but we all knew it was really taunting. Jesus certainly knew this, and maybe that is why he appeared personally to James after his resurrection. James was the oldest brother and, therefore, the leader of the other brothers. After that appearance, James was a changed man, and he and his brothers were a constant part of our group.

Over the next few days, our friends started filtering in. There had been a core group of about 120 of us followers, and now we were for the most part back together. It was nice to see everyone. They all knew how I had failed Jesus so badly with my three denials, yet everyone was kind to me. The truth was that we had all failed him in our own way.

But my failure was the worst.

BAPTISM OF THE HOLY SPIRIT

Jesus' last words before he was taken up into the clouds were still ringing in my ears. I was still trying to understand what he meant by, "Do not leave Jerusalem, but wait for the gift my Father promised, which you have heard me speak about."

Yes, we had heard him talk about the Holy Spirit, but mostly just over dinner that last night he was arrested. He had not really explained much to us. What did he mean by "gift?"

And what in the world did he mean by, "In a few days you will be baptized with the Holy Spirit?" Baptized? With the Holy Spirit? I understood baptism, or at least I had watched John the Baptizer immersing people in the Jordan, and we had done some of that ourselves with Jesus. Ritual immersing was a part of our Jewish practice. But that baptizing was a physical event—a washing, a cleansing of the body, if you will. Water. Dipping. Getting wet.

But baptized with the Holy Spirit? I asked John about it and he just shrugged. For some reason, I thought back to John's earlier comment about how bewildered Nicodemus had been by, "You must be born again." Did both statements fit together? Was being born again and this baptism of the Holy Spirit connected?

WAITING IN PRAYER

Soon, Matthew started praying, then James started praying, and soon we were all praying quietly. This went on for quite a while. It was comforting, I must say, and sweet. We were all in harmony, quietly expressing the Lord's presence in our hearts.

The silence, sweetened by the quiet praying and swaying of the followers, was a soothing antidote to our troubled spirits. There was a gentle stirring in the air and a gentle harmony of hearts. It was still; it was quiet; it was peaceful.

But one can only pray so much. At some point, someone has to actually *do* something. At least this is the way I thought back then, when I did not know what I did not know.

When I'd had enough of all this praying, I stood up and said, "Brothers and sisters, the Scripture had to be fulfilled in which the Holy Spirit spoke long ago through David concerning Judas, who served as a guide for those who arrested Jesus. He was one of our number and shared in our ministry."

Everyone looked up from their prayers, a bit surprised at my interruption. I was about to make my next big mistake. Obviously, I had yet to learn to listen. Jesus had told us plainly and directly, "Go back to Jerusalem and wait."

"Wait for the Holy Spirit," he was saying. "Do not do anything without the Spirit because you do not yet know what I want you to do."

SEE-SEEK-WANT-WAIT

Please listen to what I am about to say, and I hope I repeat it often because this is of utmost importance. The process of learning to live with Holy Spirit power follows this progression: See-Seek-Want-Wait.

SEE

We have to first *see* the Holy Spirit is real. This is akin to my earlier discussion about walking with the Spirit. We want to see he is personal. He is not an *it*, but a *he*. He is involved in the details—your details. We want to see that he is real, he is active, he is involved—and he is oh so powerful. So many Christians, and I'm talking about real, born-again Christians, are not even aware he is any of these things. Are you? Because he is, and you don't want to miss him.

I love the story of the blind man standing beside the road as we entered Jericho. When Jesus asked him, "What is it you want me to do for you?" he responded, "Lord, I want to see."

This has become my prayer every day now: "Lord, I want to see. I want to see you in everything I do today. I want to see with the eyes of the Holy Spirit. I want 'the eyes of my heart enlightened.'" This is one of Paul's favorite phrases: the eyes of your heart enlightened. My counsel to you, my dear friend, is to do the same: Each day, ask Jesus to help you to see the Spirit in every detail of your day—because he is.

My tendency is to see through the eyes of Peter. If I do not remind myself daily, I will see only what is seen, and not what is unseen. I will see only that which is temporary, not that which is eternal (Another of Paul's sayings). I will miss the Spirit, and, instead, I will see primarily Self.

SEEK

It is not enough just to be aware of the Spirit; as we "make every effort" to see the Spirit, we then must *seek* him. To seek means to look everywhere for something, so we want to be constantly alert to the presence of the Spirit. We have to look for him in every situation and seek his guidance and his action.

As I seek him, as I factor him into every situation, he becomes more and more real. The more I seek the Holy Spirit, the more I see him. The more real he becomes, the more I see with a different set of eyes—the "eyes of my heart."

WANT

The reason I seek the Spirit is I *want* his counsel; I want his guidance. For a long time, I did not want anyone's counsel but my own. I was so smart and did not need anyone else's opinion unless I knew they would agree with me. The next step in learning to live with Holy Spirit power is wanting the Holy Spirit to be involved in our details, and this is a bigger step than you may think.

Do you want the Holy Spirit to be in charge of your life? Before you give me a quick answer, think about it. Most of us really do not. It is not because we are heathens and horrible people. We do not see it as rejecting God. We simply want our way, in our timing.

We must learn to want his guidance and involvement. Perhaps your first step will be as mine: Ask the Spirit to help you *want to want*. We must really want him to take the lead. The Spirit will not shove his way in. He is not pushy, but if you want him to take the lead, he will.

And trust me, you do.

WAIT

We must then be willing to *wait*. We must be willing to wait for him to move, and to lead, and to act. We must be willing to wait for his clarity.

Again, why do you not want him to take the lead, and why will you not wait on him to take the lead? Because you want to be in charge. You want to lead. You want to act first. Why? Because you want your way, not his.

Recently, Ruth was fretting over a family situation. Her mother was very old, and Ruth was spending an enormous amount of time caring for her. She wanted her sister to help her, but Esther seemed not so inclined. After watching Ruth's frustration and seeing her growing fatigue, I had enough. It was time for Peter to step in and fix this situation.

I am a fixer, and it was time to do something, anything. Prayer might help, but doing something, taking charge, would be quicker and would likely get the result I was after faster. I knew the best solution, and I was the one to set Esther straight. Yes, I prayed about it beforehand—I gave the Holy Spirit a passing nod—assuming he was in agreement with me.

Can you see the old Peter, King Peter, raising his ugly head?

I practiced couching my words to Esther in grace and kindness. I have at least grown enough to seek first grace and kindness in these situations to avoid hurting anyone's feelings. However, I also knew I was right and this was the right thing to do. I did pray about it, but if I am honest, my prayer was really about having the Lord confirm what I had already decided to do. I was ready to approach Esther when I felt a check in my spirit. I heard the Holy Spirit say, "No, *wait.* Let me take the lead on this, King Peter. I can handle Esther far better than you. And if I decide not to move in her heart, then you just stay quiet and work harder to help Ruth."

Well, I did not like hearing that, but I did hear it loud and clear. It wasn't an audible voice, mind you, but perhaps even clearer than an audible voice. It was an inner voice from the Spirit—the kind you cannot miss or misunderstand, that is, if you want to hear him, if you want him to take the lead.

And I did. Oh, my ego did not, but because I have been living with the Spirit for so long now, I was willing to wait on his lead. In the end, I truly wanted his way over mine. I have at least learned that much. A few days later, as I waited, Esther suddenly appeared at our home with her travel bags and an abundance of food and announced, "I am here to help you, dear sister. You have been carrying too much of this load for too long. Forgive me for not coming sooner."

Can you see how I would have messed things up if I had moved to fix it, in my way? I would have caused some degree of resentment with Esther, no matter how I couched my words in kindness. But the Spirit moves perfectly, every time.

His movements are immeasurably more than anything I could have concocted or ever imagined asking for. But only if we are willing to wait on him, if we want him to lead.

Do you, my friend?

6

WAIT FOR CLARITY

IT HAS BEEN SUCH A JOURNEY FOR ME TO LEARN TO FIRST
see the Holy Spirit in all the details of my life. It took some
time for me to seek him in every situation. The process of
wanting him to take the lead looked something like this: A
situation would arise and I would take the lead, as I have
always been prone to do. The results would range from
sometimes okay, to just so-so, to outright miserable. When
the next situation arose, I would wait for the Spirit to lead,
and the results would always be the best. But then I would
tend to take over again, and the learning process had to
start again.

Finally, I came to see that waiting on the Spirit was always in my best interest, and with this realization, I began
to want him to be in charge. Now I absolutely do not want
Self to be in charge ever again. I have had enough of being
in charge. I want him to take the lead. I am willing to wait
on him because I see him and seek him first in everything.

CHOOSING A NEW DISCIPLE

Jesus wanted us to wait in Jerusalem for a reason. I can see
this now, but then, even hearing those words directly from

Jesus in such a momentous setting, I did not understand. I could not understand. I did not yet have the Spirit. So tired of all the praying and wanting, needing to do something, anything, I somehow conjured up a speech. And what a speech it was.

"With the payment Judas received for his wickedness," I began, "he bought a field; there he fell headlong, his body burst open and all his intestines spilled out. Everyone in Jerusalem heard about this, so they called that field Akeldama, that is, Field of Blood."

I then started quoting our Hebrew Scriptures: "For it is written in the Book of Psalms: 'May his place be deserted; let there be no one to dwell in it.' And, 'May another take his place of leadership.'"

"Therefore," I continued, clearly on a roll, "it is necessary to choose one of the men who have been with us the whole time the Lord Jesus was living among us, beginning from John's baptism to the time when Jesus was taken up from us. For one of these must become a witness with us of his resurrection."

Now all this sounds very spiritual, doesn't it? I was quoting Scripture like a Pharisee. I was taking charge. I was taking the leader's role, planning our next step, but do you see what I was not doing?

I was not waiting, because I did not listen.

There was nothing Spirit-filled about my words. I had no Spirit yet, so how could I be Spirit-filled? That is why Jesus told us—told me—to wait: "Wait on the Holy Spirit."

I want you to notice I was quoting Holy Scripture. I was certainly no Hebrew scholar. I was a fisherman, yet the Psalms came readily to my mind. Perhaps this was Jesus' way of showing me how misguided one can be when operating without the Spirit. Even with the best of intentions, the mistakes that come about when we move ahead of the Spirit can be very problematic.

I would not wait. I wanted to do something, to accomplish something. I quoted Scripture to back me up, and I got my way. I thought it was a good way; I thought it was a good thing to do. But I did not yet have the Spirit, so it was Peter leading the way.

CASTING LOTS

We nominated two men: Joseph called Barsabbas (also known as Justus) and Matthias. Then we prayed, "Lord, you know everyone's heart. Show us which of these two you have chosen to take over this apostolic ministry, which Judas left to go where he belongs." Then we cast lots, and the lot fell to Matthias; so he was added to the 11 apostles.

Now before I go any further, can you see the error of my ways? There it is, right in front of you: we cast lots as if we were living in the days of the Patriarchs, or with the Gentiles, who don't even know God. Instead of waiting on the Holy Spirit, whom Jesus had promised would guide us into all truth, we cast lots. Notice that never again do you see any followers of Jesus casting lots. We no longer need lots—we have the Holy Spirit.

You may be thinking to yourself, "So what? What is the big deal, Peter?"

I will tell you what the big deal is. This little mistake of mine cost my friend Paul dearly over his years out in the Gentile territories. He was obviously the one to fill the 12th spot vacated by Judas. He was clearly Jesus' choice, as was evidenced just a few years later on the road to Damascus.

Since I would not wait for the Spirit's guidance, Paul had to continually defend himself as a true apostle everywhere he went. I have read some of his letters, which, by the way, can be hard to understand, and I wince each time I see him defending his authority as an apostle of Jesus.

Here are just two examples:

In Paul's letter to the church in Corinth, he writes: "Am I not an apostle? Have I not seen Jesus our Lord? Are you not the result of my work in the Lord? Even though I may not be an apostle to others, surely I am to you! For you are the seal of my apostleship in the Lord. This is my defense to those who sit in judgment on me."

He continues: "Don't we have the right to food and drink? Don't we have the right to take a believing wife along with us, as do the other apostles and the Lord's brothers and Cephas?"

You cannot know the anguish with which I read these words. Do you see how he has to defend himself as a true apostle sent by Jesus? Paul did not mention my name by accident; he knew what I had done. And yes, he has forgiven me, as I have asked him to do many times.

Again, in his letter to the churches in the area of Galatia, Paul talks about coming to Jerusalem to see us, the "esteemed leaders."

> Then after fourteen years, I went up again to Jerusalem. I went in response to a revelation and, meeting privately with those esteemed as leaders, I presented to them the gospel that I preach among the Gentiles. I wanted to be sure I was not running and had not been running my race in vain.

> For God, who was at work in Peter as an apostle to the circumcised, was also at work in me as an apostle to the Gentiles. James, Cephas, and John, those esteemed as pillars, gave me and Barnabas the right hand of fellowship when they recognized the grace given to me.

Oh my. Paul is right to single me out. It was, after all, my fault because I would not—back then could not—wait. Here is what I have learned since then about waiting.

WHAT I HAVE LEARNED ABOUT WAITING

The Holy Spirit guides and directs us step by step with positive "yes's" and definite "no's." He even cautions us to slow down at times. When we ignore him and charge ahead, we deserve the mediocre lives we get and the messes we create.

At times, the Holy Spirit advises us to slow down and wait. My guess is, if you are anything like me, you do not like to wait on God. The weight of wait can seem like a heavy burden. It is perhaps the hardest thing for us busy, can-do, "If I don't, it won't" people to do. The complications we usher into our lives by ignoring this Holy Spirit caution can be so messy yet is so easily avoidable.

Instead of always doing, just try waiting.

Think of the collapse that would have been avoided if Adam had said to Eve, "I know the fruit looks delicious, and maybe, as the serpent says, God is deceiving us. But why don't we just wait and ask God? Is there any reason why we cannot just wait before eating this fruit?"

But waiting means I might not get my way. Here is how my mind can work: "It is obvious this person needs my advice." Maybe it is Ruth; maybe it is her sister Esther, or John, or little brother Andrew. (Please do not bring this up to Andrew. He has had enough of big brother's acting before waiting!) My mind says, "I have got to keep everybody straight. If I do not act, this might not go as I am so sure it must, and I might not get my way."

Oh my.

IT IS SAFE TO WAIT

How many decisions have you felt compelled to act on when it would have been so much better if you had just waited a while? How many comments have you made that were so utterly ineffective and unnecessary, and counterproductive—even hurtful and destructive?

Ignoring the rhythm of the Holy Spirit living within you creates complications, hurt feelings, confusion, and suffering. But waiting on the Holy Spirit to guide you will always stimulate a sense of clarity and harmony.

This is not about waiting on the Holy Spirit to do for me; it is about waiting on him to work in me.

When I wait on the Holy Spirit, I always see his best. Waiting on the Spirit's guidance brings me closer to my Lord every time. I see his movement. I see his power at work. None of this is possible when I am acting and reacting in my own power. When I am acting and reacting, all I get to see is me, Self, King Peter, and my power.

Like Andrew, I have seen enough of that.

Jesus reinforced this truth with this observation: "The pagans chase after all these things, and your heavenly

Father knows that you need them. But wait and seek first his kingdom and his righteousness, and all these things will be given to you as well."

Notice Jesus did not say, "The horrible sinners chase and charge ahead after these things." Pagans are those who do not know God, so why would they wait on him? They are scurrying. They are hurrying. They are acting and reacting. They are you and me?

But because I live in a God-saturated world, it is safe to wait. It is safe to wait because I see the Holy Spirit permeating my life. Will you, *can* you, throw off the weight of wait and learn to live freely and lightly, and follow the Holy Spirit within you?

WILLING TO WAIT

When I have waited on God's perfect timing, I have known he was directing me. Then, if I encounter trouble, I am confident I am still in his will, and whatever the trouble is, it is nothing more than a diversion, a temporary obstacle. But when I have not waited, I am unsure of myself: "Did I move too fast? Am I out of God's will? Did I make a bad decision?"

King Saul moved ahead at Gilgal and lost his kingdom. Abraham moved ahead—listening to Sarah and not God to secure a son—and Ishmael was born. The prodigal son wanted his inheritance in advance; he would not wait for it. Even Martha and Mary would have rushed Jesus to save their brother Lazarus—and they would have missed the maximum blessing of seeing their brother raised from the dead.

The Father can seem slow as molasses, but he is always right on time. Wait patiently on him in every circumstance and you will be like David, "a man after God's own heart."

David writes, "Delight yourself in the LORD and he will give you the desires of your heart. Be still before the LORD and wait patiently for him. Be still and know that I am God."

Well-meaning Christians often ask me, "How can I know God's will for me in this decision, this issue in my life? How will I know if it is God speaking to me, or just my own wishes, or even Satan?"

The answer is the same as the answer to the question young people often ask us, "How will I know if he or she is the one to marry?"

"You will just know," that is, if you want to know—if you want to know him and if you are willing to wait.

WHEN WAITING ISN'T AN OPTION

Admittedly, there are times when prolonged waiting is not an option because a deadline is approaching. In these, as in all cases, our Father wants us to seek his will through prayer and his Word, and to seek wise counsel from mature Christians. I have found he can and does speak to me through casual, unrelated comments from others. He has even spoken to me through Gentiles, as he did with Cornelius once. The Spirit has spoken to me in a host of other unexpected ways.

I then make a prudent decision and abandon the outcome to him. I know the outcome is in his hands because I waited. Typically, we really can wait. We just do not want to because we want our way.

I do not like to wait because I suffer the malady of "If I don't, it won't." You see, I want things to go my way. I want things to go the way I think they should. Why? Because I am so smart? No, because I am so selfish. Self tells me not to wait. Self tells me if I wait, things might not go as I think they must.

Wait patiently on the Holy Spirit in every circumstance and you will be amazed at his movements.

If I had only waited a few more days.

7

PENTECOST

DURING THE DAYS AFTER JESUS' FINAL ASCENSION, WE
all went to the temple daily. It seemed like the thing to do.
Jesus had always worshipped at the temple when in Jerusalem. There were about 120 of us, and we needed a larger
space than Mark's mother's big room. Each day, we gathered at Solomon's Colonnade. It was part of the temple
grounds but located on the east side of the outer court of
the temple. I do not think any of us wanted to be a part of
the normal temple worship, not after what "the temple"
had done to Jesus.

It was called Solomon's Porch because that is what it
was—a big open area with a roof over it. We prayed and
sang hymns, and either John or me and, at times, some of
the other disciples, would typically say a few words—
whatever we could remember of Jesus' teachings. We remembered much about our experiences with him, and
some of us, like Matthew, the former tax man, had taken
copious notes. However, former fishermen like John and
me, well, we did the best we could.

JESUS' WORDS DURING OUR FINAL NIGHT

One morning, we got started early. The mist was still covering part of the porch, and there was a chill in the air. Usually, someone in our group would start softly singing a psalm or a hymn of praise, and we would all join in. But today, John said he wanted to talk first. He later told me he felt compelled to talk about Jesus' words to us over dinner the night before he was crucified.

He had listened carefully that last night, and in the days after Jesus' resurrection, he had spent time each day consolidating his notes and recreating Jesus' words. I do not know how he remembered anything; I was too stunned and confused by what Jesus was saying that night. But that would be sweet John for you.

As John began, I closed my eyes and listened, reliving the scene around the table, with all of us together for the last time. The mood was somber. Jesus was tense and not his usual calm, relaxed, and joyful self. John began with Jesus' opening words:

> Now I know you have heard me say, "I am going away and I am coming back to you." If you loved me, you would be glad that I am going to the Father, for the Father is greater than I. I have told you now before it happens, so that when it does happen, you will believe.
>
> Do not let your hearts be troubled. You believe in God; believe also in me. My Father's house has many rooms; if that were not so, would I have told you that I am going there to

prepare a place for you? And if I go and prepare a place for you, I will come back and take you to be with me that you also may be where I am. You know the way to the place where I am going.

I remember thinking, "Do not let your hearts be troubled?" Jesus is talking about leaving us and he says this? That night, none of us knew where he was going, nor did we know any such way. We were dumbfounded.

PROMISING THE HOLY SPIRIT

In the midst of today's cool morning, John continued with Jesus' next words as he promises the Holy Spirit:

> If you love me, keep my commands. And I will ask the Father, and he will give you another advocate to help you and be with you forever—the Spirit of truth. The world cannot accept him because it neither sees him nor knows him. But you know him, for he lives with you and will be in you. I will not leave you as orphans; I will come to you.
>
> "All this I have spoken while still with you," Jesus said as he looked at each of us around the table. "But the Advocate, the Holy Spirit, whom the Father will send in my name, will teach you all things and will remind you of everything I have said to you. Peace I leave with you; my peace I give you. I do not give to you as the world gives. Do not let your hearts be troubled and do not be afraid."

I was so confused and conflicted, trying to figure out what in the world Jesus was talking about. An advocate? This Holy Spirit? In our Hebrew Scriptures, the Holy Spirit was given and then taken back by God to enact his plans. King Saul, for instance, was given the Spirit and then lost the Spirit.

During our years together, Jesus had mentioned the Holy Spirit a few times, but not in an emphatic way. He did not teach specifically on the Holy Spirit, or if he did, I obviously was not paying attention. Even when he did mention it … him … I never once dreamed he would be talking about this Spirit living in me. In me? What would that look like? I was about to ask Jesus to clarify what he meant when he suddenly stood and said, "Come now; let us leave."

And off we went toward the Mount of Olives, one of Jesus' favorite places.

FRUIT THAT WILL LAST

As we walked, with our little group of confused and worried band of brothers huddling behind Jesus, he led us through a vineyard. He stopped and lifted up a vine and turned to us and said,

> I am the true vine, and my Father is the gardener. He lifts up every branch in me that bears no fruit, while every branch that does bear fruit, he prunes so that it will be even more fruitful.
>
> Remain in me, as I also remain in you. No branch can bear fruit by itself; it must remain in the vine. Neither can you bear fruit unless you remain in me. I am the vine; you are the

branches. If you remain in me and I in you, you will bear much fruit; apart from me you can do nothing.

Over the years, I have learned that we remain in Jesus, first and foremost, through the Holy Spirit dwelling in us. I have learned, so often the hard way, I truly can do nothing without the Holy Spirit. Oh, I thought I could do plenty on my own. I built my fishing business on my own, didn't I? I raised a family on my own. Well, Ruth did her part, but I accomplished many things on my own—without anyone's help.

Me. Myself, or so I thought. I did it, often through sheer will and discipline and effort—*my* effort. I thought I was in control; I thought I was responsible for the outcome. What an idiot. As already stated, I have learned I do not now, nor did I ever, control the outcome. I have now learned to abandon the outcome to God.

Even as a seasoned apostle, I sometimes moved ahead of the Holy Spirit and tried to do things on my own. I have even found myself preparing sermons and various talks over the years, only to realize I was doing this on my own. I had not sought the Holy Spirit's guidance and power first—his energy, his clarity, and his creativity.

What a sad commentary. On my own, I can bear no fruit that really matters. I can accomplish many things, but in the long run, do they really matter? Will they accompany me to heaven? Do they have any eternal significance?

All these things I think I have accomplished may be memorable in the moment and seem so important, but looking back over my life, they fade into the shadows of insignificance.

I have learned that anything I do through my own effort will typically bear no long-term fruit—and isn't this what really matters, fruit that will last?

THE ADVOCATE

John continued with Jesus' next words:

> When the Advocate comes, whom I will send to you from the Father—the Spirit of truth who goes out from the Father—he will testify about me. And you also must testify, for you have been with me from the beginning.
>
> I have much more to say to you, more than you can now bear. But when he, the Spirit of truth, comes, he will guide you into all the truth. He will not speak on his own; he will speak only what he hears, and he will tell you what is yet to come. He will glorify me because it is from me that he will receive what he will make known to you.

As John finished, I recalled my thoughts of our last night with Jesus, thoughts about this word Jesus kept repeating: "the Advocate." It made a little sense to me—this Holy Spirit would act as a sort of counselor, sort of like a lawyer and advisor. But I was still confused by the idea of this Spirit, the Spirit of God the Father, being *in* me.

FLICKERS OF FIRE

John concluded his comments, and suddenly the air around me felt heavy. I do not know how to describe it any other way. It was an eerie, other-worldly feeling, strange and frightful. It was very similar to the time we were up on the mountain with Jesus and, in a burst of light, he was transfigured before our very eyes.

On the mountain top that day, God's voice came from the cloud, saying, "This is my Son, whom I have chosen; listen to him." But today this light and this voice came from *within* us. I know now, all these years later, it was the Holy Spirit. I have traveled so long with him and know his voice, but this day was different. It was all so new.

As I was saturated with this light-streaming force within, I became deeply aware of the presence of God. The air felt heavy, as though I was immersed in something like a sea of supernatural power. I could not move. I did not dare move.

Adequate words fail me. A Gentile might have thought it to be a ghost. As with all the times I have seen the Spirit arrive, there was no mistaking the rush of his power and his presence.

In a flash, this presence of power started moving through us, swirling among us like a wind. A strange light flashed around each of us, like little flickers of fire. It was all happening so fast that I could not process anything, but it was real—and it was just as equally surreal. I was not afraid, even though it felt like the earth was shifting beneath me, or, as I would later describe it to new believers, like the earth was shifting *within* me.

I felt a light within me and a sudden overwhelming sense of peace and joy. I was being filled with something, a force, and it was not of this world. I felt something like scales were falling from my eyes. I felt this supernatural presence of energy. I could suddenly see! Like the man Jesus healed who was born blind, "I was blind, but now I could see."

TALKING IN THE SPIRIT

Suddenly, with the Spirit moving, I was talking. All of us were talking, but in different languages. To this day, I could not tell you what language I was speaking. I could hear my voice saying,

> Praise be to Jesus, the master and Lord of the universe! The Son is the image of the invisible God, the firstborn over all creation. For in him all things were created: things in heaven and on earth, visible and invisible, whether thrones or powers or rulers or authorities; all things have been created through him and for him. He is before all things, and in him all things hold together.

Where was this coming from? These were not my words, yet I kept talking.

> And he is the head of the body, the church. He is the beginning and the firstborn from among the dead, so that in everything he might have the supremacy. For God was pleased to have all his fullness dwell in him, and through him to

reconcile to himself all things, whether things on earth or things in heaven, by making peace through his blood, shed on the cross.

For in Christ all the fullness of the Deity lives in bodily form, and in Christ you have been brought to fullness. He is the head over every power and authority.

Friend, there are no human words to describe what was happening inside me. If I had the words, you likely do not have the mind to fully grasp it. The Spirit had arrived, just as Jesus had promised. I never imagined his arrival would be like this, but, then again, how could I have imagined anything about this Spirit until he was in me? How could anyone imagine his overflowing sense of energy, clarity, and creativity?

Paul has a favorite saying, which I repeat often because it captures the sense of the work the Spirit does each time we wait and allow him to lead: "Now to him who is able to do immeasurably more than all we ask or imagine, according to his power that is at work within us, to him be glory in the church and in Christ Jesus throughout all generations, forever and ever! Amen."

8

THE SPIRIT ARRIVES

FOR A CELEBRATION LIKE PENTECOST, JERUSALEM MIGHT swell to as many as 500,000 pilgrims. Now, with this whirlwind of Holy Spirit power encompassing all of Solomon's Porch, many pilgrims came running up to us. They were from all over the diaspora: Parthians, Medes, and Elamites; residents of Mesopotamia, Judea and Cappadocia, Pontus and Asia, Phrygia and Pamphylia, Egypt and the parts of Libya near Cyrene; visitors from Rome (both Jews and converts to Judaism); Cretans; and even Arabs.

I quickly realized they could understand everything we were saying, each in their own native languages. The languages we were all speaking were perfectly designed for our listeners. None of us had ever spoken these languages before, nor have we since. We did not know what we were saying, but the Holy Spirit did.

He planned it all and executed it to perfection. And each ensuing experience with the Spirit has been as moving as this one—in different ways and not always as public as this one.

By this time, my mind was settling down and I could hear the crowds murmuring, saying, "We hear them declaring the wonders of God in our own tongues!" They were amazed and perplexed—who wouldn't be—and they asked one another, "What does this mean?" Some, however, made fun of us and said, "They have had too much wine."

I can understand their reaction. It did feel a little like being drunk, but instead of being filled with wine, we were filled with the Spirit. I had this new sense of clarity. I suddenly knew what to do. I knew what to say to the crowd approaching us.

PREACHING TO THE CROWD

I felt myself walking to the front of the crowd, and without any thought or preparation, I just started preaching:

> Fellow Jews and all of you who live in Jerusalem, let me explain this to you; listen carefully to what I say. We are not drunk, as you suppose. It's only nine in the morning! Don't be ridiculous. No, this is what was spoken by the prophet Joel:
>
> In the last days, God says, "I will pour out my Spirit on all people. Your sons and daughters will prophesy, your young men will see visions, your old men will dream dreams. And everyone who calls on the name of the Lord will be saved."

Here I was quoting the prophet Joel like a priestly scholar! I would ordinarily ask, "Where did that come from?" But I know where it came from: the Holy Spirit. And unlike when I was mistakenly quoting Scripture to convince the 11 we needed to add a 12th disciple to replace Judas, this time the Spirit was providing the Scripture.

On I went, totally immersed in the control and the power of the Spirit. I was in my right mind, completely aware of what was happening, but as with the miracles I would perform many more times in the future, I knew it was not me.

"Fellow Israelites," I continued, "listen to this: Jesus of Nazareth was a man accredited by God to you by miracles, wonders, and signs, which God did among you through him, as you yourselves know."

Many of those in the crowd had witnessed Jesus' miracles. They should have known he was special. I had witnessed even many more miracles, and although I knew he was indeed special, I had previously been as blind as this crowd about just how special and supernaturally unique he was.

Until the Holy Spirit indwelled me.

EYEWITNESSES

As the Spirit swelled within me, I started to drive my point home and let them see how badly they had missed it. Perhaps I was condemning myself for my own part in Jesus' crucifixion. Either way, I continued, my voice rising with passion:

"This man was handed over to you by God's deliberate plan and foreknowledge; and you, with the help of wicked men, put him to death by nailing him to the cross. But God raised him from the dead, freeing him from the agony of death because it was impossible for death to keep its hold on him."

Yes, I know now I was including myself in these accusations. It was my sinful nature—my insistence on being king of my life—that nailed Jesus to that cross. It wasn't so much my actions, although that was certainly part of it, but it was primarily my sinful *heart*. So it was with this crowd, and so it is with you.

You helped nail Jesus to his cross just as surely as this crowd did, just as surely as the Jewish leaders did, just as surely as the Roman guards did. Your self-seeking heart, like mine, pushed Jesus off your throne and onto the cross.

Do you accept *the* truth—the truth about you? Until you do, and therefore fall on your knees and surrender, you are blocking the Holy Spirit from indwelling you. This is difficult to hear, but until we see this truth, we will deny or simply ignore our desperate need for a Savior, and, thus, we will not surrender.

I started quoting King David, again, with no forethought or planning:

> I saw the Lord always before me.
> Because he is at my right hand, I will not be
>   shaken.
> Therefore my heart is glad and my tongue
>   rejoices;
> my body also will rest in hope,
> because you will not abandon me to the realm
>   of the dead,
> you will not let your holy one see decay.

As I concluded this talk, I stated, "God has raised this Jesus to life, and we are all witnesses of it. Exalted to the right hand of God, he has received from the Father the promised Holy Spirit and has poured out what you now see and hear."

Little did I know at the time, but this statement, this fact, would become a central theme in all my future preaching: "God has raised this Jesus to life, and *we are all witnesses of it.*"

Eyewitnesses!

THE ONLY FACT THAT MATTERS

"God has raised this Jesus to life, and we are all witnesses of it." Is this not the only thing, the only *fact* that really matters? Before the Holy Spirit moved within us so mightily, we had seen Jesus dead, and then we had seen him alive. Yes, it was a startling and incredible thing to see. But it took the Holy Spirit to bring it into perfect clarity. No longer was our trust just in what we believed about Jesus, but now our trust was in what we had seen with our own eyes.

We had seen Jesus dead and then seen him alive. We would never be able to deny this. What we saw with our eyes ignited the Holy Spirit's power within us. The Spirit was still leading me, so I continued,

> Fellow Israelites, I can tell you confidently that the patriarch David died and was buried, and his tomb is here to this day. We can all go look at his tomb. And if by some means we could see inside, we would see his decayed body.
>
> But I can tell you with all confidence, so much confidence I will wager my own body on the cross over this truth: You will not find Jesus'

body in any tomb. It's not there because he has
risen!

The fact of the empty tomb became our theme: He has
risen! When our feelings threatened to overwhelm us, and
our faith became shaky, we returned to this simple but
powerful fact: there was no body in his tomb. He rose from
death. We saw him dead; we saw him alive.

FACTS OVER FEELINGS

Have you built your foundation of faith on this fact? When
this world feels out of control and the Father feels so distant
and it seems he has forgotten about you, can you return to
the rock-solid foundation of this fact? You see, feelings are
okay as servants, but they are terrible masters.[1] Feelings
will cause your faith to waver. When this happens, return
to the facts: Jesus is perfectly powerful, he loves you perfectly, and he is perfectly present in all the details of your
life.

Jesus died for your sins, but he rose to a new life to
prove to you the Father loves you perfectly and to show he
is all-powerful and in perfect control—even over death.
Nothing, not one thing, can happen to you apart from his
perfect will.

My dear friend John often begins his teaching by emphasizing our eyewitness:

> That which was from the beginning, which we
> have heard, which we have seen with our eyes,
> which we have looked at and our hands have
> touched—this we proclaim concerning the
> Word of life. The life appeared; we have seen it

and testify to it, and we proclaim to you the eternal life, which was with the Father and has appeared to us. We proclaim to you what we have seen and heard, so that you also may have fellowship with us. And our fellowship is with the Father and with his Son, Jesus Christ.

The Word became flesh and made his dwelling among us. We have seen his glory, the glory of the one and only Son, who came from the Father, full of grace and truth.

We have indeed seen; we have indeed heard; we have indeed touched.

Remember, facts first, faith based on these facts, and feelings a distant third.

As I mentioned earlier, I recently wrote my second letter to the family of believers. I began this second letter, "We did not follow cleverly devised stories when we told you about the coming of our Lord Jesus Christ in power, but we were eyewitnesses of his majesty."

We did not make this up. Why would we? Some of us have been killed because we declare these things. We are simply stating the facts.

CUT TO THE HEART

I concluded my talk this Pentecost morning with my voice rising, "God has raised this Jesus to life, and we are all witnesses of it. Therefore, let all Israel be assured of this: God has made this Jesus, whom you crucified, both Lord and Messiah."

In all my years since, with all the conversions I have witnessed, this moment was the pinnacle of them all. The Spirit was moving with such overwhelming power. The hearts of the men and women in the crowd were pierced, "cut to the heart," they said. They all—yes, all—cried out, "Brothers, what shall we do?"

I looked over the crowd. These men and women were indeed cut to the heart with conviction. Their faces betrayed a desperate need to be saved from their guilt, so I softened and lowered my voice and replied, "Repent and be baptized, every one of you, in the name of Jesus Christ for the forgiveness of your sins. And you will receive the gift of the Holy Spirit."

Now here is the amazing thing: we baptized over three thousand men and women that day. Three thousand! What a day. Jesus had told us this Holy Spirit would be powerful, and he had promised us he would come, and come soon. And here he was, immeasurably more than anything we could have imagined.

SPEAKING ONLY FROM THE HOLY SPIRIT

As the crowd segregated into smaller groups, and the other disciples broke off and tended to each of the groups, I sat down, leaning against one of the columns supporting Solomon's Porch. I was exhausted, my shirt soaked through with sweat. My head was spinning. I was spent, yet oddly energized, as I pondered the events of this morning.

John soon walked over to me with a big grin on his face. "Preacher Peter!" he exclaimed. "Where did that come from? I've never heard you talk like that before. You were truly amazing, my friend."

I looked at my friend and simply said, "You know where it came from. It came from the same place, I mean the same power that was moving through you when you were speaking, what was it, Egyptian? It came from the Holy Spirit Jesus promised us."

John could not get the grin off his face as he wondered aloud, "Egyptian, huh? Who would have ever seen this coming? I was totally transfixed, Simon. The words were coming out of my mouth, but I had no control over them, nor did I have any idea what was coming next."

"I know you did not understand the language you were speaking, but did you understand what you were saying?" I asked him.

He pondered this, deep in thought, and then he said, "I think we were all saying the same thing, don't you? I think we were praising God the Father and Jesus. I think I was saying something like,

> Praise be to Jesus, the master and Lord of the universe! The Son is the image of the invisible God, the firstborn over all creation. For in him all things were created: things in heaven and on earth, visible and invisible, whether thrones or powers or rulers or authorities; all things have been created through him and for him.

"Me too!" I interrupted. "How could we have all been saying the same thing? How could we have even known what to say?"

John grinned and said, "Oh you of little faith." Then he quoted precisely what Jesus had said his last night with us: "When the Advocate comes, whom I will send to you from the Father—the Spirit of truth who goes out from the Father—he will testify about me. And you also must testify, for you have been with me from the beginning."

John was enjoying himself as he smiled and continued quoting Jesus: "When he, the Spirit of truth, comes, he will guide you into all the truth. He will not speak on his own; he will speak only what he hears, and he will tell you what is yet to come. He will glorify me because it is from me that he will receive what he will make known to you."

Born Again Through the Holy Spirit

An idea began to form in my mind, a connection between Jesus' words about the Holy Spirit and his words to Nicodemus, "You must be born again."

I asked John, "Brother, do you feel like a different person now than when you woke up this morning?"

John looked at me quizzically.

I went on. "Do you feel like a *new* person?"

John interrupted me, his eyes suddenly bright with energy and clarity, and exclaimed, "Like I have been born again? I see where you're going with this, Simon, and yes, I agree completely. With this Holy Spirit inside me, I absolutely feel like a new man, a totally different man. I feel like a child beginning a new life—born again into the Light!"

---

[1] Statement attributed to Dallas Willard.

9

CHANGED AND GRATEFUL

MAY I TAKE A MOMENT LONGER AND TRY TO PAINT A picture of what this new life, this transformed life, looks like? I quote my brother Paul again because I know his words are inspired by the Holy Spirit: "Do not conform any longer to the pattern of this world but be transformed by the renewing of your mind."

The Holy Spirit is saying through Paul that when we stop conforming to the pattern of this world, renewing our minds by changing our way of thinking, we will be transformed by him. We must learn to rethink the way we have been thinking. We are new creations, so let's think that way.

Remember, change is something we can do—as we rethink the way we have been thinking—transformation is what the Holy Spirit does in us.

"The pattern of this world" is like the Jordan River after a big rain: a rapid whitewater current sweeping through our lives. There can be no treading water in our culture. This world and its ways will pull you downriver from the life Jesus has for you and often drown you in an inescapable death.

I am not exaggerating. To think we can casually (lazily) float along in our culture, as decadent as it is, is the epitome of delusion. No! We must rethink the way we have been thinking. We must stop feeling our way through life and start thinking our way through life.[1]

A transformed person sees a God-saturated world all around. Worship and prayer become as natural as breathing, and life becomes a natural conversation with God the Father, and Jesus our Lord, as we talk intimately and constantly. All of this is joined together through the Holy Spirit within us.

"The pattern of this world" rolls out a steady and unending drumbeat of what you can buy and what you can do and where you can go to be happy. We are all subject to these illusions in one way or another. Even though we would all say money cannot buy joy, we end up trying to rent happiness.

King David wrote in one of his psalms, "Delight yourself in the LORD and he will give you the desires of your heart." To delight ourselves in the LORD will require a new way of thinking—a new focus, a focus on God the Father and Jesus our Savior, not on this world.

Brother John likes to say,

> Do not love the world or anything in the world. If anyone loves the world, love for the Father is not in them. For everything in the world—the lust of the flesh, the lust of the eyes, and the pride of life—comes not from the Father but from the world. The world and its desires pass away, but whoever does the will of God lives forever.

Amen to that.

THE DESIRES OF YOUR HEART

Have you thought about the true desires of your heart? David's psalm is one of my favorites: "Delight yourself in the LORD and he will give you the desires of your heart."

If I asked you to write down the desires of your heart, it would not take long for you to do so, would it? Most of your list would be good things, I hope. But would they be the best things?

Before I met Jesus, a successful business would have topped my list. I would have defined success as better and bigger than my competitors, and more money than I needed. Next on the list would have been a happy and healthy wife and family, although if I were completely honest, to be liked, admired, and respected would have likely ranked above them. Somewhere on the list, I would have added something about God, although that would have been simply because one should have God in their priorities, right?

A transformed person realizes he or she does not really know the true desires of their own heart. But they know Jesus knows, and they are sure he knows exactly what "Life to the Full" would look like, specifically and individually, for them.

And he does for you too.

Imagine this full life: the "desires of your heart" life. Isn't this what you have been searching for? A transformed person knows where to find this life primarily because they realize they do not have a clue what their true desires are. They thought they knew, but now they can see their puny desires will always pale in comparison to the immeasurably greater desires the Holy Spirit has for them.

"Delight yourself in the LORD and he will give you the desires of your heart." A transformed person has taken their eyes off the world's offerings and illusions and has fixed them on Jesus, the author and perfecter of our faith. They are rethinking the way they have been thinking and refusing to conform to the empty illusions of this world.

As the true desires of my heart have unfolded, I have been so surprised. I did not know, I could never have predicted, and certainly would never have had the imagination to ask God for the life he has since lavished on me. Even the painful events he has allowed have ultimately been lavish blessings. (I will tell you more about that later — if this old man does not forget!)

Now I know beyond any doubt that Jesus' life to the full is "immeasurably more than all I could ask or imagine asking." I have stopped trying to delight myself in Self and have learned to delight myself in the Lord.

If you asked me to give a description of a Christian — a true born-again follower of Christ, not a person who just attends our Christian gatherings — what would I say? I think I can capture the essence of a true born-again Christian in two words: changed and grateful.

CHANGED

I purposely did not describe a Christian as holy, righteous, loving, caring, peaceful, generous, or even humble. A true disciple of Christ will bear these fruits more and more over time, but the more telling description is that something changed in them. He or she may still be nervous, irritable, a tightwad or whatever, but they are becoming less of these.

They will be changing and transforming with more love, joy, peace, and patience over time.

To be clear, we are not talking about the kind of change that just happens as we get older: "I do not cuss as much, drink as much, or fly off the handle as much." Or, "I am getting too old to lust." Nor are we talking about getting more involved in Christian activities because it feels warm and fuzzy to have our family at our Lord's Supper evenings together.

I am talking about a real heart change: a heart shift. You and I know the difference. If you are thinking, "I have not experienced this," then you most likely have not had this real heart shift.

You are not yet born again.

GRATEFUL

The other characteristic of a born-again Christian is gratitude—real, heartfelt gratitude that pervades your day-to-day routines. This idea of gratitude reminds me of Brother Matthew, our former tax collector. Matthew has a ceaseless joy over being rescued from the trash heap of life—and hell. He is filled to the point of overflowing with gratitude. He was a hated tax collector, but now he is a saved saint.

Has anyone saved your life at the cost of their own? Have you been rescued from sure death? Do you feel as though Jesus has rescued you? Sure, we can learn from Jesus. We can study his teachings and seek to emulate him, but is he your hero? As Matthew likes to say, "Has he redeemed and salvaged your wreck of a life as he did mine?"

Perhaps I should ask the more telling question: Do you even think you need rescuing? Perhaps you think all you need is just a little polishing up. As flawed as I am, one thing I do know is Jesus took my sins upon himself. He purposely took on the Sanhedrin and the Romans, and the horror of the cross, and died so I could live his life. He marched right up to the cross, took my beating, and took my blame, my sin on himself. I am still, all these years later, so grateful.

Has this realization changed you? Do you move through life with a pervasive sense of joyful gratitude? A heart pervaded with gratitude will change your life—and the lives of those around you—especially your family and loved ones.

One friend put it this way: "If a fellow isn't thankful for what he's got, he isn't likely to be thankful for what he's going to get."[2]

Please understand I am not asking you to overlook your very real problems; I am asking you to look over them to Jesus and the peace and joy only he can deliver. I am asking you to fix your eyes not on what is seen but on what is unseen because what is seen is only temporary, but what is unseen is eternal.

Two Displays of Gratitude

I begin each day saying, "Thank you, thank you, thank you, Jesus." Gratitude has changed my life and was significant to Jesus as well. I remember so well two displays of gratitude, or the lack thereof.

PERFUME OF GRATEFULNESS

The first story is about Simon, a Pharisee, who invited Jesus to have dinner with him. While at Simon's house, a woman in that town who had lived a sinful life came in with an alabaster jar of perfume. As she stood behind Jesus, at his feet weeping, she began to wet his feet with her tears. Then she wiped them with her hair, kissed them, and poured perfume on them.

We knew this woman, or I should say we knew about her. She had been forced into making bad choices in her life. Her sins were many and easy for all to see. Looking back, I can see so clearly I had likely out-sinned her in my own life, even though it would not have looked that way to others. My former life was filled with pride and selfishness, a judgmental heart, and greed. These were likely worse sins in the eyes of my Master than anything this sinful woman ever did.

Simon the Pharisee, being one of those religious do-gooders I talked about earlier, the kind who would turn up his nose at the thought of being born again, watched with indignation as this poor woman knelt and wept at Jesus' feet. He finally said to himself, "If this man were a prophet, he would know who is touching him and what kind of woman she is—that she is a sinner."

No doubt Simon was certain he was not a sinner. Simon did not yet know what we had all learned the hard way: Jesus always knew what we were thinking.

So Jesus told Simon a story: "Two people owed money to a certain moneylender. One owed him 500 denarii, and the other 50. Neither of them had the money to pay him back, so he forgave the debts of both. Now which of them will love him more?"

Simon, in all his pride, did not yet see that Jesus was contrasting him with this sinful woman. He replied, "I suppose the one who had the bigger debt forgiven."

"You have judged correctly," Jesus said.

Simon could not help but smile. He liked to be right.

Then Jesus turned toward the woman, looking at her softly and lovingly, and said to Simon, "Do you see this woman? I came into your house. You did not give me any water for my feet, but she wet my feet with her tears and wiped them with her hair. You did not give me the customary kiss of greeting, but this woman, from the time I entered, has not stopped kissing my feet. You did not put the customary oil on my head, but she has poured perfume on my feet."

Jesus then turned from the woman, and his eyes bore down on Simon. "Therefore, I tell you, her many sins have been forgiven—as her great love has shown. But whoever has been forgiven little, loves little."

Simon was one of those religiously good people who did not think he had much, if any, sin to be forgiven, so he had little gratitude in his heart. He had earned his status. He might admit he was not perfect, but in his heart, he knew God was a lot happier with him than with this woman—or perhaps even this itinerant rabbi.

This woman, however, knew her sin and was overwhelmed with gratitude for being forgiven. She knew she needed to be saved. I hope you can see she fit the description of Jesus' words in his talk on the mount, "Blessed are the poor in spirit, for theirs is the kingdom of heaven."

She knew she was spiritually bankrupt before Jesus saved her. She knew she was in desperate need of a Savior. And she had one—Jesus.

I never encountered again Simon after that day. I hope he opened his heart to the Holy Spirit at some point because if not, he was going straight to hell. Forgive me for my bluntness.

THE GRATEFUL LEPER

The second story about gratitude is about Jesus healing 10 lepers. We were on our way to Jerusalem, traveling along the border between Samaria and Galilee. None of the disciples liked to be anywhere near Samaria because the Samaritans hated us, and we hated them. But Jesus seemed to enjoy our discomfort and often walked through Samaria, or near the borders. Perhaps he was teaching us "little faiths" something about who should be our neighbor.

As we were going into a certain village, the heat was oppressive and the air was still. I was dirty, smelly, tired, and grumpy, and I was in no mood for any interruptions. But ahead we could see 10 men who had leprosy waiting to meet Jesus. I could see them helping each other up as we approached. They were a pitiful sight. They stood anxiously at a distance and called out in a loud voice, "Jesus, Master, have pity on us!"

I had cried out to God many times before I knew Jesus, but not viscerally like the lepers. I would say something like, "Please, God, save me from this mess! If you get me out of this, if you fix this, I swear I will never do it again. I will go to synagogue like a good Jewish boy every week, and I will be better and do better." The promises would go on and on. I imagine you can relate to this kind of praying.

That particular hot, dusty day, I was secretly hoping Jesus would walk on by. He could smile at them and perhaps give them a blessing of some sort, but please don't stop. It's hot. I'm tired. I'm hungry and thirsty and I do not want to be interrupted today. But Jesus understood that ministry so often takes place in the interruptions.

Now surely you know how scary, and to be frank, how downright disgusting lepers are. Everyone was horrified of getting near a leper—everyone except Jesus. He walked right over to them, smiling that disarming smile of his, and said, "Go, show yourselves to the priests." And as they went, they were cleansed.

Nine of the 10 never returned to thank Jesus. But one did, and he was a Samaritan. Overwhelmed with gratitude for being healed, he threw himself at Jesus' feet and thanked him repeatedly. Jesus knelt and gently patted the man on his shoulders. The other nine, who were all Jews, never bothered to thank him.

Jesus noticed their lack of gratitude. He turned to the crowd following him and exclaimed, "Were not all 10 cleansed? Where are the other nine? Has no one returned to give praise to God except this foreigner?" Then he said to the man at his feet, "Rise and go; your faith has made you well." Please understand Jesus notices your gratitude, or lack thereof.

What I see in someone who has been born again is a softening heart and a grateful heart. How could I, Peter, not have both? I was plucked from a prison of certain doom. I was going to hell and did not even know it. I was rescued from the prison of Self. In fact, I am at times overwhelmed with gratitude, to the point of breaking out in praise and thanksgiving, even while doing some mundane task. I was blind and lost, but I can see and I am found.

LAVISH RICHES

We simply do not have the imagination to ask for the incredible blessings our heavenly Father wants to give us through his Spirit. As I have reflected on Jesus' parables, he so often used images of feasts, banquets, and celebrations—massive celebrations. I have come to the conclusion that we do not expect too much of God—we expect too little.

The promises of God are always about riches, true riches, which are found within. God the Father wants to lavish us with his gifts; he wants to pour out his blessings of love, joy, peace, and patience. We simply expect too little and ask and seek with the pinhole perspective of a simpleton: "Just feed me and take care of me, and please do not let me feel any discomfort."

God the Father is all about "lavish" blessings. He is not a bread and water God. He is a God of feasts. John likes to say, "How great is the love the Father has lavished on us, that we should be called children of God. And that is what we are."

Paul often said, "In him we have redemption through his blood, the forgiveness of sins, in accordance with the riches of God's grace he lavished on us."

The riches of the Spirit and his power are immeasurably, abundantly more than all we can imagine. Show me a man or woman full of gratitude and I will show you someone full of joy. Are you, my friend? If you are not, you are either an ingrate, a self-absorbed fool, or simply not born again. Again, forgive my bluntness.

---

[1] Statement attributed to Det Bowers.

[2] Quote attributed to Frank A. Clark.

10

A MEAL WITH MATTHEW

THEY DEVOTED THEMSELVES TO THE APOSTLES' teaching and to fellowship, to the breaking of bread and to prayer. Everyone was filled with awe at the many wonders and signs performed by the apostles. All the believers were together and had everything in common.

They sold property and possessions to give to anyone who had need. Every day they continued to meet together in the temple courts. They broke bread in their homes and ate together with glad and sincere hearts, praising God and enjoying the favor of all the people.

And the Lord added to their number daily those who were being saved.

This is how Doctor Luke describes our life together in the days and weeks following Pentecost. He was not yet with us back then, but he got this from interviewing all of us. I must say his description is accurate.

After Pentecost, we now had over 3,000 believers. Many of the pilgrims who had traveled to Jerusalem for the feast of Pentecost decided to stay. Can you blame them? For the first time in their lives, they were living—really living! The Holy Spirit was opening their eyes to a whole new world of joy, clarity, and positive energy.

And they did not want to lose this new life.

I remember thinking to myself, *Okay, what now, Lord? What in the world are we going to do with all these new believers?* The Twelve, as we were now being called, met together at John Mark's home to talk about our new challenge. We shared some bread and stew one of the ladies had cooked earlier that day. Someone in our new family was always cooking, and I loved that. The bread was so fresh, and the aroma of the stew made for a relaxed yet purposeful atmosphere.

I started the discussion (no surprise) by saying, "Brothers, the Lord has blessed us with this new family of believers, and he has given us this new power through the Holy Spirit. But I must tell you, I do not know what we are to do next—or how."

Matthew, who was always a most thoughtful man, said, "Well, I do not know what to do, either. But I think I know what *not* to do."

Thomas interrupted Matthew, nodding his head in agreement. "I agree, tax man."

Matthew once hated being called tax man because it reminded him of his old life. But over our time together with Jesus, he could see our tone changing from suspicion to love and affection, and his nickname became a term of endearment. I think it reminded him of what Jesus had done for him and in him. "A wretch saved by grace!" he exclaimed at every opportunity.

Thomas said, "Whatever we do, let's not copy the rule-keeping religious formality that had blinded us so badly before we met Jesus. Let's just emulate Jesus and his way of doing things: personal, relational, relaxed. My religion used to be just a checklist religion. I felt good if I could check off that I had been to synagogue, helped a widow out, or helped around the community."

"Or I felt bad when I broke a religious rule, which seemed to be often," Matthias groaned, shaking his head.

I could sense the new clarity the Spirit was starting to give us when Matthew jumped back in and said, "Yes! One of the reasons I became a tax collector, apart from my own greed and dark heart, was because I just could not connect with the religion of the temple. It seemed so dead, so full of rituals. All those sacrifices and all that rule-keeping just deadened my heart toward God."

He was shaking his head, but then his face brightened as he looked around at all of us, saying, "But when Jesus showed up that day and told me I was to follow him, I could immediately sense something was different about this man. And whatever it was, I wanted it."

MATTHEW'S LUNCHEON

All of us were smiling at the memory of that day. We had arrived back in Capernaum, having just returned from our harrowing experience with the demon-possessed man across the lake in the region of Gerasenes. This was the crazed man who was chained and living among the tombs. Jesus drove a legion of demons from him and into the pigs grazing nearby, and the pigs all ran off the cliff into the water.

That was a harrowing experience. We were exhausted and ready for a rest, but Jesus stopped and engaged Levi, the tax collector. I was not happy and not in the mood to be interrupted by a hated tax collector. But as I said before, the Master understood that ministry so often occurs in the interruptions.

We could not believe Jesus was even talking to this despised traitor—a tax collector for the hated Romans—and we were even more shocked when Jesus said, "And by the way, Matthew, we are going to your house. We are all hungry and you are rich, so have your servants prepare a meal for us."

Well, you could have knocked us over with a feather—even more so Matthew. His eyes were as big as saucers, but he quickly collected himself and stammered incredulously, "Master, if you are coming to my house, may I invite some of my friends?"

Jesus nodded, smiling that huge smile of his. We were all tired and hot, and this was a little too much for me, so I said, "Jesus, are you sure this is a good idea? What will people think?" Remember, I considered myself Jesus' advisor back then.

He just looked at me, but instead of condemnation or even disappointment, I could see the mischief in his eye. He said, "Oh you of little faith."

And with that, I turned to John and the others, shrugged my shoulders as if to say, "Well, I tried," and off we went.

By the time the meal was ready, Matthew had about a dozen of his friends gathered around his huge table. These were mostly other tax collectors, but some were just rich, greedy businessmen whom everyone knew cheated people. One thing they all had in common: not one ever darkened the doors of the temple or a neighborhood synagogue. Religion and God were dead to them.

The Pharisees labeled these men "sinners," so when a few Pharisees saw us marching off to Matthew's house, they followed us. This was nothing new, for they followed Jesus often—some out of fascination, trying to figure this new rabbi out; others out of hatred and jealousy, hoping to catch Jesus in a misstep with Rome or some temple heresy.

During the meal, Jesus was having a raucous conversation with Matthew and his friends. He was engaging them with questions and responding to their various questions and comments. They, in turn, were totally connecting with him. I could see from their expressions they liked this rabbi, Jesus, and wanted to hear what he had to say.

This was Jesus' style, you know. Everyone who met him liked him. Everyone, that is, except the religious men. If you had an agenda when you encountered Jesus, you often left angry or hurt, and almost always disappointed. But if you were open to what he had to say, with no hidden agenda, you left with a big smile and a new, fresh outlook about God the Father, and often about life.

HYPOCRITES

The mood around the table was positive, and the energy was palpable. The "sinners" would say something like, "But what about all your religious hypocrites? Why would anyone want to be like them?" To which Jesus would reply, "I am with you. I do not like hypocrites either. Not one bit. But you know what the funny thing about hypocrites is?"

They shook their heads, looking at Jesus expectantly.

"Everyone is one at one time or another, and yet no one thinks they are," Jesus continued. "Why do you look at the speck of sawdust in your brother's eye and pay no attention to the plank in your own eye?"

The men sat in silence, not sure what Jesus would say next.

"How can you say to your brother, 'Let me take the speck out of your eye,' when all the time there is a plank in your own eye? You hypocrite, first take the plank out of your own eye, and then you will see clearly to remove the speck from your brother's eye."

I thought for sure this would offend them, but instead of being offended, one of the tax collectors leaned toward Jesus and said, "This does not feel like a religious session; this feels more like just an honest discussion. I like this! I do not like organized religion at all, but I am a very spiritual man."

I do not recall exactly how Jesus answered this man, but it was something like this: "I do not like that kind of organized religion either, my friend, but are you sure you are not just using that as an excuse to avoid God altogether? When you say you are a very spiritual man, to whom is your spirit talking?"

These men loved this kind of blunt honesty from Jesus—no pretending, just transparent truth.

CALLING THE SINNERS

As their conversation continued, it was clear to these "sinners" that Jesus had no interest in perpetuating meaningless or ego-driven organized religion. There is no more secure hiding place from God, from ourselves, or from the world around us than within the religious structure. Everything Jesus taught and said called his listeners out from behind its walls.

The 12 of us had stepped away from the table after the meal, partly to give the men more access to Jesus and partly because we were uncomfortable being seen with them. Remember, at this point, we were almost as blind as they were; we just did not know it.

But these sinners had no illusions as to their righteousness, or lack thereof, which gave them a distinct advantage over us—and certainly over the Pharisees and all the other religious do-gooders. These men knew they were outcasts in the eyes of the people, and certainly with God. Yet most of us just assumed we were right with God. We were Jews, his chosen people; we were right with God.

The Pharisees were absolutely convinced they were. Speaking of whom, a few were now approaching us with scowls on their faces. They asked us, "Why does your teacher eat with tax collectors and sinners?"

Jesus, who always seemed to hear everything, said, "It is not the healthy who need a doctor, but the sick. But go and learn what this means: 'I desire mercy, not sacrifice.' For I have not come to call the righteous, but sinners."

I could describe to you the angry look on the faces of the Pharisees, but what was so much more interesting was the look of the men around the table. They had just heard Jesus call them "the sick" and "sinners." There was a sudden silence around the table as their smiles faded and a look of consternation spread across their faces.

GRACE AND TRUTH

I wondered what would happen next. Had Jesus gone too far? They looked insulted and deflated, and they began to murmur.

Matthew then spoke up, "Rabbi, are you calling us sick and sinners?"

As soon as Matthew asked his question, he knew the answer—Jesus was. How could it be otherwise? Every one of us is sick. Every one of us is a sinner. And yet here Jesus was, so clearly loving Matthew and his friends in the midst of their sickness and immersion in their sin.

Since then, Matthew has imitated Jesus several times, imagining what Jesus must have been thinking when he asked him, "Rabbi, are you calling us sick and sinners?" With that contagious grin of his, Matthew would answer as Jesus did: "I am, Matthew. You are, aren't you?"

Matthew would continue impersonating Jesus, and Jesus would often laugh as he did. "Look at yourselves: you're tax collectors and dishonest businessmen, but understand I am not condemning you. In fact, I like you—all of you. But let's face the facts." Still imitating Jesus, Matthew would then turn his smile to us, the other 11, and say, "And so are they. They're sinners just like you!"

As we sat around the table that day, there was a moment of uncomfortable silence, but then Matthew smiled and started laughing. One by one, each of the men started to laugh, and so did we. Ours was a nervous laughter, but theirs was a belly laugh.

"It's true," one of them bellowed. "We are sinners. I am, that is for sure, and for the first time in my life, I don't mind admitting it. Yes, I'm sick, but I believe this man can make me right."

Another man joined in, "Me too! Come on, friends, let's face it, we are all sick sinners. But this man Jesus does not make me feel bad, rejected, or like a failure. In fact, I do believe he likes us. He is definitely convicting us with truth, but I feel nothing but grace from him—and no condemnation."

This was the essence of Jesus—full of grace and truth.

Can you imagine this scene? A bunch of grown men, dressed in their finest clothes, proud, rich, and accomplished, suddenly giggling, each looking intently at Jesus, some even crying? All the while, I watched this play out, wondering, "Who is this Jesus, that even the hated tax collectors feel comfortable around him?"

A New Beginning

Thinking back to that day, we were all smiling. Thomas then brought us back to the present by repeating his earlier comment: "Whatever we do, let's not copy the strict religious formality that had so blinded us before we met Jesus. Let's just emulate Jesus and his way of doing things."

John said, "Yes, I see what you mean, Thomas. Let's emulate Jesus and how he lived and taught each day he was with us. He was calm and relaxed—full of grace and full of truth. Let's just start meeting together and sharing meals together. Let's invite anyone and everyone to join us, regardless of their background."

I was now starting to see with the clarity the Holy Spirit always brings, and his energy was gaining momentum in all of us. "Okay," I said, "let's start telling everyone that we are gathering together tomorrow morning at Solomon's Porch. We will then figure out who has homes and meeting places and all those other details."

Thomas jumped in, "I'm sure Mark's mother will offer this big room upstairs for meals and gatherings. And at least a few more of our new converts have suitable homes. But what about food, and what will we talk about?"

I responded, "The food will come, Thomas, as will the teaching. Jesus promised us this when he said, 'But when the Spirit of truth comes, he will guide you into all the truth. He will glorify me because it is from me that he will receive what he will make known to you.'"

I continued, "Let's just start meeting together and let the Holy Spirit guide us. We will talk about Jesus, testifying to all that he said and did. This is what he told us to do on his last night with us: 'When the Advocate comes, whom I will send to you from the Father—the Spirit of truth who goes out from the Father—he will testify about me. And you also must testify, for you have been with me from the beginning.'"

John smiled and nodded.

ORGANIC, NOT AN ORGANIZATION

And that is what we did. You see, we did not know exactly what to do; we just knew what *not* to do: not to be formal, not to be rigid, not to lord it over our new brothers and sisters. No hierarchies. No memberships. No programs. No fixed rules.

We were not going to be about rituals but about relationships. We wanted to be organic, not an organization. We wanted a priesthood of *all* believers. After all, this is how Jesus was with us. Rituals can dull us, but relationships drive us. Jesus was always about relationships over rules.

No one would be in charge, lording it over the others. The Holy Spirit is the only one with the authority to be in charge. We would have no memberships; this was to be a family, not a club. Having members and memberships would only serve to make some feel in and some feel out. Those who feel *in* may develop a false sense of security in their salvation, and those who feel *out* may feel like they are less important.

None of that.

Our plan was to gather together as a family and learn to experience Jesus together, and to learn to experience this new Holy Spirit presence and power within each of us. The Holy Scriptures, as well as Jesus' words, would serve to guide us. As the Psalmist said, "Your word is a lamp for my feet, a light on my path."

That night, I laid on my bedroll thinking about what this new gathering of believers was going to look like. How many people would join us? Would anyone even show up? Would we be successful? Then I caught myself, realizing I was venturing back toward the kingdom of Peter, worrying about numbers and success.

I just relaxed and said, "Holy Spirit, you are going to have to help us. We do not know what to do or say. You are the teacher. You have the wisdom. We ... I ... am so unworthy and so flawed. Give us the words to say. Show us what to do and we will do it."

I felt a sense of comfort and could sense Jesus' presence. Suddenly, peace washed over me, and I knew we would be alright tomorrow morning. I did not know the what; I just knew the why—we wanted everyone to know Jesus. We wanted them to know what a great friend he can be. We wanted them to know the peace and power that comes from knowing him personally and intimately. We wanted them to know him as their Savior.

That is all I needed to know. The Holy Spirit knew the rest. I closed my eyes, picturing Jesus' smile and his warm, joyful, and accepting heart, just like he was with Matthew and his sinner friends. I knew this was how we wanted to be as well.

11

A New Family:
A Community of the
Redeemed

THE NEXT MORNING, WE GATHERED AT SOLOMON'S
Porch. The sun was not yet up, so it was still cool, with a
mist floating in the air, causing fog to dim our view of the
surrounding temple grounds. The 12 of us and the larger
group of 120 had arrived early to start praying. No one else
was there yet, and as I knelt to pray, my old Self whispered
a warning that no one else would be showing up.

Satan whispered that we were fools—incompetent and
incapable. Who did we think we were, representing Jesus?
Satan attempted to distract and discourage us, but I told
him to flee as I turned to the Holy Spirit, and he calmed my
fears.

You can do this too, you know. You can tell Satan to go
away, to get out of your face. Do not allow him to discourage you. Be alert and of sober mind. Your enemy the devil
prowls around like a roaring lion looking for someone to
devour. Resist him, standing firm in the faith, because you

know that the family of believers throughout the world is undergoing the same kind of sufferings.

The sun was slowly starting to break through the mist while we were praying. I looked up and my heart filled with joy—hundreds of men and women were gathering around us. All those we had seen on Pentecost were arriving. Everyone was smiling. We started hugging the new arrivals, and everyone started hugging everyone else. Someone started singing, and soon we all joined in. I had my arm around a Greek Jew from Alexandria, and he had his arm around one of Matthew's tax collector friends. John was hugging an entire family of Parthians. Smiles were everywhere. Joy was as pervasive as the morning mist.

What a sight—a new family joined together not by blood relations but by the blood of our Master, Jesus. This family would reflect the love, joy, and unity Jesus had always possessed with the Father and with the Holy Spirit. This family was not of official membership but of Brothers and Sisters.

This is what Jesus wanted. This is what the Father had planned all along. This is what the Holy Spirit was bringing together—a family that "sold property and possessions to give to anyone who had need. Every day they continued to meet together in the temple courts. They broke bread in their homes and ate together with glad and sincere hearts, praising God and enjoying the favor of all the people."

None of this was because anyone felt they had to or because they wanted to gain favor with man or God. No, this was love and joy and peace overflowing from the hearts of these new believers, hearts filled to all the measure of the fullness of God.

WELCOMING THE NEW FAMILY

In that moment, the Spirit told me what to say—or, more accurately, the Spirit *moved* me to speak. The Spirit has rarely dictated to me what to say, at least not in advance. He does not seem to work that way.

The Spirit guides me, filling me with words as I speak—my words, my voice, but his heart. Suddenly, I knew what to talk about: our new family. I wanted them to experience the family Jesus had created among the Twelve. I wanted them to know Jesus like we knew him. I wanted them to understand with their hearts as well as their minds who he was, what he cared about, and how he did things.[1]

I called out to everyone, and a hush fell over the crowd. "Brothers, sisters, welcome to the family of God. This is the day the LORD has made; let us rejoice and be glad in it."

A chorus of "Amens" and "Hallelujahs" went up from the crowd, and more smiles and more hugs. Speaking by the Spirit I continued,

> We were with Jesus for almost four years, and we came to love him, but we did not really know him until the Holy Spirit came to us, as he did to each of you on Pentecost.
>
> So let us all understand from the start, we are not superior to you, not one bit. We are all in this together. Greeks, Jews, converts, rich, poor, educated, or working men like us. Slaves and freedmen, women and men and even children. Greek-speaking, Hebrew-speaking, and Aramaic-speaking. We are all equal. We are all now children of God Almighty.

> In Christ Jesus, you are all children of God
> through faith, all of you who were baptized into
> Christ have clothed yourselves with Christ.
> There is neither Jew nor Gentile, neither slave
> nor free, nor is there male and female, for you
> are all one in Christ Jesus.

As I concluded, my voice raised with passion: "We are all sinners, and we are all saved by the grace of his Son, our Lord and Savior, Jesus."

John, Matthew, Thomas, and the others were spreading out among the crowd, encouraging them to sit in groups of 10 to 20. John turned back to me and said, "Preach it, Brother!"

Joyous laughter broke out among the group: a loving laugh, an encouraging laugh, full of joy and enthusiasm.

I continued. "Jesus came to us from heaven. He came from the Father, and he has now returned to the Father. But he promised us he would send the Holy Spirit in his place, and so he has."

People were looking at each other and nodding.

THE FULL LIFE

Little brother Andrew, who rarely speaks out in public, surprised me by breaking in and saying, "One of the first things Jesus said to us was 'Do not think that I have come to abolish the Law or the Prophets; I have not come to abolish them but to fulfill them.' Please know, my friends, that Jesus loved the Law, our Torah, and he loved the Holy Scriptures. Jesus also said, 'For truly I tell you, until heaven and earth disappear, not the smallest letter, not the least stroke of a pen, will by any means disappear from the Law until everything is accomplished.'"

"At the time, I did not know what Jesus was trying to tell us, but I can see now he was being very purposeful with his words when he said, 'I have come to fulfill the Law and the Prophets.' He meant he was going to 'fill out' the true meaning of the Law and the Prophets. He was going to live it out so we could see the Father's heart behind the Law."

Andrew kept talking, as he walked among the group.

"Jesus wanted us to see the Torah is not a set of rules predicated on performance, but the Father's teachings and instructions on how to live the full life—his life, life in the flow of the kingdom among us.[2] As most of you know, Torah means 'teachings and instructions,' not law and rules."

"He would show us the relationship behind the rules, and this is precisely what he did with his words and with his actions—with his grace and with his truth."

Everyone was smiling and nodding toward one another. My fellow apostles started to talk among the smaller groups, so I had a moment to reflect.

Have you thought about it this way? God the Father told Joseph to name his baby "Jesus" because he would save man from his sins. John the Baptizer said, "Look, the Lamb of God, who takes away the sin of the world." My fellow apostle John teaches that Jesus came to destroy the devil's work.

They are all correct, but Jesus said it this way: "The reason I have come is so you may have life, and I am talking about life to the full."

It was obvious to us Jesus was driven, compelled to show us how much we were missing life, and how much more there was to life with him—much more than religion, much more than just attending synagogue or "church," as people have started calling it recently.

Today, as I write this, it is just as obvious to me that so many are still missing this life to the full because they are missing the Holy Spirit—the missing link.

When there was a lull in the conversations, I continued, "Jesus gave life to the Scriptures. He showed their meaning to us in bodily form, and in the day-to-day details of life. He showed us how to live, really live. He taught us and he showed us the heart of the Father. He wanted us to know the Father as he knew him. And this is what we now want for all of us. We want you to know who the Father is, what he cares about, and how he does things."

LIVING IN THE FAMILY OF THE TRINITY

I paused and reflected for a moment, struck by a new thought: "It's like God the Father wants us to live in partnership with him, collaborating together as we walk through the details of life. He gives us space to live out our lives, but he wants and intends to be in partnership with us."

This was an original thought from the Spirit that I have reflected on many times since. Yes, we are his children; yes, we are his creation; and yes, he is our Father and Master. But Jesus seemed intent on showing us that God Almighty, El Shaddai, would and could live in partnership with us, through us, by the Holy Spirit in us.

My point is the Father sent the Spirit so we could live within the Trinity, led by and powered by the indwelling Holy Spirit. What a concept: tucked into the Trinity!

I turned back to the crowd, my voice rising, and said, "Through Jesus, we came to see God Almighty, the maker of the heavens and the earth—as our Father, not as some grand impersonal force out there in the heavens, looking down on us with constant disappointment and disgust. Jesus showed us the Father cares about us—that's right, he cares about each of you. You are now his child. He adores you. He is proud of you. You are now part of his family."

"And Jesus showed us how the Father does things, by 'filling out' the Scriptures through compassion, caring, and a warm, welcoming heart. He was full of grace and truth."

Revealing Jesus to the World

The Holy Scriptures from Isaiah and the Psalms then began pouring out of me as a stream flowing over rocks in a riverbed, cascading and building up speed.

> As you come to him, the living Stone—rejected by humans but chosen by God and precious to him—you also, like living stones, are being built into a spiritual house to be a holy priesthood, offering spiritual sacrifices acceptable to God through Jesus Christ. For in Scripture it says:
>
> > "See, I lay a stone in Zion,
> > a chosen and precious cornerstone,
> > and the one who trusts in him
> > will never be put to shame."
>
> Now to you who believe, this stone is precious. But to those who do not believe,

"The stone the builders rejected has
become the cornerstone"

and

"A stone that causes people to stumble
and a rock that makes them fall."

They stumble because they disobey the message—which is also what they were destined for.
But you are a chosen people, a royal priesthood,
a holy nation, God's special possession, that you
may declare the praises of him who called you
out of darkness into his wonderful light. [10] Once
you were not a people, but now you are the people of God; once you had not received mercy,
but now you have received mercy.

I concluded with, "We are the community of the redeemed, so we are to glorify God the Father. 'Glorify'
means we are to *accurately reveal* him to the world—starting
with loving each other, here and now. Then we are to love
those around us here in Jerusalem, throughout Judea, and
even Samaria, and then to the ends of the earth."

The crowd was mesmerized, as was I. I did not know
in advance what I was saying from one sentence to the next,
but my words flowed naturally—or should I say supernaturally? As I spoke, it all became so clear to me, as it did to
the crowd. I have learned this is how the Spirit moves in us.

He gives us a sense of clarity and even a new creativity
in the way we present the truth to others. Along with this
clarity and creativity coming moment by moment, he gives
us a new energy—fueled by the Spirit within.

John's Turn

John stepped up and said, "Peter is right. We want you to know Jesus, just as he wanted us to know the Father. We want you to know what a great friend Jesus is, and to know him both personally, and yes, even intimately, even as you know him to be God Almighty. And we are all going to have to get to know this new Holy Spirit together. He is as new to us as he is to you."

John always had a way of smiling when he talked, and he continued with something I had never heard Jesus actually say, but, clearly, John's words were Jesus' words, powered by the Spirit:

"The Father and the Son and the Spirit were together in holy communion, a sweet fellowship and a holy community, before the beginning of time. In the beginning was the Word, and the Word was with God, and the Word was God. He was with God in the beginning.

"Through him all things were made; without him nothing was made that has been made. In him was life, and that life was the light of all mankind. This life is lit up by the light that shines in the darkness, and the darkness has not overcome it."

John continued, his own energy and confidence growing. "And this light that is the light of all mankind, yes, this incredible life, was part of the Trinity before the beginning of time. Jesus, the Word, the Logos, the divine reason for and the divine reason behind everything, came to this earth so we could live this life with him—this life he called, 'Life to the Full.'"

John paused for a moment, surveying the men and women, then he said, "You see, he died for our sins; he paid the price for our sins, actually becoming sin for us so that, through him, we might become the righteousness of God. Isn't this amazing: that we can actually become the 'righteousness of God?' With this new righteousness, we join the family of the Trinity. With this new righteousness and the indwelling of the Holy Spirit, *you* are part of the Father and the Son and the Holy Spirit's communion and fellowship and community."

John's smile was so big, he was almost laughing with joy. "You are now a family member!" he bellowed, "and with this comes the same love, joy, and adoration the Trinity enjoyed before the creation of the world. Don't you all want this?" The crowd responded with another chorus of "Amens" and "Hallelujahs."

"We are the community of the redeemed, so we are to glorify God the Father," he continued. "This means we are to *accurately reveal* him to the world—starting with loving each other, here and now. Then loving those around us here in Jerusalem, then throughout Judea, and even Samaria, and then to the ends of the earth."

THE RIGHT TO BECOME CHILDREN OF GOD

I remembered this is what Jesus had said to us that day on the hillside just outside Jerusalem, before he ascended to heaven for the last time. As I said before, we are just the mirrors, but he is the Light. I wanted to point this out, but John was on a roll and I was not about to interrupt him.

"The true light that gives light to everyone was coming into the world, but the world did not recognize him. He came to that which was his own—us Jews—but his own did not receive him. Yet, and this is for all of you, my brothers and sisters, to all who did receive him, to those who placed their heart's trust in him to be their Savior, he gave the right to become children of God—children born not of natural descent, nor of a human decision or a husband's will, but born of God."

I could hear some of my fellow Jews in our new family of believers asking each other, "What does he mean, 'the right to become children of God?' We Jews are God's chosen people. We were *born* children of God."

Most people do not understand that no one is born a child of God—no one, not you, not me, not even your saintly grandmother. We must be *reborn* into God's family. I know this shocks many of my fellow Jews, yet I have also encountered this sort of bewilderment from Gentiles and God-fearers alike over the years.

Many have said to me, "I thought your Scriptures say God created us and loves us perfectly, even while in the womb?" To which I reply, "Yes, he does love you perfectly and did knit you in your mother's womb, but you are not born his child. You are born in his love, but not in his family. Your sinful nature prevents that. That is why he sent his Son to sacrifice himself, so when you surrender to Jesus and are born again, you become a child of the Father. He sent Jesus precisely because he does indeed love you so much."

THE HOLY SPIRIT COMPLETES WHAT JESUS STARTED

John continued, "The Word became flesh and made his dwelling among us. We have seen his glory, and what a glory it is!—the glory of the one and only Son, who came from the Father, full of grace and truth—his amazing grace and his life-giving truth."

Then John started walking among the crowd, saying, "You remember John the Baptizer, the one who called us out to the Jordan in the wilderness, challenging us to repent? Well, John testified concerning Jesus. He cried out, saying, 'This is the one I spoke about when I said, 'He who comes after me has surpassed me because he was before me.'

"Out of Jesus' fullness, we have all received grace upon grace. For the law was given through Moses; grace and truth came through Jesus Christ. No one has ever seen God, but God the one and only, our Jesus, who is at the Father's side, has made him known."

John took a deep breath, looked out across the crowd, and said, "Let me conclude with this. Jesus wanted to make the Father known to us, and we want to make Jesus known to you. Jesus told us the Holy Spirit would have to complete what he had started. He made it clear to us that without the Holy Spirit, we couldn't possibly understand what he was saying.

"But now we have the Spirit in us, and so do you. If anyone does not have the Spirit of Christ, they do not belong to Christ. But if Christ is in you, then even though your body is subject to death because of sin, the Spirit gives life because of righteousness. And if the Spirit of him who raised Jesus from the dead is living in you, he who raised Christ from the dead will also give life to your mortal bodies because of his Spirit who lives in you."

John concluded, "For there is no difference between Jew and Gentile—the same Lord is Lord of all and richly blesses all who call on him, for, everyone who calls on the name of the Lord will be saved. Together, powered by the Holy Spirit, we are all going to grow together and learn together to live with this incredible power of the Holy Spirit."

Amen to that.

What Was to Come

On our last night with Jesus, he had warned us of what was to come:

> All this I have told you so that you will not fall away. They will put you out of the synagogue; in fact, the time is coming when anyone who kills you will think they are offering a service to God. They will do such things because they have not known the Father or me. I have told you this so that when their time comes, you will remember that I warned you about them.
>
> Yes, I have told you these things, so that in me you may have peace. In this world you will have trouble. But take heart! I have overcome the world.

We did not comprehend what he was telling us back then. But now we were about to experience firsthand the warnings and the troubles.

---

[1] Statement attributed to Doug Greenwold.

[2] Statement attributed to Dallas Willard.

PART TWO

THE ENEMY STRIKES BACK

12

A New Beginning

WE BEGAN EACH DAY AT THE TEMPLE, AT SOLOMON'S
Porch, and most days we ended at someone's home, enjoying a common meal together. We did this by breaking our
large morning group into smaller home groups, typically
letting the people decide who would gather with whom. I
think we reasoned the less we got in the way, and the more
we let the Spirit guide and direct us, the better off we were.

The old Peter would have likely insisted on organizing
the groups myself because of my superior understanding. I
would have tried to pair people up according to who I
thought fit the best or who was most likely to get along—
or some other purely human rationale.

But how could I know what the Spirit wanted to accomplish in their individual lives? How could I know how the
Spirit would speak to, or speak through, someone, who
might then speak into someone else's heart? We let the
Spirit take the lead, which is part of learning to live with the
power of the Holy Spirit.

When we let the Holy Spirit take the lead, he does. And
he always—and I mean always—does it the right way.
When I take the lead, maybe it turns out right, but there is
certainly no guarantee. How many times when I insisted on

taking the lead did problems or even some degree of disaster arise?

Don't ask.

TRANSPARENCY

As for food, there was never a shortage. The Jerusalem believers pooled their resources. The former pilgrims from around the empire who had stayed in Jerusalem after Pentecost also contributed by picking up jobs and pooling their new incomes with the rest of us. Some property owners even sold their property and contributed the proceeds to our new family.

I was amazed at the lack of selfishness among our group, and the rest of the city noticed this as well. Many joined us, and many others wanted to join us but were afraid of the Sanhedrin. However, just about everyone treated us with kindness. We even had a few temple priests secretly join us.

Our unity, love, and compassion for each other, as well as for those around us, was just what Jesus had prayed for. It gave me such a sense of peace to know we were fulfilling his plan, just as he had fulfilled the Scriptures for us.

In the evenings, we gathered at individual houses, sang a song or two, and then listened to stories from the group of how the Spirit was working in their lives. I loved these times. It was so encouraging to see the Lord moving in such a mighty way.

We would hear about a man who had been a very angry, bitter husband, treating his wife and children poorly or treating them as his own property. But after he heard about Jesus, and the Holy Spirit had captured him, everything would change. During these stories, I would often see the children tearing up as their father talked about how Jesus had saved him, and saved his family, from his old self, and his lost, blind ways. I would see his wife nodding quietly, her eyes filled with a new love.

I could hear Isaiah's words in my heart: "What no eye has seen, what no ear has heard, and what no human mind has conceived—the things God has prepared for those who love him." These are the things God was revealing to us by his Spirit.

Grown men would cry like babies as they got down on their knees and surrendered their lives to Jesus. Many women who had led lives of prostitution and sin turned from their former lifestyles and joined our way. We would hear about families being reunited and divorces being stopped. Change. Transformation. A new life. A new beginning. What a joy those evenings were.

No one judged the other. We knew we were all sinners, saved by the same loving grace. My wife Ruth's sins may not have been as obvious as the prostitutes', but she knew her heart was just as sinful. I knew I was no better than anyone else, and so did James and John, Andrew and Matthew, and all the other apostles.

The Fruit of a Believing Community

This is the way the community of believers should always be—full of compassion and grace, void of judgment and condemnation. Relaxed and informal, not rigid and formal—and transparent. Transparency is all-important for a community of believers. When everyone feels free to be transparent, several things happen.

We learn we are not alone in our problems and that others are struggling with the same issues and sins we are. Most importantly, we see we are all sinners—lost, blind, fragile, and insecure, and in desperate need of Jesus. If everyone is transparent, there is little judgment of others. Why would there be?

I fear if we do not continue to emphasize Jesus and his Way, we will someday be just like the former temple, with her fixed and formal Sanhedrin, and the teachers of the Law, who placed such a heavy burden upon the people, never caring to help them with their burdens—stiff, prideful, and afraid to show or share their mutual weaknesses.

After all these years, watching our fledgling church grow across the world, I fear we will lose this informal community of grace and compassion as we continue to grow. We will lose this transparency. People will start hiding their sins and acting like they are better than others. If this happens, if the church becomes an organization, with buildings and programs, we will surely lose this new life, the life that is truly life.

In the mornings as we gathered at the temple, one of us would start the teaching, and then others would join in with a word from the Lord. Everything we did was so that this new community, this fellowship of believers, would be encouraged and built up in Jesus.

Not built up in the apostles or the leaders, but in Jesus.

During our time together in the mornings, two or three apostles might speak, and the others would weigh carefully what was said. If a revelation came to someone who was sitting down, the first speaker would stop. We all spoke the word of the Lord in turn—what many call prophesying—so that everyone could be instructed and encouraged.

Remember, prophesying is not always about the future; it actually means to speak the Word of God. This word could be about the here and now, about the future, or both, as we see so often in our Hebrew Scriptures.

We learned over time that the spirits of prophets are subject to the control of the Spirit, so we were comfortable opening up the time to any Believer who wanted to share their heart. For God is not a God of disorder, but of peace. It took time for the new believers to open up, but because we were intent on developing a transparent fellowship of family, not a fixed, formal meeting, we encouraged anyone who felt the Lord speaking to them to share this with the group.

What did we, the Twelve, teach in our morning gatherings at Solomon's Porch? Mostly what Jesus taught. We did not feel the need to complicate things, just share the Master's heart. Again, we wanted them to know who Jesus is, what he cares about, and how he does things.

We wanted them to know he is the single greatest friend we could ever hope to have.

13

RECEIVE

DURING ONE MORNING AT THE TEMPLE, I FELT THE SPIRIT
prompting me, so I stepped up next to John and began,
"Can you see it now? Jesus has made God known; he is
your Father. Jesus fulfilled—filled out in bodily form—the
Scriptures. Jesus came to expand to us the life he had enjoyed with the Father and with the Spirit before time, before
even the creation of time. He came to provide a way for us
to join this cosmic One-In-Three-God fellowship by creat-
ing a community, a family, of Brothers and Sisters here on
earth.

"When we are in his family, we understand what King
David was saying in his wonderful Psalm,

> You have searched me, LORD,
> and you know me.
> You know when I sit and when I rise;
> you perceive my thoughts from afar.
> You discern my going out and my lying down;
> you are familiar with all my ways.
> Before a word is on my tongue
> you, LORD, know it completely.
> You hem me in behind and before,

and you lay your hand upon me.
Such knowledge is too wonderful for me,
too lofty for me to attain.
Where can I go from your Spirit?
Where can I flee from your presence?

I continued, "Jesus is the light of the world, about which our brother John so often speaks. Each of us, all of us!—received this light when the Holy Spirit indwelled us. We received it as a gift. We did nothing to earn it, that is for sure. Now I want you to think about this idea of receiving a gift."

PARALAMBANO THE HOLY SPIRIT

But Matthew interrupted me and repeated what John had said earlier: "He came to that which was his own, but his own did not receive him. Yet to all who did receive him, to those who believed in his name, he gave the right to become children of God."

Matthew then said, "When my brother John used the word 'receive,' it brought to mind the Greek word *paralambano*. Perhaps you Greek-speaking friends fully understand its meaning, but we Hebrews might well miss it." (As a tax collector, Matthew understood Greek better than most of us.)

"*Paralambano* means 'to take with' or 'to join one's self to.' This is what receiving this gift of life looks like: we join ourselves to the giver, Jesus. We take the Holy Spirit with us, within us, into our hearts. Now, what if I gave you a gift, and you took it but never opened the package? Did you *receive* this gift?"

The people shook their heads. I thought to myself, Either Matthew is a lot smarter than I realized, or he is filled with the Holy Spirit—or both.

Matthew continued, "What if I gave you a gift and you opened it but then set it aside, rarely or never using it. Did you receive my gift? Of course not. Please understand what the Spirit is saying through John—for us to become a child of God, we must 'join ourselves to Jesus,' embracing him and absorbing him, and living with the knowledge and understanding of the heart-felt love with which the gift was offered. This is what *receiving* the gift of eternal life looks like."

Matthew then turned to me and nodded, as if to say, "Okay, I'm done. You can continue now."

GATHERING AS ONE

I continued, saying, "Do you see, my friends, that this world is God's plan to create an external structure—the universe—so that he might replicate in man the internal workings of the Trinity? God's plan from the beginning was to expand the fellowship of the Father, the Son, and the Holy Spirit into a community of believers here on this earth—an external, material creation created for our internal, spiritual new creation.

"We are to glorify God, which, as I have said, means to accurately reveal him to the world. Jesus spoke of this idea of revealed glory on his last night with us:

> I have revealed you to those whom you gave me out of the world. I have given them the glory that you gave me, that they may be one as we

are one—I in them and you in me—so that they may be brought to complete unity. Then the world will know that you sent me and have loved them even as you have loved me.

Father, I want those you have given me to be with me where I am, and to see my glory, the glory you have given me because you loved me before the creation of the world.

"My dear friends," I continued, "We will gather here at the temple grounds each day. We will also gather at each other's homes and have our meals together. We will fulfill Jesus' prayer for us: 'Then the world will know that you sent me and have loved them even as you have loved me.'"

This was the beginning of our new family. Some have taken to calling it a church because the word for church, ecclesia, means "a gathering of called-out ones." That is certainly what we were—called out of an impersonal, performance-based religion into a new Trinitarian community of family, faith, and fellowship.

How beautiful is that?

14

A GOD-SATURATED WORLD

I STARTED MY TEACHING RIGHT WHERE JESUS STARTED his. From the beginning, Jesus went throughout Galilee, teaching in our synagogues, proclaiming the good news of the kingdom. What was this gospel, this good news? I think I can capture Jesus' heart and his message with two words—freedom and confidence.

Jesus' good news of the kingdom was simply that the kingdom had arrived. He was bringing the kingdom of God to us, right into our very lives. He wanted us to know we could start living in the kingdom now, today. We all thought we had to wait to die to go to heaven, but Jesus' message was, "If you want to go to heaven, you can go now!"[1]

Jesus was telling us his kingdom is not a physical one, at least not yet. Instead, his kingdom is all-pervasive. This physical world in which we presently live is, in reality, a God-saturated world. His is a spiritual kingdom now but will become a very physical one when Jesus returns.

I remember vividly the day we were traveling back to Galilee from Jerusalem and stopped midday in a village in Samaria to rest and buy more supplies. In a conversation with a Samaritan woman just outside Sychar, next to

Jacob's well, Jesus spoke of this spiritual kingdom among us, saying, "Believe me, a time is coming when you will worship the Father neither on this mountain nor in Jerusalem. My kingdom has now come," he told the woman. "True worshipers will now worship the Father in the Spirit and in truth, for they are the kind of worshipers the Father seeks. God is spirit, and his worshipers must worship in the Spirit and in truth."

Once, on being asked by the Pharisees when the kingdom of God would come and what it would look like, Jesus replied, "The coming of the kingdom of God is not something that can be observed, nor will people say, 'Here it is' or 'There it is,' because the kingdom of God is in the midst of you—and it will be *within* you."

I want you to stop and ponder this idea of a kingdom for a moment. What would it be like to live in a kingdom with a king who is all-powerful, generous, benevolent, and compassionate? Living under the rule of Rome, we know what this is *not* like. But Jesus wants us to know we live in his kingdom, not the kingdom of Rome.

We live in a God-saturated kingdom.

KINGDOM LIVING

Jesus often used this word kingdom, and he just as often used the word "reign," as in, "The reign of God has arrived," and, "The reign of God is among you." He was saying we live with and under his reign, his authority, not the rulers of this world—demonic or human. They are all subject to his authority.

This is why, when he stood before Pilate on his last day, facing a cruel crucifixion, Jesus chose to remain silent in response to Pilate's repeated questions. Jesus knew Pilate had no real power over him and didn't *reign* over him in any way. He knew he lived in the kingdom of his Father and under the reign, the power, of his Father.

When Pilate asked him, "Are you the king of the Jews?" Jesus responded, "Is that your own idea or did others talk to you about me?"

This irritated Pilate. He was not accustomed to being asked questions and certainly not from some Galilean itinerant rabbi. He spat out, "Am I a Jew? Your own people and chief priests handed you over to me. What is it you have done?"

Jesus said, "My kingdom is not of this world. If it were, my servants would fight to prevent my arrest by the Jewish leaders. But my kingdom is from another place."

Pilate was growing more and more agitated, both from the idea that this Jesus might be a true king and the fact that he would not kowtow to him. He finally snapped, "Do you refuse to speak to me? Don't you realize I have power either to free you or to crucify you?"

I will never forget Jesus' response to Pilate: "You would have no power over me if it were not given to you from above."

Pilate had no power over Jesus. None. Zero. Jesus knew this, and you can bet Pilate sensed it. This is why he washed his hands of the affair. He was frightened by this power and wanted no part of it.

I continuously reminded the people each morning at Solomon's Porch, "You live in a world saturated with God's power and love and presence—a God-saturated world. His reign is total and complete, his power is unequaled, and his

THE MISSING LINK

love is unconditional. Therefore, there is no need to worry about anything."

Freedom and Confidence

James, Jesus' little brother, would often say, "Jesus came so you could now turn from this empty worldly kingdom and begin to live, really live, in his kingdom. His good news of the kingdom of God is you can be freed from your kingdom of Self, which has imprisoned each of you, far more than anything Rome could ever do. Now you can learn to live with freedom and confidence under the reign of your heavenly Father."

I want you to know you can too, my friend. You can live with freedom and confidence, knowing your King is in total control—and that he loves you perfectly. One morning I offered this example: "What would it be like to live in a kingdom with a king who is all-powerful, generous, benevolent, and compassionate? What might your day-to-day life be like, living in such a kingdom, under the reign and authority of such a great and loving king?"

One man in the crowd said, "It would feel safe." Another nodded and said, "That is just what I was thinking, what a safe, secure life that would be." A Greek woman stood up and said, "I would be free to pursue my day-to-day life, my hopes and dreams, with no fear. I could have the confidence that if anything or anyone, any outside force, threatened me, my all-powerful king would take care of me. I would feel safe. I would not have to worry," she concluded.

I nodded enthusiastically and said, "Yes! The good news is all about freedom and confidence. Now the Lord is

—138—

the Spirit, and where the Spirit of the Lord is, there is freedom. This is what Jesus meant by the good news of the kingdom. He wants you to know his Father, who is now *your* Father, and that he is indeed all-powerful, and he is all-loving, compassionate, and even generous—lavishly generous.

"You can be confident in the love and power of your King," I said, my voice rising with enthusiasm. "And please don't miss this," I concluded. "With this freedom and confidence, you are free to live your life to the full, the life that is truly life."

By the way, my friend, so are you when Jesus is your King. But if you insist on being the king or queen of your own castle, you are on your own and you deserve what you get. (Ruth would not like me saying it so harshly.)

Safe in Father's Will

One day when we disciples were worried and uptight about something, Jesus told us this parable: "Are not two sparrows sold for a penny? Yet not one of them will fall to the ground apart from the will of your Father. And even the very hairs of your head are all numbered. So do not be afraid; you are worth more than many sparrows."

Do you understand what Jesus is promising—what he is guaranteeing? Nothing, not one thing, happens to you apart from your Father's will. He knows about everything and anything that is happening to you, right now, in the details of your life. He is in control always, and he loves you perfectly."

I wanted our new family to fully grasp this truth, so I continued talking that morning. "If something is happening to you, God allowed it, at the very least. And if he allowed it, then he plans to use it to grow you and bring you closer to Jesus. Calm your worries. Jesus is in control. He knows all the details of your life—every one of them."

I continued, "Nothing, not one thing, happening to you or your loved ones is out of his control. Rest assured, your Father is not now or is he ever wringing his hands saying, 'What are we going to do about this situation? I didn't see this coming. This caught me by surprise.'"

I could hear some quiet laughter at this silly image, which is kind of humorous, isn't it? Yet we actually act like this happens when we worry. Don't you?

A GOOD FATHER

The Spirit must have reminded Andrew of another time Jesus emphasized the goodness and greatness and the generosity of the Father, so my young brother looked out to the crowd and said, "Some of you were with us when Jesus took a large crowd up to the side of a high slope in Galilee and spent several hours teaching us.

"Jesus said something that day that fits perfectly with what we are talking about today. He said, 'And when you pray, do not keep on babbling like pagans, for they think they will be heard because of their many words. Do not be like them, for your Father knows what you need before you ask him.'"

Andrew paused for a moment and then asked, "Do you believe this? Really, do you believe you can trust Jesus when he promises that your Father knows what you need before you ask him? Because I am here this morning to assure you that, yes, you can. With this trust and assurance, and the freedom and confidence it brings, surely you can see how this will change your prayer life."

Andrew was on a roll. How proud I was, how surprised I was, to see my little brother speaking with such boldness and truth. I kept my mouth shut as he continued: "No longer should you feel compelled to babble on like the pagans you once were, the pagans we all once were. Pagans are people who do not know God the Father. They do not know he loves them perfectly. They do not know that he knows exactly what they need long before they ever ask him."

Andrew's eyes were blazing as he continued, "People who do not know God as their Father cannot understand that he knows the true desires of their heart, so they live with nervous insecurity that he might not take care of them. People who do not know Jesus simply and sadly do not know that in all things, God works for the good of those who love him and are called according to his purpose."

WHY WORRY?

At this John jumped in, "People who do not know God as their Father will never live with the freedom and confidence that is the good news of the kingdom! But you, dear friends, can now know God Almighty, El Shaddai, as your Father, your Abba. You now have his Holy Spirit living within you. Please never forget what Jesus assured us: 'Greater is he who is in you than he who is in the world.'"

I stepped aside because John was prophesying now, speaking the Word of God. This is what I was referring to earlier when I described our meetings as having one or two prophets sharing a word the Spirit put on their heart.

John kept talking, a smile spread wide across his face, "My dear brothers and sisters, can you see why we should never worry about storing up for ourselves treasures on earth, where moths and vermin destroy, and where thieves break in and steal? But instead, we want to store up for ourselves treasures in heaven, where moths and vermin do not destroy, and where thieves cannot break in and steal. For where your treasure is, there your heart will be also."

John was quoting Jesus from that day on the hillside in Galilee.

> Therefore I tell you, do not worry about your life, what you will eat or drink; or about your body, what you will wear. Is not life more than food, and the body more than clothes? Look at the birds of the air; they do not sow or reap or store away in barns, and yet your heavenly Father feeds them. Are you not much more valuable than they?

Thomas stood up, continuing to quote Jesus:

> And why do you worry about clothes? See how the flowers of the field grow. They do not labor or spin. Yet I tell you that not even Solomon in all his splendor was dressed like one of these. If that is how God, your Father, clothes the grass of the field, will he not much more clothe you? And take care of your deepest felt needs?
>
> Do not worry, saying, "What shall we eat?" or "What shall we drink?" or "What shall we wear?" For the pagans run after all these things,

and your heavenly Father knows that you need them.

"He knows!" Thomas bellowed. "But instead of seeking these material things first, seek first his kingdom and his righteousness, for this is all that really matters, and all these other things will be given to you as well."

Thomas sat down and nodded at me as if to say, "Okay, you can wrap this up."

APPROACHING THE THRONE OF GOD

I cleared my throat, getting everyone's attention, and said, "Do you see how this new freedom and confidence, this good news of the kingdom, can and will transform your lives? Do you see you are now free to pursue the life to the full Jesus came to give you? You are safe. You can approach the throne of God with confidence because we have a great high priest who has ascended into heaven, Jesus the Son of God.

"So let us hold firmly to the faith we profess. For we do not have a high priest who is unable to empathize with our weaknesses, but we have one who has been tempted in every way, just as we are—yet he did not sin. Let us then approach God's throne of grace with freedom and confidence, so that we may receive mercy and find grace to help us in our time of need."

What powerful truth. I only hope all our people will believe this truth and absorb it into their lives. I know they believe in Jesus, but too many do not actually believe what Jesus believed. They still live according to the flesh and have their minds set on what the flesh desires, but those who have now begun to live in accordance with the Spirit have their minds set on what the Spirit desires. The mind governed by the flesh is death, but the mind governed by the Spirit is life and peace.

Remember, the Lord is the Spirit, and where the Spirit of the Lord is, there is freedom and confidence.

After this, we sang a hymn, John led us in prayer, and everyone left to go about their workday.

---

[1] Quote attributed to Dallas Willard.

15

SURRENDER

WE TAUGHT AND TALKED ABOUT TOPICS THAT WERE DEAR
to Jesus' heart. As he sought to fulfill the Scriptures for us,
to actually live them out, he often talked about what his Father cared most about—trusting and obeying. He would
talk to us about how our love for the Father would naturally
lead to obedience and surrender.

Can you see how trust and obey and surrender are in-
tricately tied together? We surrender because we see how
much God the Father loves us, and how desperately we
need a Savior. As we grow to love the Father through the
power of the Holy Spirit, we will naturally begin to understand more fully his love for us. Learning to live within this
kind of love will naturally lead us to want to obey the Father's commands—his Torah, his teachings, and instructions for living.

PROTECT NOT PROHIBIT

We learn to know with absolute certainty that God always
has our best interest in mind. Always. We learn to obey precisely because we begin to see his commands not as rules

meant to prohibit us from having fun or getting our way, but to protect us from making mistakes.

He protects us from making selfish and stupid choices that harm us as well as harm our families. Regrettably, I know all about this. I wish I had understood this protective nature of God the Father a long time ago. Just as a loving king seeks to protect the subjects of his kingdom, so the Father's commands are about protecting us, not prohibiting us.

As we begin to see this, we naturally see the logic in surrendering our will and our way to God's will and God's way. We also see the safety of humbling ourselves under his mighty hand, that he may protect us and lift us up in due time. And as we live more and more with his freedom and confidence, we begin to understand what Jesus meant when he said, "My commands are not burdensome."

Jesus talked about how he was bringing good news—the good news of the kingdom among us. The Holy Spirit has shown me that any command I see as burdensome or see as a rule that appears to be bad news, the fault lies within me, in my dark heart. Everything Jesus taught us about living his life to the full is *good* news—always.

It is only when selfish and stupid Peter wants his way that the Lord's commands may appear to be bad news—because I think he is trying to prohibit me from getting my way, yet all the while, he is simply seeking to protect me from getting my way.

SEEING HIS KINGDOM

Obedience is all about love—understanding God's perfect love for us. On our last night together, Jesus said to us,

"Whoever has my commands and obeys them, he is the one who loves me. The one who loves me will be loved by my Father, and I, too, will love them and show myself to them."

At the time I did not understand what he meant by, "and I will show myself to them." But with the Spirit's clarity, I now know exactly what he meant. As we see with his eyes and absorb his love, we more naturally surrender and obey. His kingdom among us becomes more and more real. The Spirit gives us a newfound clarity to see through the lens of Jesus, with the eyes of our heart enlightened. We can practically *see* the kingdom. We see the world around us as a God-saturated world. But if you are not yet born again, you cannot see the kingdom of heaven, as Jesus told Nicodemus.

You may remember the story about Elisha and the king of Aram. The king of Aram sent his army to kill Elisha. The king was fed up with Elisha warning the Israelites about his every move, so he sent horses and chariots and a strong force to Dothan. They went by night and surrounded the city.

Early the next morning, the servant of the man of God got up and went outside and saw that an army with horses and chariots had surrounded the city. "Oh no, my lord! What shall we do?" the servant cried out to Elisha.

"Don't be afraid," the prophet calmly answered. "Those who are with us are more than those who are with them." (I must admit if I am Elisha's servant, I am troubled by his math skills in that moment!)

The Scriptures then say, "And then Elisha prayed, 'Open his eyes, LORD, so that he may see.' Then the LORD opened the servant's eyes, and he looked and saw the hills full of horses and chariots of fire all around Elisha."

I want you to notice Elisha did not pray for the Lord to *send* chariots of fire; he simply prayed his servant would *see* the chariots that were already present. Elisha could see them because he was obedient to the Lord's commands — out of love for him. He knew he lived in the kingdom of a powerful and loving Father. He did not have to pray for God to come to the rescue; he could see God the Father was already there rescuing them.

This, my friend, is what Jesus means by, "I will show myself to you."

THE UNFORCED RHYTHMS OF GRACE

One day Jesus turned to the crowds and said, "Come to me, all you who are weary and burdened, and I will give you rest. Take my yoke upon you and learn from me, for I am gentle and humble in heart, and you will find rest for your souls. For my yoke is easy and my burden is light."

His burden is light because we obey out of love, not fear. His burden is light because he is about protecting us, not prohibiting us. We no longer have to try with gritted teeth to obey a set of rules out of fear, or out of a need to perform. No, we trust his love for us, and so we naturally surrender to his will and his way.

One of our Gentile prophets, Eugene, paraphrased Jesus' words like this: "Come to me. Get away with me and you'll recover your life. Walk with me and work with me — watch how I do it. Learn the unforced rhythms of grace. Keep company with me and you'll learn to live freely and lightly."[1]

Learning to live freely and lightly, with his unforced rhythms of grace, is exactly what Jesus' life looked like each day we were with him. He was free on those dusty Galilean paths, sweat dripping down his face, or being harassed by the never-ending questions and challenges from the Jewish establishment who opposed him with such fervor. I wish you could have witnessed how he lived. It was a beautiful thing to see. He moved with such grace, with such confidence. He was so relaxed. He was purposeful but relaxed in his purpose.

We learn to live with his unforced rhythms of grace as we learn that in him, we live and breathe and have our being. It is his easy yoke and unforced rhythms of grace with which I am learning to live, through the presence and power of the Holy Spirit inside me.

And you can too.

But you must first see his protective love. You must then learn to trust and surrender.

This is, after all, the entire biblical message—trust and surrender.

SELF-SURRENDER

I know now that learning the unforced rhythms of grace, learning to live freely and lightly, can only be found through surrender to Jesus Christ. I realize this is an offensive idea to many, and to us men especially. Surrender is not a word men like. We were not raised to surrender. We were raised to win, to conquer!

But the truth is, you ladies struggle with surrender as well. Do you know why? Because, like men, you are human. We like our independence. It is part of the Fall. We like being in control because we want to get our way. But to experience these unforced rhythms of grace, we must surrender our familiar and constant companion: Self.

This is precisely what Jesus was talking about when he said, "Whoever wants to be my disciple must deny themselves (deny their Self) and take up their cross and follow me. For whoever wants to save their life will lose it, but whoever loses their life (their Self) for me will find it."

You have to give up Self. Release Self. Lose Self. Loosen your grip on Self. Jesus, through the Holy Spirit, will then give you real life, but not if you go to him for just a little help improving Self. This is not a Self-help program. As long as you are trying to save your own life on your terms, you are not going to get Jesus' full life in any way.

The very first step is to try to forget about my Self altogether. It is not like my Self has done such an outstanding job anyway, has yours? So why am I trying so desperately to hold on to my old life? If I want to find my new, true self, the one I know the Holy Spirit wants to bring out in me, I surely will not find him as long as I am looking to benefit Self. I will find him only when I am looking for Jesus.

I have to abandon my Self for Jesus.

ABANDON SELF

I have found this works in all areas of life. For instance, in my marriage, if I try to hold on to my rights, Ruth and I inevitably argue. The harder I try to win, the more we spiral downward. But if I humble my Self and surrender any claim to getting my way, we come closer to each other, growing in harmony with each other and with the Lord.

But I have lost already if I think I have to win.

Why is surrender so hard for me? Why do I continue to revert to serving and protecting Self? Ruth is so much more important than my Self. She deserves so much better than the old King Peter. Perhaps you can relate.

If you promote Self, you promote stress. If you surrender Self, you promote harmony.

This was true in my former fishing career. If I was pushy and demanding, trying to control the outcome, which was a typical day in the kingdom of Peter, I ended up white-knuckling everything, making everyone more tense and agitated. Andrew, James, and John, and even their father Zebedee, had to endure this more than I want to remember. And even if I made more money in the process, in the end, was it really worth the stress and hassle?

Because I think I have to win, I lose every time.

The bottom line is this: If I push and control to get my way, I lose in the long run. If I try to 'save' my desired outcome, to get my way, then I 'lose'—as do the people most important to me. But if I am willing to lose, to let go, to loosen my grip on my control and let the Spirit have his way, then the outcome is always better.

Ruth and I may agree that my way is the better way at times, but it will only be because we decided together, not because I won. My way may or may not render good results, but my way will always be far inferior to the Holy Spirit's way.

Always.

This principle runs through all of life. If I give up my Self, I will find my true self—the one my Father created me to be, the one I have been getting in the way of all my life. If I will lose my old life, the silly make-believe life of King

Peter, I will find Jesus' new life to the full, the life that is truly life.

I am astounded, looking back over my life, how I could have been so blind to this obvious truth. If I have a purpose of my own, I typically tighten my grip, thus losing my calm, relaxed pace, which should be obvious in a follower of Jesus.[2]

I must surrender it all. Even I, "the great Apostle Peter," have to do this day in and day out. I can hold back nothing. Anything that I am not willing to lose, anything I am holding onto, will just hold me back from Jesus. And the silliness of it all is nothing—not one thing—is really mine anyway.

Satan loves to hear us talk about what is "mine." In the end, we will see that nothing was ever mine to call mine,[3] and the joke will be on us. It was all an illusion. Satan duped us.

Trust and surrender are the keys to life that is truly life. Trust. Surrender. Obey out of love. We were about to find out just how much we trusted Jesus and just how much we were willing to surrender our will to his.

---

[1] Quote attributed to Eugene Peterson.

[2] Statement attributed to Oswald Chambers.

[3] Statements attributed to C. S. Lewis.

16

React in Fear or
Respond in Faith

IN MY PROLOGUE, I BEGAN THIS ENTIRE CONVERSATION
with the story of the healing of the lame man at the temple
gate called Beautiful. Please allow me to return briefly to
the story so I may tell you what happened next.

Healing in Humility

John and I were on our way to the temple for the 3:00 p.m.
Tamid sacrifice and prayer time. After Jesus returned to be
with the Father, we made it our practice to follow our Jewish customs of worship, just as Jesus had done. After all, we
were still Jews. All the first followers of Jesus were Jews, a
fact sometimes lost now that the Gentiles have become such
an integral part of the family of believers.

As we were approaching the gate that afternoon, a lame
man looked at us as if to ask for money. In that moment, I
felt the Spirit stirring inside me. You remember the story: I
reached down and, just by my touch—the touch of the
Spirit moving through me—the man was healed and stood
upright on both feet.

Now this man, Abell, followed us into the temple courts, walking and jumping, and praising God. All the people saw him dancing around and could see it was the same man who begged at the temple gate for all those years. I wish you could have seen their faces. They were filled with wonder and amazement at what had happened to him. Some were laughing at his happy, or perhaps silly, antics, but everyone was mesmerized.

As soon as we could slip away, John and I walked into the temple. We had seen Jesus perform miracles and then walk away as if nothing spectacular had just happened, and we inherently understood this was how he would want us to respond. We had not planned this miraculous healing; we had done nothing, not one thing, in our own power, so we naturally moved away from the miracle, focused on our upcoming worship.

Does that seem extraordinarily humble to you? Nonsense. Yes, I was learning to be more humble, but I had a long way to go. It is only natural to be humble when you know you have done nothing yourself. Anything else would be silly and foolish pride. I have plenty of experience with silly and foolish pride, and I am sure you do too.

I once thought I was responsible for my fishing success, and I was equally sure it was someone else's fault when I was not. But as the Holy Spirit grows in me, I see with such clarity how silly my foolish pride was.

If you knew me back then, you would know I would even take pride in growing more humble! I know many who still do, but now that the Spirit is giving me new eyes to see, and a new perspective, I could see this miracle for what it was: a movement by the Spirit to glorify Jesus—not Peter.

MIRACLES GLORIFY JESUS

Abell followed us in and kept dancing around, and I was a little worried we would not be able to properly prostrate ourselves in the temple, as was customary during the 3:00 prayer time. Finally, he calmed down enough to lie down and be quiet while the priest performed the sacrifice, and we celebrated with song. But as soon as we made our way over to Solomon's Porch, he was at it again.

He jumped around and called out to everyone within shouting distance, "Look, a miracle! I can walk! God Almighty has healed me! Look at my legs—how strong they are. Don't you wish your legs were this strong?"

All the people were astonished and came running toward us. When I saw them gathering around, their eyes as big as saucers, I felt the Spirit move in me again. I said to them: "Fellow Israelites, why does this surprise you? Why do you stare at us as if by our own power or godliness we had made this man walk? The God of Abraham, Isaac, and Jacob, the God of our fathers, has glorified his servant Jesus through this miracle."

I wanted to be sure they understood I had done nothing in my own power to perform this healing. I wanted to be sure they heard the name Jesus and that Jesus received all the glory. But then I felt the Spirit moving me with growing energy and clarity to speak to this crowd, to convict their hearts, to wake them up.

REPENTANCE THROUGH CONVICTION

I continued, trying not to have a condemning scowl on my face, but with conviction rising in my voice. "You handed him over to be killed, and you disowned him before Pilate, though he had decided to let him go. You disowned the Holy and Righteous One and asked that a murderer be released to you.

"You killed the author of life, but God raised him from the dead. We are witnesses of this. By trust in the name of Jesus, this man whom you see and know was made strong. It is Jesus' name, not anything I have done, and the trust that comes through him, that has completely healed this man, as you can all see."

I could see their countenance falling as my words pierced their hearts. Yes, a few of them had been part of the crowd that yelled for Barabbas' release instead of Jesus' release that fateful morning before Pilate. But most were just bystanders, not yet understanding the cosmic ramifications of Jesus' execution.

I softened my voice and said, "Now, fellow Israelites, I know that you acted in ignorance, as did your leaders. But this is how God fulfilled what he had foretold through all the prophets, saying that his Messiah would suffer. Repent, then, and turn to God, so that your sins may be wiped out and times of refreshing may come from the Lord, and that he may send the Messiah back to us, who has been appointed for you—my Lord and Master, Jesus."

PEACEFUL PASTURE

Even as I said these things, I could see their hearts lifting and hope returning to their eyes. Someone asked, "What do you mean by 'times of refreshing may come from the Lord?'"

I was reminded of Jesus' words about finding peaceful pasture with him wherever we are. This idea of "refreshing" is in perfect keeping with Jesus' words: "I am the gate; whoever enters through me will be saved. They will come in and go out and find pasture."

Have you ever thought about what Jesus meant by, "They will come in and go out and find pasture"? Only the Spirit can deliver the peaceful pasture about which Jesus so often spoke. But with the Holy Spirit inside us, for the first time, we now can live a life in harmony with our Father, wherever we are. The times of refreshing grow and grow, so that no matter our circumstances, we are refreshed within the gate of his green pastures of harmony and peace.

Whether we "go in" to be with other believers or "go out" into the secular world of culture and commerce, we can sense his peaceful pasture all around us. What a promise! Wherever you are, whatever you are doing, whoever is around you, if you see Jesus with you and see the Holy Spirit in you, you will be as centered and as balanced as if lying in a green and luscious pasture, having a quiet conversation with Jesus.

A huge crowd of men and women cried out, "Please, we want to be saved. Help us find this pasture. We did not know Jesus was the Messiah. What are we to do?"

The other apostles had gathered around Solomon's Porch, so we all fanned out and started to speak to the men and women about the gospel, the good news of salvation through Jesus, and his grace and peace. I could see the Spirit moving mightily through the smaller groups.

Their hearts were convicted, and the Holy Spirit was moving like the wind. I could not see the Spirit, but by him, I could see hearts melting. This is the kind of conviction

Jesus said the Spirit would accomplish: "When he comes, he will convict the world about sin and righteousness and judgment."

I had retained some of what Jesus had told us on his last night with us, but now the Spirit was reminding me of everything he said. I needed to remember his words of assurance because, as I surveyed the crowd, I suddenly saw a nasty looking group of men quickly approaching. The Sadducees and the temple guards, along with some very angry priests, were headed our way. They did not look like they wanted to congratulate us on our new converts.

ARRESTED

I have seen Doctor Luke's written version of what happened next, and he was very precise:

"The priests and the captain of the temple guard and the Sadducees came up to Peter and John while they were speaking to the people. They were greatly disturbed because the apostles were teaching the people, proclaiming in Jesus the resurrection of the dead. They seized Peter and John and because it was evening, they put them in jail until the next day. But many who heard the message believed; so, the number of men who believed grew to about five thousand."

John moved over to me as they approached. We could both sense trouble was coming, but we felt unnaturally calm. One of the priests called out while still 10 feet away, "Who do you think you are making such a ruckus here at God's holy temple?"

I wanted to say, "Whose God are you talking about, certainly not yours? Your god is your ego and your rituals and your precious establishment." John could sense my anger, and he nudged me and shook his head discreetly. He was communicating, "Not now, Peter. Keep it in check."

John stepped forward and replied, "We do not think we are anybody. We are simply servants of the Messiah, Jesus of Nazareth."

Oh boy, that set them off. Then Abell jumped—literally jumped—into our midst and practically shouted out, "Yes, they must be prophets of this Jesus, and he must surely have been the Messiah! Look what they just did. I've been lame all my life, and they healed me!"

With Abell's unintentional distraction, and before anyone could say anything else, the top Sadducee motioned to the temple guards and we were suddenly being marched off to prison.

JESUS' PEACE

I have been in worse situations since that night, but this was our first persecution after Jesus had left, and I could not help but think about the fact that this is the very same group that had recently orchestrated Jesus' death. They could easily do the same to us.

Was I afraid? Yes. Was I panicked? Not at all. Since my ridiculous blustery proclamation on Jesus' last night, "If all else abandon you, Jesus, I will stand by your side," I've learned to rest in Jesus' promise that he will always be with me, even to the end of the age.

In my previous life, I did everything in my own power, which I can assure you is the path to anxiety and fear. How could it not be? When you are trying to operate in your power, the outcome is always up to you. When you think the outcome is up to you, you will experience anxiety and stress. But when you learn to rest in the power of the Holy Spirit and abandon the outcome to God, his peace and assurance abide in you as you go in and out of times of stress.

The need to control things around you cannot coexist with peace, and certainly not with a calm, relaxed pace. Back when King Peter thought he was in control and the outcome had to go his way, Ruth endured many a night with a husband completely out of sorts. I would pace the floor, toss uneasily in bed, grumbling, sweating, and far too often snap at Ruth for nothing.

This always leads to unhappiness, to say the least, and more often anger and frustration. Jesus said the Father was always in control. He said he would never leave us, even to the end of the age.

This night in jail might be the end of Peter's "age," but I was ready to face it if it came to that. Remember, Jesus told us, "Peace I leave with you; my peace I give you. I do not give to you as the world gives. Do not let your hearts be troubled and do not be afraid."

REACT IN FEAR OR RESPOND IN FAITH

This was one of those moments I could choose to find pasture, even if I felt outside his safe gate, or I could choose to allow fear to overwhelm me.

Is not this our choice in any difficult situation—to choose to trust or choose to not trust? It is a choice after all. "Do you react in fear or respond in faith? Whenever you see the word *faith*, I want you to think of *trust*. That is, after all, what Jesus means by faith.

There John and I sat, our feet and legs shackled, sitting in a cell in the guards' barracks, just to the side of the temple grounds. If we tried to shift our position on the hard dirt floor, the rough edges of the iron shackles would dig into our skin. It was damp and dark.

John looked at me and said with his usual smile, "Well, this has been quite a day, hasn't it, my Brother? You heal a lame man, dance around like a little girl, hundreds of men and women are converted, and we end up in this filthy cell."

I just nodded and said, "You really know how to win friends, my young Brother, with that declaration about Jesus being the Messiah."

John laughed and replied, "Would you have it any other way?"

I laughed. "No, Brother. There is no other way."

We sat in silence for a moment, and I continued thinking about reacting in fear versus responding in faith.

I used to *react* to everything, good or bad. My feelings were my master; therefore, reacting was all I knew. As I have grown in my trust and the Spirit has filled me with the rock-solid awareness that I live in a God-saturated world, my feelings are no longer in control, and my faith, my trust, is now leading the way.

Reacting conjures up images of being overwhelmed, of a quick, emotion-filled, knee-jerk reaction. But to respond is more like a quiet peace, a calm and measured thoughtful response. I have learned to hold back my desire to quickly react and not allow my feelings to lead the way. I instead try to respond in trust. I try to remember Jesus' promises as well as the way he always seemed so relaxed, especially in difficult situations.

This was surely a difficult and dangerous situation we found ourselves in. Could I follow Jesus' example of faith ruling over my feelings? I would soon find out.

17

FACTS, FAITH,
AND FEELINGS

FAITH, FEELINGS, AND FACTS—HOW SHOULD A FOLLOWER
of Jesus prioritize these? Most would automatically place
faith first, then muddle around with their answer between
feelings and facts. Many of you would place facts last because you think faith trumps facts. I once thought this way
too. With such an emphasis on faith among Jesus' followers, many think facts are anathema to faith.

No doubt, many outsiders think we are even afraid of
the facts, that we hide behind "blind faith" because we have
no facts to support our faith. They are wrong. We are not
only not afraid of the facts, but my order of priority is facts
first, then faith, then feelings a distant third. Feelings are
okay as servants, but they are terrible masters.[1]

If John and I allowed our feelings to move front and
center sitting in this dark cell, fear would have overwhelmed us. Remember, these are the same men who had
Jesus crucified. Instead, we both knew the facts—Jesus said
he would never leave us or abandon us; he said the Holy
Spirit would be with us in times such as this. He said,
"Nothing happens apart from the will of your Father."

We trusted Jesus, and we trusted his promises, which became the truth for us.

Not one thing happens apart from, or outside, the will of my Father. That is a fact. I know I can trust this. God is not suddenly surprised that John and I are here in this cell. I can assure you he is not saying, "Oh, no, I did not see that coming. They have really gotten themselves in a mess. I am not sure what to do now."

I know that sounds laughable to you, but think about it—isn't this what worrying is all about? When you think this way, you are reacting in fear because you are letting your feelings lead the way. Feelings are disastrous masters. They can certainly be positive as servants, but disastrous as masters.

BELIEVING SATAN OVER GOD?

Now, this is going to sting a bit, and I am certainly not judging you. I can only say this because I have seen it in myself. When we fear, we might as well say to Jesus, "I have decided not to trust you and instead to trust Satan. I find you to be untrustworthy, Jesus, and I find Satan to be much more trustworthy."

I know it stings, but do not sluff it off. It is you and it is me when we worry.

In the Garden of Eden, this is exactly what happened. God actually walked with Adam and Eve in the cool of the evening. I love that picture—in the cool of the evening. Can you imagine that? Well, I can because he walked with me too, in the form of Jesus. Adam and Eve walked with God the Father, John and I walked with God the Son, and now we can all walk with God the Spirit.

God promised Adam and Eve anything and everything. But Satan came along and said, "You cannot really trust God. You cannot really trust he has your best interests in mind. God is trying to prohibit you from having fun."

Adam and Eve believed Satan over God. That is precisely what you are believing when you fear. Your feelings take over and you totally ignore the facts: the promises of both Jesus and God the Father. I understand this process only too well because before I learned to live with the power of the Spirit, fear was a stronghold for me as well.

TAKE CAPTIVE THOUGHTS

Brother Paul likes to say, "For though we live in the world, we do not wage war as the world does. The weapons we fight with are not the weapons of the world. On the contrary, they have divine power to demolish strongholds. we take captive every thought to make it obedient to Christ."

As I sat in this cell, looking at the weapons of the world—the guards with their swords and daggers, this cell, and the iron chains around our hands, I heard the Holy Spirit saying, "Fear not, Peter and John. I am here with you; I am here *in* you. I can demolish this prison anytime I choose. But allow me to first demolish your prison of fear. Allow me to first demolish your prison of feelings, your prison of doubts."

This is why I place the facts first, then my faith. I am a mere human, just like you. I can and I do feel fear. However, I now choose—it is my choice and it is your choice— to focus on the facts instead of my feelings. As I do this, my faith and trust strengthen and my fear and anxiety diminish.

I can only do this by "taking captive every thought to make it obedient to Christ." As I sat in this cell, my feelings wanted to take over. The thoughts in my head reminded me of Jesus' gruesome death at the hands of these same men. Satan was telling me I was a nobody and these powerful men held my absolute fate in their hands.

Satan whispered in my head that God is not involved in these kinds of details, that God likely does not even know—or care—that I am in this cell.

Can you see this is what Satan wanted me to believe? But who would I *choose* to believe?

When these thoughts of fear start to overwhelm me, and my feelings try to take over, I have learned to grab those thoughts, wrestle them down, take them captive, and cast them aside.

In my first letter to the believers, I said, "Humble yourselves, therefore, under God's mighty hand, that he may lift you up in due time. Cast all your anxiety on him because he cares for you."

My word for "cast" is the same word we fishermen use to throw our nets away from the boat out into the water. Take captive your thoughts of fear and cast them far away from you and onto the broad, loving shoulders of Jesus. He will take them from you because he cares so much for you. In fact, he will take your anxieties and bury them deep in the ocean and then place a "No Fishing" sign in their place.

In Due Time

When I wrote "that he may lift you up in due time," I understood fully that this "in due time" might not be in my timing. This is the part none of us like—in due time. But God's timing is always the best timing.

John and I could be sitting in this cell longer than I wanted, maybe forever. To be transparent with you, that scared me, and I could feel panic wanting to take over.

Instead of reacting in fear, I could choose to calmly respond in faith. I looked at John and smiled, and raised my eyes and said, "Thank you now, Lord, before we see what you are going to do here because we know we will be thanking you later."

John smiled and said, "Peter the rock."

John then started to hum a psalm quietly. I joined in, and the next thing we knew it was morning, and we had slept soundly and peacefully through the night, even though surrounded by the dangerous weapons of the world.

TESTIFYING IN THE TEMPLE

The next day, the rulers, the elders, and the teachers of the law met in the temple area. Caiaphas, the high priest, was there and so were Annas, John, Alexander, and others of the high priest's family. Annas had been high priest first but was deposed by the Romans. He was succeeded by his son, Eleazar, then by his son-in-law Caiaphas. They were all alike—hypocrites and fakes, motivated by power, prestige, and money.

They did not love the LORD with all their hearts; they loved their position and their power with all their hearts. Jesus loved them, as only he could, but he disdained their lives. The guards marched into the cell, unchained us, lifted us up, and brought us before these men. They began to question us: "By what power or what name did you do this?"

They were truly agitated. Their expressions were filled with hatred and disgust. It was a scary situation that could go bad quickly. My pulse was quickening, so I clenched my fists to regain control. John remained calm, keenly aware these men were driven by fear.

They were afraid of what they could not understand, or control. They were afraid of uncertainty. They were afraid of Jesus. Even though we knew they had the worldly power to cause us great harm and bodily pain, we were unafraid. Now understand we did not know with any certainty how this would turn out. We were uncertain of the next step, but we were certain of Jesus and his promises.

Then, filled with the Holy Spirit, I said to them: "Rulers and elders of the people! If we are being called to account today for an act of kindness shown to a man who was lame and being asked how he was healed, then know this," and I pointed my finger at them, "you and all the people of Israel—it is by the name of Jesus Christ of Nazareth, whom you crucified but whom God raised from the dead, that this man stands before you healed."

Their faces were distorted with anger, but I was undaunted. "Jesus is 'the stone you builders rejected, which has become the cornerstone.' Salvation is found in no one else, for there is no other name under heaven given to mankind by which we must be saved."

John was looking at me with a smile, standing right with me, and repeated, "Yes, salvation is found in no one else." We both expected to be slapped, or worse. The men staring at us were filled with hatred, and the room was charged with negative energy. But then an unexpected thing happened. After a moment of silence, Caiaphas, with an angry scowl on his face, motioned for the guards to escort us out of the room. What happened next, we know only because Nicodemus told us later.

As you might know, Nicodemus had become a follower of Jesus, albeit a quiet one. He had maintained his place in the Sanhedrin—in part, because of his wealth and influence. As time went on, he and Joseph of Arimathea would be ongoing sources of what went on behind closed doors in the Sanhedrin, and we were grateful for both their insider information and their wisdom and warnings.

When the Sanhedrin saw our courage and realized we were unschooled, ordinary men, they were astonished and took note that we had been with Jesus. Nicodemus later told us there followed heated discussion and debate. Some wanted to sneak us off and stone us. Others wanted to whip us, and still others voted in favor of just leaving us in jail for a while.

RESPONDING BASED ON FACTS

Nicodemus boldly stood up and said, "Men, since we have the lame man, Abell, healed and standing right here with us, how do you propose to explain this away? Everyone living in Jerusalem knows they have performed a notable sign, and we cannot deny it."

They could not deny it precisely because everyone had seen this miracle. In all these years, they have still been unable to deny it. Many people saw it happen, eyewitnesses, and not just our own followers.

Annas interrupted Nicodemus and said, "We better decide quickly what we are going to do with these men. To stop this thing from spreading any further among the people, we must warn them to speak no longer in the name of Jesus."

This seemed to carry the day, and they all nodded, murmuring among themselves. Then they called us in again and commanded us, with threats, not to speak or teach at all in the name of Jesus.

Now I want you to put yourself in our place. What would you say in response to their order? Remember, these are the same men who had Jesus crucified, and there was plenty of reason to think they could orchestrate the same for us.

Would you react in fear, overwhelmed by your feelings, or would you respond in faith, trusting the facts? If you think we are giants of the faith, you would be wrong. Yes, we have grown greatly in our trust, but again, at this point, so early on, we simply responded based on the facts—we had seen Jesus dead and buried. We had seen his dead body, and we had then seen him very much alive—living and breathing, eating with us, and laughing with us.

John stepped forward and said, in a matter-of-fact manner, "Which is right in God's eyes—to listen to you or to Jesus? You be the judges! As for us, we cannot help speaking about what we have seen and heard."

"What we have seen and heard" had become the facts for us. Brother John loved this theme and would come back to it again and again. "What we have seen and heard." Many times, I have heard him begin his teachings with,

"That which was from the beginning, which we have heard, which we have seen with our eyes, which we have looked at and our hands have touched—this we proclaim concerning the Word of life. The life appeared; we have seen it and testify to it, and we proclaim to you the eternal life, which was with the Father and has appeared to us."

BOLDNESS FROM WHAT WE HAD SEEN

This is what compelled John that day in front of this murderous crowd of religious men. We were not yet bold because we were such great men of courage; we were not yet bold because of what we believed; no, we were bold and undaunted because of what we had seen.

It reminds me of Job's last words to God: "My ears had heard of you, but now my eyes have seen you." Job was a righteous man—a man God singled out as a man pleasing to him. Had any of us known Job before the story began, we would have been surprised to hear him say, "My ears had heard of you but now my eyes have seen you."

But what Job is saying is he knew about God, but he did not know God. Before his trials, he had a head knowledge of God, but after his trials, after he had been sifted, he had a new heart knowledge, and then "the eyes of his heart had been enlightened."

If it took a beating from this Sanhedrin for me to see Jesus in a new light, I was ready for it. In fact, I would welcome it! After Jesus rose from the dead, we had seen him several times. We had heard his voice; we had touched him; we had seen him eat. But it was not until the Holy Spirit indwelled us that we were we able to truly *see* him. Therefore, to deny him now would be a cowardly and despicable thing to do.

Those were the facts, and we simply could not deny them. In the ensuing years, many of my Brothers and Sisters have died because of what we had seen—Jesus very much dead and then very much alive. But when a Roman guard has a gladius sword at your throat, belief can be overwhelmed by feelings of fear. But even with a sword at your throat, how could you deny what you have seen, what you had experienced, what you had touched with your own hands?

We simply could not.

JOY COMPLETE

Right there in front of the Sanhedrin, John shouted out, "We proclaim to you what we have seen and heard, so that you also may have fellowship with us. Our fellowship is with the Father and with his Son, Jesus Christ. We say all this to make our joy complete."

There it was, "To make our joy complete." John was indeed full of joy, with streams of living water flowing from within him, just as Jesus had promised.

Caiaphas and his friends were certainly not full of joy. All their joy had drained out completely, and they were even more agitated, and an angry restlessness pervaded the room. They continued to threaten us, but they could see we were unafraid, so they let us go. They could not decide how to punish us because all the people were praising God for what had happened, for Abell had been lame for 40 years—and was still dancing around the temple area.

THE RUMBLING POWER OF GOD

After the guards walked us out and gave us a nice shove to the ground, we stood up, dusted ourselves off, and set off to see our family of believers, who were no doubt praying for us with fear and trembling. As we walked, Jesus' promises echoed in our ears,

> All this I have spoken while still with you. But the Advocate, the Holy Spirit, whom the Father will send in my name, will teach you all things and will remind you of everything I have said to you. Peace I leave with you; my peace I give you. I do not give to you as the world gives. Do not let your hearts be troubled and do not be afraid.

We went back to our own people and reported all that the chief priests and the elders had said to us. Upon hearing all this, they raised their voices together in prayer to God. "Sovereign Lord," they said, "you made the heavens and the earth and the sea, and everything in them. You spoke by the Holy Spirit through the mouth of your servant, our father David, 'Why do the nations rage and the peoples plot in vain? The kings of the earth rise up and the rulers band together against the Lord and against his anointed one.'"

Thomas then stepped in front of the crowd and said, "Indeed, Herod and Pontius Pilate met together with the Gentiles and the people of Israel in this city to conspire against your holy servant Jesus, whom you anointed."

A hush fell over the group as he continued, "Father, they did what your power and will had decided beforehand should happen. Now, Lord, consider their threats and enable your servants to speak your word with great boldness. Stretch out your hand to heal and perform signs and wonders through the name of your holy servant Jesus."

We all fell to our knees together and started praying, and as we did, the building started shaking—yes, rumbling and shaking. As I prayed and the timbers shook, my thoughts went back to the Israelites and the rumbling Mount Sinai:

> On the morning of the third day, there was thunder and lightning, with a thick cloud over the mountain, and a very loud trumpet blast. Everyone in the camp trembled. Mount Sinai was covered with smoke because the LORD descended on it in fire. The smoke billowed up from it like smoke from a furnace, and the whole mountain trembled violently.

Back then, the people were terrified of God. The voice of God Almighty, El Shaddai, boomed as if a roaring earthquake was toppling the great Mount Sinai. Yet here we were, with this same God Almighty, creator of the universe, and the same mighty display of rumbling and shaking, yet his mighty voice was now a soft, sweet whisper in our innermost hearts.

Isaiah said it like this, "What no eye has seen, what no ear has heard, and what no human mind has conceived."

These are the things God has prepared for those who love him. These are the things God has revealed to us by his Spirit. We were all filled with the Holy Spirit and spoke the Word of God boldly each day at the temple and each night over dinner with the brothers and sisters.

---

[1] Statement attributed to Dallas Willard.

18

ANANIAS AND SAPPHIRA

TRUST AND SURRENDER ARE THE KEYS TO A LIFE THAT IS truly life. Trust in Jesus' perfect love, his perfect power, and his perfect and constant presence. I must surrender my way—my claim to my right to my Self.[1] This is the path to peace.

Nowhere in our lives does trust and surrender meet a greater challenge than with our money. During these early days, it seemed all the believers were one in heart and mind. No one claimed any of their possessions as their own, but we shared everything we had. People didn't necessarily sell everything they had, but, rather, when one of our family saw a need, and the Spirit moved them, they would sell or give or do whatever it took to address that need. The Holy Spirit was so powerfully at work in all of us, there were virtually no needy persons among our new family of believers.

It was a wonderful thing to behold. We were so encouraged by everyone's love and generosity. John and I were talking one afternoon about the finances and welfare of our new community, when James, Jesus' younger half-brother, joined us. James was fast becoming a leader in our group.

JAMES, JESUS' HALF BROTHER

In some strange way, having him with us helped us feel Jesus' presence a little more. There was definitely a family resemblance. Yes, it is true he was skeptical of Jesus during his earthly ministry, but that was fading into the background these days. I remember the time when Jesus chose to stay in Galilee instead of going with his brothers and his family to the festival in Jerusalem.

He did not want to go about in Judea because the Jewish leaders there were looking for a way to kill him. He was not afraid of them in the sense you and I would be afraid. No, everything Jesus did was for a reason. He did not react to the plans of men, but, instead, he responded to the direction of the Holy Spirit.

Fear never set his agenda; faith did.

This episode of James' skepticism was near the time of our Jewish Festival of Tabernacles. We were in Capernaum at the time, and the 12 of us were talking with Jesus one morning when his brothers, Jude and James, sarcastically said to him, "Leave Galilee and go to Judea so that your disciples there may see the works you do. No one who wants to become a public figure acts in secret. Since you are doing these things, show yourself to the world."

Even his own brothers did not believe in him, but I can certainly see why. They had grown up with him. Andrew would certainly have a hard time believing his big brother was the Messiah. Jude told me later that growing up together, they could see Jesus was special, but he was still their brother. Their father Joseph would not tolerate any derision among his boys, but after Joseph died, the brothers asked their mother Mary several times about Jesus' odd birth story.

They had heard stories about a virgin birth, which was both embarrassing and perplexing to them. I think the embarrassment fueled their skepticism. As a young man, Jesus would ask a controversial question in the synagogue, which, to his brothers' chagrin, was a little too often. James told us they had to endure the common refrain from their neighbors, "Is this not Jesus, the son of Joseph, whose father and mother we know?"

Yes, they were skeptics, but after Jesus appeared to James following his resurrection, everything changed for James. It took us a while to fully trust his sincerity, but his passion and sense of purpose were now winning us all over.

THE HOLY SPIRIT CAN

"What are you two talking about?" James asked as he sat down next to me, stretching out his legs. The other apostles were off visiting with their home groups, so it was just us three. It was mid-afternoon, and the sun was high and hot, so John and I were sitting in the shade of a tree near Mark's house to escape the direct sun.

"John was just remarking on how smoothly things were going with our financial and food needs," I answered. "Do you realize, James, how incredibly generous and enthusiastic everyone has been with their money and resources?"

Before James could answer, John added, "When the 12 of us first met, just after Pentecost, we had no idea how to set all this up." He smiled at the memory of how clueless we were back then. "We knew we couldn't possibly pull together a plan to organize our 3,000 new converts, but we knew the Spirit could, and we trusted he would."

I added, "We just started doing the next right thing, with our hope—our confident expectation—in the Spirit."

James laughed and said, "Oh, I know all about that. I was watching you and thinking to myself, "Jesus, big brother, you better show up and show off because this motley crew does not have a chance without you!"

"Hey now!" John laughed, raising his fists in feigned aggressiveness.

James held up his hands in mock surrender, saying, "But, but, but," he paused for the effect, "I knew you had the Holy Spirit, although, admittedly, I did not understand anything about the Spirit back then. I knew your hearts were pure, so I was completely confident things would work out."

"Well," I said, "I am glad you were so full of faith because I was still operating in the realm of my own power and my faith in me. That is probably why your big brother used to chide us with, "Oh, you little faiths!" We all laughed together at this and reflected among ourselves how our community was evolving.

Most of our new believers, and certainly the ones who had been with Jesus from Galilee, were contributing what they could, as best they could. Some contributed more than others, but we were grateful for any assistance, no matter the amount. The Holy Spirit was showing us that the heart behind the gift was what mattered, and, more importantly, he was showing us he could do more with a little than we could ever do in our own power with a lot.

BARNABAS

From time to time, those who owned land or houses sold them, and the money from the sales was used to help our brothers and sisters in need. We never asked anyone to do this, or even imagined asking, but the Spirit clearly moved in their hearts. One such was a Levite from the island of Cyprus named Joseph, whom Thomas, Matthew, and Nathanial had started calling Barnabas, which means "son of encouragement."

BARNABAS: ENCOURAGER

Barnabas was the perfect name for Joseph because he was always smiling and encouraging those around him. Just being around Barnabas was uplifting. We all liked him. He had traveled to Jerusalem from Cyprus for the Feast of Pentecost and was among the first new converts that fateful day.

He was full of the Holy Spirit. You did not have to see him doing anything to know this. You just sensed it. Barnabas had such a strong air of love, joy, peace, and patience. He was so positive, so full of hope—full of confident expectation in his newfound Savior. As I have already mentioned, in our language "hope" means confident expectation. Followers of the Master do not hope for things as those who do not know Jesus do; we have confident expectation in his perfect love and the Holy Spirit's perfect power within us.

When I thought about Barnabas, I could not help but think of Jesus' words, "Let anyone who is thirsty come to me and drink. Whoever believes in me, rivers of living water will flow from within them."

By this Jesus meant the Spirit, whom those of us who believed in him were later to receive. Up to that time the Spirit had not been given to us permanently, since Jesus had not yet been glorified. But at Pentecost, Barnabas had received the Holy Spirit, and the fruit of the Spirit was strong in him.

In one of my long-winded discussions with my fellow apostle Paul—and believe me when I say there was no other kind of discussion with Paul except long-winded—we debated whether encouraging was a spiritual gift from the Holy Spirit. Paul seemed to think it was, but I suggested it was more a personality trait.

Surely, it is some of both, but either way, encouraging people is a gift to them. Even if it does not come naturally, we can all make every effort to add this to our daily walk with Jesus. It is so easy to do, and it is such a great gift to the receiver.

Try it. Be purposeful and intentional about encouraging others. You will, in fact, be encouraged yourself. It is one of those gifts we can easily manufacture in our own power, which is then joined by the Spirit to become a true spiritual gift.

At our morning gatherings at Solomon's Porch, Barnabas walked around greeting the newcomers with his infectious smile and introducing them to the other believers. He always acknowledged them when they asked a question or made a good point. Give me more men like Barnabas for every scriptural scholar, and I guarantee you any gathering of believers will thrive.

BARNABAS: GIVER

Barnabas sold a field back on his home island of Cyprus, and one day he walked into a meeting of the Twelve and put the money at our feet. It was more than I earned in a year back in my fishing business! You could have knocked me over with a feather. My little brother Andrew later kidded me that my jaw dropped six inches.

As I stared at Barnabas with a quizzical look, he just smiled and said, "What good will it be for a man to gain the whole world yet forfeit his soul? For whoever wants to save his life will lose it, but whoever loses his life for me will find it."

He gave a little mock bow, looked around the group, and said with a mischievous grin, "Isn't that what you told me the Master taught you? I'm only following what I learned from you giants."

There was a momentary silence as we pondered Barnabas' wit and wisdom, then Matthew burst out laughing. The next thing you know, we were all standing up and hugging Barnabas, slapping him on the back and thanking him profusely. It was one of those joyful moments when the Holy Spirit shows up and surprises you—shocks you—and I will remember it forever.

GENEROUS EYES

Perhaps there is a link between the Holy Spirit gift of encouragement and generosity. I am sure this is at least part of what Jesus meant when he said, "The eye is the lamp of the body. If your eyes are good—generous—your whole body will be full of light. But if your eyes are bad—stingy—your whole body will be full of darkness."

Barnabas was generous in all ways and, therefore, was so full of light as to be contagious. He later traveled up to Antioch, Syria and helped guide that gathering of Gentile believers. He is the one who brought Paul to Antioch, and then he brought him to Jerusalem to meet us for the first time. What a gift he was to all of us.

Although Barnabas asked us not to tell anyone about his gift—he was modest and humble in that way—word got out and spread among our community of fellowship. How could it not? A few others also sold their property. The money was so helpful, and our family of believers continued to grow, adding to our numbers weekly.

During this time, there was such a sense of peace among us, and we all reveled in the power of the Holy Spirit among us and the love and generosity of our Father in heaven. But, alas, not all was well. We were about to experience a whole different side of the Holy Spirit's power—what some might mistakenly think of as a dark side. I, and our family of believers, would never be the same after.

ANANIAS

A man named Ananias, together with his wife Sapphira, sold a piece of property and brought the money and put it at the apostles' feet, much the same way Barnabas had. But I can tell you it was not the same as Barnabas' gift—I could sense there were going to be strings attached to this gift.

Ananias was not a bad man; in fact, he was a good man. He was a leader in the community, always attending our meetings, as he had always attended the temple before

Pentecost. He prayed often and did many good things for the community. But I sensed he did these things to be seen by others.

I was sure neither he nor his wife was born again. He did not have the Holy Spirit; therefore, he could not even begin to understand Jesus. His prayers were flowery and fancy, and I got the sense early on that he was more interested in the approval of man than of God.

Jesus taught often about this type of misguided motive: the approval of man. I can remember his words as though he said them today: "Be careful not to practice your righteousness in front of others to be seen by them. If you do, you will have no reward from your Father in heaven."

This fit Ananias perfectly. But as I said, he was not a bad man; he just had a hole inside his heart. Instead of looking to Jesus to fill it, he looked to the approval of man. He had that "checklist" sense of religion. All his good works in the temple, as well as his community, gave him the false confidence of being right with God.

I can imagine if he stood before Jesus on Judgment Day, he would be quick to list everything he had done, and among them would be the selling of this piece of land. He would be sure he was good enough to qualify for heaven, and he would be absolutely wrong.

Ananias was one of those men who just did not get it, no matter how many times we taught that good works would count for nothing unless one was born again. He would nod in full agreement, even throwing out a few "Amens" and "Preach it, Brothers." But I knew he was missing it.

Ananias and his wife Sapphira, and so many "good people" like them, will say to Jesus on Judgment Day,

"Lord, Lord, did we not prophesy in your name and in your name drive out demons and in your name perform many miracles?" Sadly, they will experience the shock of their lives when Jesus says to them, "I never knew you. Away from me, you evildoers!"

Jesus told many parables that concluded with some people making it to heaven, but many, many more ending up in hell. What always fascinated me was the common reaction from everyone in his stories who ended up in hell—surprise, even shock and dismay. Each story Jesus tells about Judgment Day ends with shock and dismay and gnashing of teeth by those in hell. I am not altogether sure what gnashing of teeth looks like, but I know I do not want to be doing it.

Do you? Are you certain *you* will not be surprised on that Day? All those folks in Jesus' parables were sure they were good with God—or at least good enough. Even those who did not think much about God were sure they were good enough, at least a lot better than the dregs of society.

LYING TO THE HOLY SPIRIT

Ananias did not have evil intentions, in the sense he would ever want to hurt someone or cheat them, but he did not know Jesus. He never took the time to get to know him. All his good activities distracted him from the one and only thing of which we must all be sure: "Do I know Jesus, and even more importantly, does he know me?" Not, "Do I know about him," but "Do I know him personally and intimately?"

Ananias' lack of personal knowledge and relationship with the Master ultimately got him in trouble. With his wife's full knowledge, he had kept back part of the money from the sale for himself and brought the rest to us. I do not know exactly how I knew this at the time, but I did. The Holy Spirit made it obvious to me, and he compelled me to confront Ananias.

"Ananias, how is it that Satan has so filled your heart that you have lied to the Holy Spirit and have kept for yourself some of the money you received for the land? Didn't it belong to you before it was sold? And after it was sold, wasn't the money at your disposal? What made you think of doing such a thing? You have not lied just to us, but you have lied to the Holy Spirit."

I was not angry with Ananias; I felt sad for him. I did not feel like he had lied or cheated me personally, or even our family of believers. No, for some reason my heart was wounded because he had lied to and cheated the Holy Spirit, who was such an intimate and very real part of our community. If asked, Ananias would not have thought he was lying at all.

THE CONSEQUENCES OF LYING TO THE HOLY SPIRIT

My words were meant to convict Ananias, and hopefully to direct him back to Jesus, not to condemn him. I did not care about the money; I cared about his heart and his ultimate eternal damnation. Yes, he had lied to the Holy Spirit, but the Spirit could take care of himself. I hoped this public embarrassment might be the thing to wake Ananias up so he could see the hole in his heart and turn him back to salvation.

I wanted him to recognize his spiritual poverty apart from Jesus. He needed to see that even with all his money and all his good works, he was spiritually bankrupt without Jesus. With Jesus' first Beatitude echoing in my ears, I said, "Ananias, do you not remember the Master saying, 'Blessed are the poor in spirit, for theirs is the kingdom of heaven?'"

Ananias looked at me confused.

"When are you going to stop this charade and see you are a spiritual pauper without Jesus—that you are spiritually bankrupt without the Holy Spirit? It is time for you to humble yourself and surrender to Jesus and receive the Holy Spirit!"

But when Ananias heard this, he fell down and died. I was shocked, and a great fear seized all who were in the room. Up to this point, the Holy Spirit had been a Helper, a Counselor, and a great asset to us all. We had not yet experienced this kind of power, and we simply did not know how to respond. The man was dead, right there before us.

John looked at me and I looked back at him, both of us stunned. I then looked down at Ananias' dead body, then again back at John. We were both dumbfounded. The Spirit's presence was still heavy in the room, and the aftershock was palpable.

My body was frozen, but my mind was racing. I simply did not know what to do next. Did I cause Ananias' death? Was I a murderer? But Matthew, ever the sensible one, motioned to some of the younger men to come forward, so they wrapped up his body, carried him out, and buried him.

I was so uneasy, and my spirit was restless and agitated, so I did the only thing I knew to do—I knelt down and prayed. All of us did. We asked the Lord to show us what to do about Sapphira. I needed the Spirit's guidance, and I was not going to get up off my knees until I was sure of what he wanted me to do.

I was learning to wait on the Holy Spirit's clarity and guidance.

SAPPHIRA

About three hours later, Sapphira came in, not knowing what had happened. Without planning in advance, relying solely on the prompting of the Holy Spirit, I showed her the money and asked her, "Tell me, is this the price you and Ananias got for the land?"

"Yes," she said, "that is the price."

"How could you conspire to test the Spirit of the Lord?" I cried out, exasperated at this point by her stubborn heart. "Listen! The feet of the men who buried your husband are at the door, and they will carry you out also."

At that moment, she fell down at my feet and died. Then the young men came in and, finding her dead, carried her out and buried her beside her husband. In the days following this, a great fear seized our family of believers and all who heard about these events. Can you only imagine? I struggled to understand what seemed to me to be an unnecessarily brutal harshness on the part of the Father.

Why would he take the life of these two people? What they had done was not that bad, was it? I just could not reconcile a death sentence for someone who was just being greedy. As I prayed and pondered this, the Holy Spirit took me back to our Hebrew Scriptures and the story of the emerging Israelite nation.

THE YEAST OF SIN

Back during those early days as God's people struggled to establish themselves in the Promised Land, God told them to wipe out their enemies, every man, woman, and child. They did not follow his command, and, ultimately, the sinful people from the surrounding nations infiltrated the Israelite community and saturated it with their gods and their idols and their sin.

Furthermore, God told Solomon to stay away from foreign wives, but he did not listen nor obey. Solomon's disobedience is summed up succinctly in the book of Kings in our Hebrew Scriptures. It reads like an epitaph:

> King Solomon, however, loved many foreign women besides Pharaoh's daughter—Moabites, Ammonites, Edomites, Sidonians, and Hittites. They were from nations about which the LORD had told the Israelites, "You must not intermarry with them because they will surely turn your hearts after their gods."
>
> Nevertheless, Solomon held fast to them in love. He had seven hundred wives of royal birth and three hundred concubines, and his wives led him astray. As Solomon grew old, his wives turned his heart after other gods, and his heart was not fully devoted to the LORD his God, as the heart of David his father had been.
>
> He followed Ashtoreth the goddess of the Sidonians, and Molek the detestable god of the Ammonites. Solomon did evil in the eyes of the

LORD; he did not follow the LORD completely, as
David his father had done.

Unbelievable. What a collapse; what a complete fall
from grace.

The yeast of Solomon's wives with their foreign cultures and foreign gods cost Solomon dearly, as well as all
of Israel. Sin is like yeast in dough: a little will work its way
through until it infiltrates and affects every fiber of the
dough—and every fiber of you.

I remember the Master talking about yeast several
times. Once, as we were crossing the Sea of Galilee, we disciples forgot to take bread. I was irritated with Andrew and
let him know it with a roll of my eyes. Why Andrew? Well,
I could not be irritated with me. It had to be someone else's
fault, and little brothers are the easiest to pick on.

The old king Peter—ugh.

But Jesus said to us, "Be careful; be on your guard
against the yeast of the Pharisees and Sadducees."

We were so stupid back then. After Jesus said this, we
discussed it among ourselves and said, "It is because we
didn't bring any bread." But after Jesus exposed our dull
faith, we understood he was not telling us to guard against
the yeast used in bread but against the teaching of the Pharisees and Sadducees.

The yeast of the Pharisees and Sadducees was the sin
of a rigid, rules-based religion—doing religious things to be
good and be seen by others. Not much has changed in that
respect with organized religion, I am afraid.

KEEPING THE SPIRIT IN THE DETAILS

As for Ananias and Sapphira, I believe the Spirit was telling me, just as he told the emerging Israelites, our new community of believers could not tolerate such greed and deceptive sin among us. As with the sinful nations in the Promised Land and Solomon's foreign wives, the yeast of Ananias and Sapphira had to be removed. It was a harsh lesson about the dark side of the greedy heart and the sin that so often emanates from within such a heart.

It was also a harsh lesson in the power of the Holy Spirit, yet another reminder that he, the Spirit, is so intimately involved in the details of our lives. Ananias and Sapphira would have been a dark yeast among our new family of believers, sowing stinginess and half-truths. The Spirit would not allow this to happen, at least not at this early time.

This Holy Spirit is active, involved in the details, personable, and, man oh man, is he powerful. I wonder if you are starting to see him this way and if you are starting to see him in your details?

---

[1] Phrase attributed to Oswald Chambers.

19

ARRESTED

TYPICALLY, THE TWELVE WOULD GATHER AT SOLOMON'S
Porch early each morning to pray together before the family
of believers arrived. We cherished this time together. With
so many new believers crowding around us, our time together was limited. During these times, we would share
what was going on in our personal lives, often encouraging
each other, at times challenging each other, and, on rare occasions, calling each other out by speaking truth.

If one of us was drifting, or perhaps speaking to our
wives in a manner unfit for a follower of Jesus, we would
bluntly but lovingly point it out to our Brother. John was
the sweetest and Matthew the most blunt—I guess besides
yours truly. Andrew was typically quiet, but when he had
something to say, we knew he had thought it out before
speaking.

A MORNING INTERRUPTION

One morning, Thomas was telling us about a new family
who had joined us, and the wonderful transformation of
the husband, when the temple guards showed up without
warning and surrounded us.

I was tempted to repeat Jesus' words to the guards the night of his arrest, "Am I leading a rebellion, that you have come out with swords and clubs to capture me? Every day I sat in the temple courts teaching, and you did not arrest me. But this has all taken place that the writings of the prophets might be fulfilled."

But the Spirit checked me. There was no reason to antagonize these men. They did not look particularly happy to be arresting us. By this time, some of them were even secret admirers. At least two of them had wives who openly followed Jesus. No, this arrest was not their idea.

Originally, the temple guards were priests and Levites whose duty it was to guard the temple at night, as set forth in our Hebrew Scriptures. The guards were not originally intended to be militaristic, and they certainly were not intended to be intimidating and threatening.

But as the temple became more and more a business, the role of the temple guards became more military in nature. These days, they could be rough and intimidating, but only if they knew their masters—the chief priest, Annas, and his crowd—wanted them to be.

These men obviously did not want to be nasty to us, so they arrested us quietly and marched all 12 of us off to the public jail. We sat there all day, singing hymns and talking about Jesus. I assured my friends Jesus was right here with us, and the Holy Spirit would direct us, just as Jesus had promised. But they did not need my reassurance. No one was frightened, at least not yet.

We were not in any pain, but we were not exactly comfortable either. We had some anxiety, but no one was going to show any fear. I think we all assumed we would have yet another confrontation with the Sanhedrin, angry words would be spoken, threats made, and then we would be released.

Of course, with this temple crowd, there was always the potential for things to go awry, and we were all aware of this. I thought about Ruth and hoped she would not be too worried. I could take the anxiety and the unknown, and so could Ruth—her trust and faith were at times far stronger than mine. But she is my wife and worrying about Peter could be a full-time job, especially in the old days!

MY BEST FRIEND

As darkness settled in, I was fully expecting to spend the entire night in the jail cell. The guards were asleep in an adjacent room because we had assured them we were not going to cause any trouble. I could hear Thomas snoring, and one of the guards tossing and turning.

I was alone with my thoughts and did what I have often done in the ensuing years—talked to my best friend. I missed Jesus. I missed his smile. I missed his joy. I missed his calm, relaxed manner. I missed his self-confidence in any situation. At least, back then I thought it was his self-confidence, but now I know it was his confidence in his Father.

Jesus' assurance that he would always be with us was because the Holy Spirit would always be *in* us. I know this now, in both my heart and in my head, but that night it was still mostly head knowledge, and I was still getting accustomed to Jesus being gone. Yes, it had been a while since his departure, but when one experiences his deep friendship and unconditional love, it is hard to replace, even with the power of the Spirit indwelling you.

My experience with Jesus as my best friend has always compelled me. I want everyone to know Jesus as I know him. My Savior, yes; God Almighty, yes; but also my best friend and constant companion—even now. I want you to know he is always right there with you. With all the confusion and competing ideologies as well as the different ethnic backgrounds and world cultures, the real Jesus can get lost in the fog.

I find myself saying the same thing repeatedly to anyone conflicted or confused by all the details and distractions, religious hypocrisy, or just a hard life: "For now just ignore anything that confuses you and just get to know Jesus. If you get to know him, I guarantee you will like him."

My friend, you will learn he likes you too. As I have said before, this was my biggest surprise, that Jesus actually liked me—liked us. He spent time with us, laughed with us, ate with us, and started the day with us.

Is it too much to understand that you, too, can live this way with Jesus, even now? He absolutely can be your best friend. You can share your day-to-day life with him. You can laugh with him. You can cry with him. You can share your most intimate hopes and dreams and your most frightening worries.

Jesus wants you to know that when the Father peers into your soul, he sees every thought, every past hurt, every present longing, every void, and yes, even every fault and frailty. He still says, "Look at my son; isn't he wonderful? Look at my precious daughter, so beautiful and alive. I just adore her."

This is what your soul is thirsting for, isn't it?

Sitting there that night in the darkness, I said, "Master, my Savior, my best friend, I miss you. I love you. I want nothing more than to glorify you, to accurately reveal you to the world. I want the world to see what you can do inside an ordinary man like me. I want them to know you. Thank you, dear friend, for always being here for me."

HE NEVER LEAVES

Tears were streaming down my face as I thought of my dear friend and his warm, contagious smile. Jesus. I could feel him with me, right next to me. He was right there beside me — *in* me — through the Holy Spirit.

I could almost audibly hear him saying, as he did on his last night with us, "Do not let your heart be troubled, Peter. Peace I leave with you; my peace I give you. I do not give to you as the world gives. Do not let your hearts be troubled and do not be afraid."

I remember so vividly the peace that washed over me that last night as he continued, "You believe in God; believe also in me. My Father's house has many rooms; if that were not so, would I have told you that I am going there to pre-pare a place for you? And if I go and prepare a place for you, I will come back and take you to be with me, that you also may be where I am. You know the way to the place where I am going."

I smiled as I recalled Thomas' response, "Lord, we don't know where you are going, so how can we know the way?" We were all so blind back then.

Jesus answered Thomas with a declaration I still hold dear in my heart: "I am the way and the truth and the life. No one comes to the Father except through me. If you really know me, you will know my Father as well. From now on, you do know him and have seen him."

Philip interjected, "Lord, show us the Father and that will be enough for us."

Jesus answered with a bit of incredulity: "Don't you know me, Philip, even after I have been among you such a long time? Anyone who has seen me has seen the Father."

He did indeed show us the Father, in so many ways. He showed us the Father's compassion, his forgiveness, his joy, and most of all, his unconditional love. Jesus did indeed "come back" as he promised. Over these past 30 years, he has come back repeatedly. Anytime I have sought him, each time I have asked him to be with me, he has come back.

In fact, he never left.

FREED BY THE ANGEL

Tonight, in this jail cell, it was dark and cold, with just the faint light of a torch casting shadows. As the light from the flame flittered across the cell, I could see flash images of the other disciples. I was at peace, and so were they.

As I sat in the cell pondering all this, suddenly the area lit up like lightning. My friends immediately awoke, and we sat there startled and dumbstruck as the light intensified. Because of my prior experience with Jesus on what people now call the Mount of Transfiguration, I knew either Jesus or an angel was going to appear. Whatever was getting ready to happen, I knew in my gut it would be big.

In an instant, an angel of the Lord stood before us. He was as white and as bright as Jesus was that day up on the mountain, when his true glory was shown to James, John, and me. If I tried to describe exactly what he looked like, I would not have the words, and you simply would not have the mind to see it.

Trust me—if it ever happens to you, you will be dumbstruck and overwhelmed with a power that is not of this world. These glimpses of the real Jesus and his kingdom, as overwhelming as they are, are just pinholes of light into true reality. These pinholes show us just how awesome his kingdom truly is. If we are blinded by just these glimpses, can you imagine the real thing?

The angel immediately opened the doors of the jail and led us out. No one was saying a word. No one dared to talk. We were all in a trance of sorts, not sure if this was real or if we were dreaming. As we stepped out into the early dawn, the angel pointed to the temple and said, "Go, stand in the temple courts and tell the people all about the good news of the kingdom."

Suddenly he was gone. It was daybreak, and we looked at each other, not sure what to do next. After a moment, Thaddaeus shrugged and said, "Well, let's go to the temple." We entered the temple courts, just as we had been instructed. We told the people all about the good news of the kingdom and this new life Jesus came to give us.

RESURRECTION LIFE

This new life is the resurrection life. Some call it resurrection power, which simply means learning to live with the same power that raised Jesus from the dead—Holy Spirit power. It is called resurrection power because when you are born again, it is like being resurrected from the dead—in essence, you were. The Spirit indwells you and you are no longer the old you. A new power is at work. Brother Paul says it like this: "I have been crucified with Christ and I no longer live, but Christ lives in me. The life I now live in the body, I live by faith in the Son of God, who loved me and gave himself for me."

This new life is all about freedom, peace, joy, contentment, gratitude, and confident expectation. May I comment for just a moment on each of these?

Freedom: A freedom from and freedom to. Freedom *from* the bonds and the prisons in which we have put ourselves. The bad habits and dark heart issues to which we have surrendered. But a freedom *to* experience the fullness of God the Father's riches. For the first time in our lives, we are free to pursue the life to the full Jesus brought us.

Peace: A peace that comes from knowing your Father is all-powerful, all-knowing, and all-loving. Because of this heart and head knowledge, fixed and secured by the Spirit, you know you are perfectly safe in his care.

Joy: the joy that brings a pervasive sense of well-being;[1] a sense deep in your soul that everything is as it should be and will be because the Father is in control.

Contentment: The contentment that flows naturally from this joy, this sense of well-being, this sense that, "The LORD is my Shepherd and I shall not want for anything." For the first time in my life, I lack nothing.

Gratitude: The gratitude that comes from this freedom, peace, joy, and contentment. From knowing you are saved from the agony and suffering of eternal hell. This alone should be enough to live gratefully forever! But Jesus also saved you from your Self. He saved your loved ones from your old Self as well. Finally, the eternal and overwhelming sense of gratitude for his grace and goodness and generosity to you personally.

Hope: The confident expectation that your Father is perfectly loving, perfectly powerful, and perfectly present in the details of your life. You can view any situation with so much confidence in his perfect character that you can sincerely say, "Thank you now, Father, before I see how you are going to work this out because I know I will be thanking you later."

This is the heavenly Father we serve.

------

[1] Definition attributed to Dallas Willard.

20

WHO DO YOU SAY I AM?

IT WAS MORNING, THE ANGEL HAD FREED US, AND WE were at Solomon's Porch sharing the story of the angel's miraculous deliverance. People were crowding around us to hear the details. They were awe-struck by the image of the angel's power, and they clamored for more.

Nicodemus tells us when the high priest and his associates arrived at the Hall of Polished Stones that same morning, they called together the Sanhedrin—the full assembly of the elders of Israel—and sent to the jail for us. On arriving, the officers did not find us there, so they went back and reported, "We found the jail securely locked, with the guards standing at the doors, but when we opened them, we found no one inside."

The captain of the temple guard and the chief priests were at a loss, wondering what this might lead to. Then someone came in and said, "Look! The men you put in jail are standing in the temple courts teaching the people."

The captain and his officers found us at Solomon's Porch and asked us to accompany them. They did not use force because they feared the people would attack them. It was clear they were themselves in wonderment and in a semi-state of shock about what could possibly have happened. The very men they had arrested and thrown in jail were somehow free? I could hear them whispering among themselves. They were a bit unnerved and suddenly plagued by the realization they were not in control.

Because they were not.

STANDING TRIAL ... AGAIN

They brought us in and made us stand before the Sanhedrin to be questioned by the high priest. You see, the Sanhedrin judged accused lawbreakers, but a minimum of two witnesses was required to convict a suspect. There were no lawyers. Instead, the accusing witnesses stated the offense in the presence of the accused, and the accused could then call witnesses on their own behalf. The court then questioned the accused, the accusers, and the defense witnesses. We did not need any defense witnesses. There were 12 of us ready to testify and answer any questions they might have.

The 70 men sat in a semicircle facing Annas and Caiaphas and our little group. Annas glared at us and said accusingly, "We gave you strict orders not to teach in this name, yet you have filled Jerusalem with your teaching and are determined to make us guilty of this man's blood."

You can hear their fear, right? When they saw Jesus dying on the cross, they mocked him and hurled insults at him. They were proud to have silenced this heretic rebel. They celebrated their success and were quite proud of themselves. But Nicodemus tells us even back then, in the immediate afterglow of their victory, it was evident they were nervous. There was anxiety present even in their celebration. Nicodemus said he could tell that deep within them, they had a nervous sense of unease, a conviction they just could not shake.

They could not rid themselves of this haunting sense they had killed an innocent man. They were even more haunted by the growing awareness that Jesus controlled the entire affair. That truly rattled them.

Now, in all their religious garb, and even surrounded by their weapons of the world, they were afraid of being associated with the killing of Jesus. Yes, these powerful men were afraid, but we were not.

This unsettled them even more. What do people like these men, who are accustomed to being in total control, do when they are unsettled? They try to tighten their control even more.

I started to talk first, but then each of us joined in at various times. Dr. Luke summed up the essence of what we all said quite nicely: "We must obey God rather than human beings! The God of our ancestors raised Jesus from the dead—whom you killed by hanging him on a cross."

That made them squirm.

"God exalted him to his own right hand as Prince and Savior that he might bring Israel to repentance and forgive their sins," I continued. "We are witnesses of these things, and so is the Holy Spirit, whom God has given to those who obey him."

Well, they did not like hearing that. They were furious. The murmuring among them grew to an uproar. Their red faces were contorted with anger. Their eyes burned with hatred. They wanted to put us to death, and I was sure they would figure out a way to do so.

GAMALIEL

But then another surprise—a Pharisee named Gamaliel, a well-respected rabbi and teacher of the law who was honored by all the people, stood up and ordered the guards to take us outside. This was the famous rabbi under whom our brother Paul studied.

He then addressed the group of angry men: "Men of Israel, consider carefully what you intend to do to these men. Some time ago, Theudas appeared, claiming to be somebody, and about four hundred men rallied to him. He was killed, all his followers were dispersed, and it all came to nothing. After him, Judas the Galilean appeared in the days of the census and led a band of people in revolt. He too was killed, and all his followers were scattered.

"Therefore, in the present case I advise you: Leave these men alone! Let them go! For if their purpose or activity is of human origin, it will fail. But if it is from God, you will not be able to stop these men; you will only find yourselves fighting against God."

Do you think the Holy Spirit was directing Gamaliel's wisdom? Apparently, Gamaliel's speech persuaded them, but they were so angry and so scared of us, they were not about to just simply let us go. The high priest and his cronies waited until Gamaliel and some of the others had left and then called us back in.

ANNAS' ORDER

None of us knew at the time what Gamliel had said, so we had no idea what would happen next. Annas glared at us for a moment and then said, "You ignorant fishermen have overstepped your authority and attacked us for the last time. But because we are holy and righteous, and want to extend mercy when we can, we are going to let you off."

Holy and righteous. His face and his tone certainly did not match his words, but I must admit I breathed a sigh of relief.

But then his face contorted and he sneered, with a sick sort of glee, "As a parting gift, we are going to leave you with a reminder of just who you are defying."

With that, he called in a different set of guards—former military men who carried out the dirty work of the Sanhedrin. I knew we were in trouble, and sure enough, Annas ordered us to be flogged.

Flogged.

His order sent a shiver down my spine. I knew the others were inwardly reeling as well. Annas ordered our flogging like it was a child's spanking, but if you know anything about floggings, they are extraordinarily painful. I have seen many die from floggings. It is a horrible punishment. The pain is unbearable, and the public humiliation as you are stripped of all your dignity and the skin off your back renders you an unclean outcast, as alienated as a leper in the eyes of the people.

John had seen the Master flogged. His back was ripped to shreds. His sides and chest were gashed. It was sickening. Blood was everywhere as bits of his skin flew off his back.

For a moment, I was paralyzed with fear. Everything in me said, "Run! Save yourself!" I know my brothers were experiencing the same horror and abject fear. Suddenly I saw Jesus. I do not know if I actually saw him or if it was an image in my mind, but I immediately felt a sense of peace. Jesus was looking at me intently, with a questioning expression. He was smiling, but I could tell he wanted me to see something—to grasp something.

JESUS—SON OF MAN OR SON OF GOD?

Suddenly, in my mind, I could see us standing on the hill in the region of Caesarea Philippi. Jesus turned to us and asked, "Who do people say the Son of Man is?"

Matthew said, "Some say John the Baptist; others say Elijah; and still others, Jeremiah or one of the prophets."

I remember thinking Matthew's response pretty much summed it up,

Then Jesus looked at each of us and said, "But what about you? Who do you say I am?"

Can you see this is the real question each of us has to answer? I cannot answer this for you. Your wife or husband cannot answer it for you. Your parents, your teacher, your rabbi, or priest, none of these can, either. You must answer Jesus' question in *your* heart. Please do not fool yourself with an answer only from your head.

Standing here today, facing this flogging, I had better already have answered this question in my own mind and heart, or else I would not be able to stand up under this coming trial.

Head knowledge counts for nothing if there is no penetrating heart knowledge. Who do *you* say Jesus is? Is he a great teacher, a prophet, or perhaps a godly guru? Is he a soulful ambassador for God? Perhaps someone from whom you want to learn, or even emulate?

Hear this, my friend, he did not leave you with any of those options. He said, "I am God." He said, "I and the

Father are one and the same." He said, "I can forgive sins." Now understand in our Jewish culture, no one can say such a thing and be taken lightly. In our worldview, there is only one God, and only he can forgive sins.

When Jesus told someone, "Your sins are forgiven," he said it with an authority only God Almighty has. Now understand the contrast: I can forgive you for a wrong you commit against me, but I have no authority to forgive you of your *sin*. That kind of forgiveness is between you and God.

You can forgive someone who wrongs you, but wouldn't you reject any notion that I could forgive that same person for his sins against you? Wouldn't you vehemently object to my doing such a thing? You would naturally be offended and aggravated at such an arrogant assumption of authority. Would you not say something like, "Who are you to forgive him? Are you God? He sinned against me, not you."

This is exactly the way the Sanhedrin reacted to Jesus saying he could forgive sin. It was blasphemy. He was equating himself with God, which was heresy of the highest order.

NO IN-BETWEEN

When Jesus asks, "Who do you say I am?" There is no room for a lukewarm, ambiguous response. He is either a lying manipulator, a lunatic, or he is who he said he is.[1]

There is no in-between. I have never met anyone who knew Jesus who would say he was a lying manipulator, nor have I met anyone who would say he was a lunatic unless, like this Sanhedrin, they had a narcissistic, Self-agenda. But

I have met many who would say he was a good man, a prophet, a holy man, but not necessarily God incarnate.

Hogwash.

These are the ones of whom the prophet Isaiah spoke when he said,

> You will be ever hearing but never understanding; you will be ever seeing but never perceiving. For this people's heart has become calloused; they hardly hear with their ears, and they have closed their eyes.

That day back in Caesarea, Jesus asked us this soul-penetrating question: "Who do you say I am?" I answered without even thinking, compelled by the Holy Spirit, "You are the Messiah, the Son of the living God."

Today as I faced this flogging, I could sense Jesus wanted me to remember how he had responded to us that day. He explained that he must go to Jerusalem and suffer many things at the hands of the elders, the chief priests, and the teachers of the law and that he must be killed and on the third day be raised to life.

GET BEHIND ME, SELF

Well, Jesus' prediction was too much for me to take, and since I was the self-appointed leader of the disciples and the self-appointed caretaker of Jesus, I took him aside and began to rebuke him. "Never, Lord!" I said. "This shall never happen to me, uh … I mean you!"

There it was. I had said what I felt, but not what I meant to say. I did not want anything like that to happen to Jesus because of how it would affect *me*. Oh, please know I loved Jesus and cared deeply for him, but back then, I was operating in the kingdom of Peter. In the kingdom of Peter, it is all about Peter. Can you relate?

I had meant to say, "This cannot happen to you, Lord." But the true desires of my heart instead blurted out "me." I recall Jesus saying many times, "For out of the overflow of the heart the mouth speaks." Oh my, does it ever. You see, I knew whatever happened to Jesus happened to me. Back then, I was too self-absorbed and too focused on "what is in it for me" to see it any other way.

I will never forget Jesus' response. He jerked his arm loose from me and wheeled around and said, "Get behind me, Satan! You are a stumbling block to me; you do not have in mind the concerns of God, but the concerns of your Self."

There I was, exposed. This is what happens when we are face to face with Jesus—we are exposed for who we really are. In such a moment it is uncomfortable, embarrassing, and even distressing. But this is not the Master's intention. He wants us to see ourselves for who we are so we can then begin being transformed more and more into his likeness.

This is, after all, what humility is truly all about—being realistic about who we are: dark-hearted, selfish, self-absorbed, fragile people. Once you see yourself with this type of raw clarity, the joy and freedom that comes from this self-awareness is practically exhilarating. We can finally stop pretending to be something or someone we are not.

Humility does not mean thinking less of oneself but to stop thinking about oneself as much as we all do,[2] and to just relax in the confidence Jesus knows all about you yet loves you anyway. As I say so often, he even likes you.

Jesus then turned to the other 11 and said, "Whoever wants to be my disciple must deny themselves and take up their cross and follow me. For whoever wants to save their life will lose it, but whoever loses their life for me will find it."

---

[1] Statement attributed to C. S. Lewis.

[2] Statement attributed to C. S. Lewis.

21

FLOGGED!

HERE WE WERE, GETTING READY TO TAKE UP OUR
crosses with this flogging. With Jesus' words ringing in my
ears, I lost all sense of fear and stepped forward. I said to
Annas, "Sir, let these men go. I will take this punishment
on myself."

Annas looked at me with a questioning smirk. He was
trying to process what he had just heard. Just a moment before, he had felt such great power. Now with my request,
his power had slipped.

Then I heard Thomas clear his throat and say, "No, sir.
I will take this punishment for my brothers. I am responsible. Let it be me."

Silence.

There was a thickening of the air, a heaviness. It was
the Spirit. We all felt it … him, even Annas and Caiaphas
and the guards. Only we knew exactly who was with us.
They had no idea. They only knew something heavy was
happening.

Suddenly, the sons of Zebedee—James and John—both
stepped forward and said, "Sir, we are the Sons of Thunder.
We will take this punishment on ourselves. Let these other
men go. We are, in fact, the true instigators."

Suddenly, all 12 of us were clamoring to be the ones to take the lashing. Philip, Simon, Matthew, Thaddeus, James, and Nathanael were all exclaiming, "Do not rob me of this blessing. Let it be me!"

Annas was stunned. "Do not rob me of this blessing?" A beating now a blessing? Now all his power had been usurped. His body language was closing up, shrinking before our eyes. He was defeated. For all his temple and earthly power, and his weapons of the world all around him, he knew he was facing a divine power—a power able to demolish any and all strongholds, physical or spiritual.

Any stronghold fear may have had on us was gone. Demolished! But I want you to understand our motive. We were not trying to shame Annas and Caiaphas. We were not seeking to establish ourselves as heroes. No. We simply wanted to take the beating ourselves. We wanted to protect our brothers. We wanted to glorify Jesus.

I *wanted* to suffer for Jesus. He had suffered for me, and I had betrayed him in his hour of need. I would not betray him now. I would not let him down this time. I wanted to take this beating. I was proud to suffer for my Master Jesus.

Caiaphas, seeing the situation was getting out of hand, stepped in and said, "Quiet! You all want to suffer? Well, so be it. You will." His face was contorted with hatred. The Spirit was stirring in the room, but Satan was strong in Caiaphas. Any reasonable approach Gamaliel had previously offered was gone. Hatred and fear had won the day.

WHEN WE COULD NOT FOLLOW JESUS

The guards took us out and, two by two, they tied us down, ripped the shirts off our backs, and prepared to whip us. I will spare you the details of this beating, but I will share with you my thoughts as I was on my knees, awaiting the first blow.

As the guards were preparing to flog us, I was transported in my mind back to our last night with the Master. Judas had just left. Jesus then said, "Now the Son of Man is glorified and God is glorified in him."

Remember "to glorify" in our language carries with it the sense "to accurately reveal." Jesus was telling us that his next 24 hours would accurately reveal the Father in him and accurately reveal who he truly is—the Son of Man.

"My brothers," he continued, "I will be with you only a little longer. You will look for me, and just as I told the Jews, so I tell you now: Where I am going, you cannot come."

At this point, I asked Jesus, "Lord, where are you going?" (Is that the best I could come up with?)

Jesus replied to me, "Where I am going, you cannot follow now, but you will follow later."

Now that did not make any sense to me, not at all, so I asked, "Lord, why can I not follow you now? I will lay down my life for you."

Can you now see why I could not follow him back then? I loved Jesus, and I was devoted to him. In any ordinary situation, I would have proudly fought alongside him. In any ordinary situation, I would have been proud to protect him. I had been in fights before. I was not afraid of any man. I was bigger and stronger than most men.

But this was not an ordinary situation. Cosmic forces were at work. As Paul so often teaches, "For our struggle is not against flesh and blood, but against the rulers, against the authorities, against the powers of this dark world and against the spiritual forces of evil in the heavenly realms.

"Be strong in the Lord," Paul continues, "and in his mighty power. Put on the full armor of God, so that you can take your stand against the devil's schemes."

I had no spiritual armor that night of Jesus' arrest because I had no Spirit yet. I was operating in Peter's power, in the kingdom of Peter. Yes, I was bigger and stronger than most men, but without the power of the Holy Spirit, I was puny and pathetic against Satan.

SUFFERING SIFTS THE DROSS OF SELF

Why could I not lay down my life for Jesus back then? Because I could not even lay down my own agenda, my own personal plans for Peter. I could not even begin to lay down Self. Why could I not follow Jesus that last night of his arrest? Because I was too focused on following Peter.

These days, I live with the power of the Spirit—the same power that raised the Master from the dead. I now have that power. So do you—if you are born again.

I am not afraid of Satan. I am aware of his evil power, and I certainly am not going to look to pick a fight with him. But I do not have to look. Our enemy the devil prowls around like a roaring lion looking for someone to devour. Yet I am not afraid of him because greater is he, the Holy Spirit, who is in me than is Satan.

Do you believe this? The Master said it was so. You might believe in Jesus, but do you believe what Jesus believed?[1] I do. I do not just believe it, I trust it. I rely on it. I make my life decisions based on this trust. If Satan attacks me, if he is seeking to sift me like wheat, I can resist him, standing firm in my trust. One thing I know: Satan cannot attack me unless the Father has given him permission. He had to ask God for permission to sift me like wheat on Jesus' last night. God allowed it because I so needed it, and then he used it for good.

Remember, he had to ask permission to attack Job as well.

Can you see that God used both attacks by Satan to further his plan? Can you see how Job and I were strengthened by our experience? The sifting process exposed me to myself, and it was not pretty. But suffering sifts out the dross of Self. After that experience, I was no longer under any illusion that I was big, strong Peter. I knew I needed a Savior, and I knew I needed my Lord's strength, not mine.

As our patriarch, Joseph, said to his brothers, "You meant it for harm, but God meant it for good." Satan always means it for harm, but your heavenly Father always means it for good. The harm he allows to come your way is God's way of sifting out the old you and leading you forward, deeper into his kingdom.

I needed sifting. I needed the old Self sifted, but I did not know it back then. You need sifting too, but do you know it? You think I am some great man of God, the great Apostle Peter, leader of the church of Christ. No. I am just a man, a human like you—or I was. Now I have learned to look to the power of the Holy Spirit instead of Peter. I have learned to ignore the kingdom of Self, and my own pitiful power, and to seek first his kingdom and his righteousness—and his Holy Spirit power. As the Master promised, "All these other things, these things you worry about or need, will be provided to you."

BLESSED ARE THOSE WHO ARE PERSECUTED

Today, as the first lash hit my back, the pain screamed through my brain. It was a pain I had never experienced before. My back was on fire. I wanted to cry out and a gasp escaped my mouth. I could not contain it. The guard laughed at me and said, "Where is your Jesus now, fisherman?"

I started praying. I was going to glorify Jesus through this pain. I was going to accurately reveal him, right here, right now. I was going to be a witness for him because I knew I had the power of the Holy Spirit within me.

I heard John cry out, "Be strong, brothers! Jesus is here with us. The victory is already his!"

We all responded, "Blessed are those who are persecuted because of righteousness, for theirs is the kingdom of heaven!"

Thomas cried out, "Blessed are you when people insult you, persecute you, and falsely say all kinds of evil against you because of me."

Matthew yelled, "Rejoice and be glad because great is your reward in heaven, for in the same way they persecuted the prophets who were before you."

I WANT TO KNOW YOU

At this point, the pain was burning so badly, I started tuning everyone and everything out and started going deeper. Another lash and I think a bit of my own flesh flew past my eyes. But I was digging in with Jesus. Going deeper. My prayer in this moment was this: "I want to know you, Jesus. I want to know the power of your resurrection and I want to participate in your sufferings. If this suffering can bring me closer and take me deeper, then I want it. I want to become like you in your death, and somehow attain to the resurrection from the dead."

As the flogging continued, the Spirit took me back to Jesus' prayer in the garden that last night: "My Father, if it is possible, may this cup be taken from me. Yet not as I will, but as you will."

As you know, while Jesus was praying, John, James, and I had fallen asleep in the garden. When he returned to us, he said, looking directly and only at me, "Couldn't you men keep watch with me for one hour? Watch and pray so that you will not fall into temptation. The spirit is willing, but the flesh is weak."

Back then, my spirit thought I was willing, but my flesh was still so weak. But not today. Now it was not my spirit that was willing, but the Spirit inside me, welling up with a force of power so strong the blinding pain was all but blocked out.

Back then, in that moment of searing pain, and even now, I want to know my Master and Savior. I want to go deeper. I want everything he wants for me. Everything. I know now that what he wants for me, and for you, is to be conformed to his likeness, to abandon our Selfs and live the life to the full only he can provide. In my journey, and in yours, there will be times when being conformed is going to involve pain. The pain is not his desire; it is our growth he desires, our holiness.

I was not about to ask the Father to take away this beating or this pain. I was asking only not to waste it. I closed my eyes and concentrated on Jesus, not the pain. "Take me deeper, Father. I will be your witness, and I will be a faithful one. With your Holy Spirit empowering me, I will take this pain and capture it, subdue it, and use it to get closer to you."

FUELED BY SUFFERING

After the lashing, the guards untied us and pushed us to the side. I was about to lose consciousness, so I am groggy on what was happening with the other apostles. But the sound of the whips tearing apart flesh will never leave me.

The next thing I knew, we were dragged and pushed back into the room with Caiaphas. Annas apparently did not have the stomach for the gruesome, bloody sight we presented. Caiaphas ordered us again not to speak in the name of Jesus, and then he let us go.

We left rejoicing because we had been counted worthy of suffering disgrace for Jesus. Do you think we were out of our minds to celebrate our suffering? We were not. If you had experienced the love of the Master, the years of his deep abiding friendship, and then abandoned him like we did, you would understand.

Jesus did not demand we suffer as some sort of penance for our failures. We knew we were totally and completely forgiven. We knew there was no penalty to pay for abandoning him. But it just felt so good to suffer for him. In some small way, we had been able to repay him, to share in his suffering.

After that, day after day, in the temple courts and from house to house, we never stopped teaching and proclaiming the good news that Jesus is the Messiah. We were fueled by our suffering. We were propelled by the Spirit. We would never give up. We knew now we could endure anything with the power of the Holy Spirit resonating through our bodies.

Therefore, since Christ suffered in his body, arm yourselves also with the same attitude because whoever suffers in the body is done with sin.

---

[1] Statement attributed to John Ortberg.

22

DISTRACTIONS

WE HAD JUST ENDURED AN EXTRAORDINARY PHYSICAL
challenge from the scourging we received from the Sanhedrin, but that terrible ordeal, from those outside our family,
soon faded into the background as we faced a new challenge from *within* our family—distractions and busyness.

The persecution we were experiencing from the outside
was easy to identify and, therefore, at least for me, easier to
combat. The Jewish establishment hated us; that was plain
to see. Anything we can see is easier to combat, to take a
stand against. Yes, they could hurt us physically, but because the Holy Spirit was moving so mightily with us and
through us, I was not worried about their outside, physical
attacks.

But this new persecution from within could prove to be
much more debilitating because it was not so obvious. You
see in those days, when the number of disciples was in-
creasing, the Hellenistic Jews among us, Nicanor and Timon, came to the Twelve and complained against our
Hebrew Jewish brothers because they felt their widows
were being overlooked in the daily distribution of food.
Nicanor and Timon were both level-headed and both loved

the Lord. Their manner was not aggressive, but they were determined.

Maybe they were accurate and maybe they were not. I was not focused on food distribution. My focus was on feeding spiritual food to our new family of believers. But these brothers had stayed with us in Jerusalem after Pentecost, and they felt it was an issue, so we had to address it. I was frustrated with this and might have shown it. I hope not, but all I wanted to do was what I knew I was called to do—preach and teach about Jesus. This kind of administrative detail could distract me from the Spirit's top priority for us.

DISCOURAGE AND DISTRACT

Over all these years, the Holy Spirit has helped me to see the real villain in these situations is Satan. Satan's primary strategy is destroy, distract, and discourage.[1] If he can keep you out of a saving relationship with Jesus, he will destroy your soul. This is his top priority to be sure. But if he loses that battle and you are born again, he will spend the rest of your life seeking to distract you and discourage you.

He is relentless, and his destroy, distract, discourage strategy is so effective. Please keep this in mind the next time you are feeling distracted or discouraged. This is not from the Holy Spirit. Any discouragement you ever feel is from Satan. There is now no condemnation for followers of Jesus.

The Holy Spirit convicts but never condemns. Please do not miss this. Conviction is a reminder from the Spirit within you that you are off track. Condemnation is an accusing voice saying you are a failure, a hopeless sinner. This kind of degrading negativity is always from Satan.

Discouragement and distraction are Satan's tactics. See it for what it is. See him for who he is: "a liar from the beginning," as Jesus said. Rebuke him; refuse to be his victim. Absolutely refuse! You can, you know. Resist the devil and he will flee. Yes, he is like a lion prowling around looking to devour, but with the Holy Spirit empowering you, his growl is much worse than his bite.

In fact, Satan has no real bite. He can only bluff.

BUSYNESS

Satan's number one weapon against us is busyness. I have witnessed many a soul lost to Satan through busyness. Sadly, I have also witnessed many a man or woman find salvation but miss the life that is truly life because of busyness. As our Way has grown and spread, our slower and more meditative Hebrew culture has mixed and assimilated with the other cultures of the world. The busier cultures of the larger cities have promulgated this busyness weapon of Satan quickly.

The Holy Spirit brings peace, and God is a God of order, not distraction.

I see men and women scurrying around all week, trying to get it all done. I see these same folks scurrying around on our days of worship, trying to get all their worship activities done. During the week, they are busy and distracted with work and activities. Even though most of our believers honor the Lord's Day by not working at their profession, some still busy themselves with church activities on the Lord's Day.

They are missing the one thing that is most important: knowing Jesus. It is much easier to work for God than to know God.[2] The truth is many people would rather serve God than get to know him personally and intimately. Perhaps this is because serving God is tangible, and therefore measurable, so this is where they find their reward. But it is a fleeting and temporary reward.

I am reminded of the Psalm:

> Unless the LORD builds the house, the builders
>   labor in vain.
> Unless the LORD watches over the city, the
>   guards stand watch in vain.
> In vain you rise early and stay up late, toiling
>   for food to eat—
> for he grants sleep to those he loves.

I know many men, and even some women, who struggle to find peaceful sleep because they think they are in charge of "building their houses and watching over their personal cities." They stay up late and get up early in a frenetic urgency to get it all done. This, my friends, is not the life to the full Jesus wants for you.

FUTILE MOTIONS VERSUS TRUE MOVEMENT

Busyness mistakes motion for true movement. People imprisoned by busyness have much motion in their lives, but they are not moving closer to Jesus. They are producing much worldly fruit, but not fruit that will last.

Getting closer to the Father, digging deeper with Jesus, abiding with him, and learning to live with the power of the Holy Spirit are not tangible, and the world does not reward this—not at all, not in any way. I urge you to be on guard against this all-too-human tendency to measure your spiritual life by your activities.

A tragic life is a life that seeks things that are measurable in the moment instead of things that are measurable eternally. I have found that things that are measurable in the short term are often neither measurable nor memorable in the long term.[3] Let us fix our eyes on what is unseen instead of what is seen because what is unseen produces fruit that will last. But what is seen is all too often no true fruit at all. Holiness is an inward harmony and unity with the Father, not an outward display of activity and religion.

You may remember Jesus' dear friends—Lazarus, Martha, and Mary—who lived in Bethany. Jesus loved all three siblings equally, but he seemed to truly relish his quiet time with Lazarus. I think he felt he could be himself with Lazarus. Lazarus' home was quiet, and the two of them would often sit all afternoon just talking about the Scriptures. Lazarus asked many deep questions, questions I would never have even thought to ask. Jesus enjoyed asking Lazarus challenging questions in return.

That kind of give and take debate gave Jesus great joy.

Their conversations, and sometimes debates, could go on for hours. The younger sister Mary would sit near them and listen to all they said, absorbing their words deep into her heart. She had such a peaceful way about her. Neither she nor Lazarus ever seemed to be in a hurry, and Mary would not let anything distract her from listening intently to Jesus.

MARY'S PERFUME

You may recall Mary was the same one who poured perfume on the Lord and wiped his feet with her hair. She did this six days before the Passover, after we had just arrived in Bethany. A dinner was given in Jesus' honor at the home of Simon the Leper, a man Jesus had previously healed. Simon was the father of Martha, Mary, and Lazarus, and Martha helped prepare and serve. She was the hostess in her own home, you can be sure of that. Besides, Martha could never just sit still.

Lazarus was among those reclining at the table with Jesus and Simon. Mary took an alabaster jar filled with expensive perfume and poured it on Jesus' feet, wiping his feet with her hair. The house filled with the fragrance of the perfume. It was such a beautiful moment.

But Martha was just the opposite of Mary. Don't get me wrong—she was a pleasant person, friendly and welcoming. She loved to have Jesus visit and would always prepare great meals for us. The 12 of us loved it when Jesus said we were stopping in Bethany!

But Martha could be difficult. She would get distracted by all the preparations that had to be made. I remember the time she worked herself into a frenzy, cleaning the house and getting the food ready. When she got into this mode, I would be sure to stay out of her way. I had been bossed around by Martha before and even snapped at when I did not do something the way she wanted it done.

Mary typically got the brunt of Martha's frustrations. I have no doubt Martha considered Mary lazy. She certainly thought of her as inefficient and a timewaster. Martha reminded me of … me, back in my fishing days. Rushed, hurried, and harried, temper rising and patience falling.

Distracted by all my important activities.

I was watching her get worked up, and I elbowed John and said, "Watch out. Martha is getting frustrated." John looked her way, saw her face reddening, and quietly walked outside. So did Nathaniel and Philip. They knew better than to get in Martha's way when she was pressing and stressing.

I saw her finally drop her spoon and march over to Jesus and Lazarus. She cried out, "Lord, don't you care that my sister has left me to do the work by myself? Tell her to help me!"

I have to say I was trying my best to suppress a smile. Poor Martha. She was, after all, doing all the work. She was hot and weary, but the truth is she liked being this way. She thrived on being busy. Some of us had tried before to help her out and she pushed us out of the way, murmuring, "If you want something done right, you have to do it yourself."

Are you possibly a Martha?

---

[1] Idea attributed to Search Ministries.

[2] Idea attributed to Cubby Culberton.

[3] Statement attributed to Andy Stanley.

23

BE STILL AND KNOW
THAT I AM GOD

THAT DAY, JESUS HAD TOLD MARTHA NOT TO BUSY
herself preparing a meal. We had brought with us fresh
bread and even some honey and dates. Jesus wanted her to
relax, sit with him, and listen to what he had to say.

But Martha did not like just sitting. In fact, I do not
think I ever saw her just being still. She couldn't, don't you
see? Busyness made her happy. Busyness made her feel important. Busyness made her feel needed—and busyness
made her feel necessary.

Busyness defined her, and she liked it that way.

Does this sound a little too familiar?

Martha simply could not sit still. That day, she was so
distracted and disjointed, and just so miserable as she complained to Jesus. She was about to make everyone else miserable. This is often the way of busy people. No one can
really relax around them. Jesus looked at Martha with a
look I had experienced many times before, when I was being busy and distracted King Peter.

Jesus loved her, and he was not in the least bit irritated
with her. But he was also saddened because he knew that

with all her busyness, she was missing the important things in life. Martha knew a lot about Jesus and had spent a lot of time around him. But she did not know Jesus like Mary knew him. Mary had a deeper knowledge of Jesus—a relationship saturating her heart.

Mary's relationship was personal, visceral. Martha's was surface—sincere, but still surface.

ONLY ONE THING

Jesus turned to Martha and said, "Martha, Martha, you are worried and upset about many things, but only one thing is needed. Look at Mary. She sits here quietly, listening to what I am saying. She is soaking in my words, but you are too busy and distracted to spend time with me. Mary has chosen what is better, and it will not be taken away from her."

Martha did indeed look at Mary, but it was with a frenetic frown.

"But you, my dear, sweet friend," Jesus continued with a smile, "you are missing the things that are truly important. Martha, do you remember King David's psalm?

> One thing I ask from the LORD,
> this only do I seek:
> that I may dwell in the house of the LORD
> all the days of my life,
> to gaze on the beauty of the LORD
> and to seek him in his temple.

Martha did not respond. Jesus then said to her, "You are worried about so many things, but only one thing is needed. I want you to just be still for a while. Come, sit down next to me."

Jesus smiled with his warm, infectious smile and opened his arms toward Martha. I watched as she at first began to turn back toward her food, but then she stopped, hesitated, and slowly turned and sat down next to Jesus. Her beet-red face softened as Jesus lovingly placed his hand on her shoulder.

He then looked directly into her eyes with love and affection and said "Good. Now, just be still and know that I am God."

"Only one thing is needed," Jesus had said. For Martha, for you, and for me, this one thing means going deeper in your relationship with Jesus. Everything else is periphery. All your good activities, all those things that "if I do not do them, who will?", all your church service—they mean nothing if you are not getting to know your Savior personally, intimately.

Just the two of you.

That, my friend, is the one thing.

The value of our public service for God flows from our private intimacy with him.[1] I have to remember this over and over. Trust me, I, too, can get busy and distracted and lose sight of the Holy Spirit. I, too, can be distracted by all that must get done and, therefore, bypass my quiet time with my Lord.

It's hard to be still when there is so much to be done. It's harder still when I am the one to get it all done!

SIN OR SERVICE

Whether you miss Jesus because of sin or because of service, you still missed him. What does it matter to a dying man lost in the desert if he missed the only water source by 100 feet or by a mile? He missed it, the only source of his salvation.[2]

One day, Jesus was speaking to a crowd, many of whom had been present when he fed the five thousand. He told them, "Do not work for food that spoils, but for food that endures to eternal life, which the Son of Man will give you."

They then asked him, "What one thing must we do to do the works God requires?"

Now please do not miss Jesus' answer: "The work of God is this: to believe in the one he has sent."

The crowd asked about works; Jesus instead pointed them to the only work: believe, trust, surrender. The crowd—perhaps you?—asked for a checklist of things to do. Jesus instead pointed them to what he has *done*. His work—to believe, to trust and surrender—is the only fuel that fans the flame of the Holy Spirit into fire. All our other works must emanate from this source.

Please remember Jesus' high priestly prayer on his last night with us: "Now this is eternal life: that they may know you, the only true God, and Jesus Christ, whom you have sent." The work of God is to believe, to trust Jesus. Eternal life, beginning now, is knowing Jesus.

You see, service is not what we do; service is who we are. Service is our worship. To Jesus, service is getting to know him, learning to believe in him, which means learning to trust him. That is the one thing he was trying to get across to the crowd, and to Martha, and to you.

I have heard Brother Paul put it this way, "Therefore, I urge you, brothers and sisters, in view of God's mercy, to offer your bodies as a living sacrifice, holy and pleasing to God — this is your spiritual act of worship. This is your true service."

Service is a good thing but not the best thing. Service as worship, worship as service, this is the best. It is not sin or service — it is surrender. Are you missing your Savior because of your busy service?

Choosing the Seven

After the Hellenistic Jewish Brothers approached us with their concerns about their widows being treated fairly, we gathered all the disciples together and said, "It would not be right for us to neglect the ministry of the Word of God in order to wait on tables. Brothers and sisters, choose seven men from among you who are known to be full of the Spirit and wisdom. We will turn this responsibility over to them and give our full attention to prayer and the ministry of the Word."

Slipping Back into Old Ways

Before we met with the larger assembly of disciples, the Twelve had discussed this among ourselves and decided this was the obvious solution. What was not so obvious was how to choose the seven. My inclination was for us to do the choosing. I can assure you this is how I handled everything before learning to live with the Holy Spirit, and, sadly, I can slip back into this control mode anytime.

I said to the other 11, "Brothers, I have given this some thought," which I had not really, "and I have a list of names I think would be good for this role. Most of them are our Galilean brothers because they have been with us from the beginning."

As I paused, James, John's older brother said, "Maybe we should pray about this and seek the Holy Spirit's clarity before we decide. Do you think we should include a few of the Greek Jews? Perhaps Philip, Nicanor, or Timon should be considered?"

I did not particularly like James butting in like this, but I think I hid it well. Why did I not like it? Because I thought I was right, and I did not appreciate James not going along with my obviously sound judgment. Does this surprise you? The great Apostle Peter, irritated because he was not getting his way?

Well, it should not. Back then, I was just learning to live with the Holy Spirit. I had not yet learned to see-seek-want and ...*wait*. Remember wait? At that moment, I wanted to control the outcome because I was sure I was right. I was not seeking the Holy Spirit for guidance because I did not truly want his guidance. Therefore, I was not planning to wait for his guidance.

I would never have admitted this to the others, nor would I have admitted this to myself. Self had taken charge, and Self was not interested in Spirit. Please understand this was not intentional on my part. I just slipped back into my old ways, and it would not be the last time.

It can happen in the blink of an eye, can it not? Be aware, alert, and of sober mind. Again, our enemy the devil prowls around like a roaring lion looking for someone to devour. He will do it with pride, and he will do it with busyness. So often our pride feeds our busyness.

We are proud of being busy!

With James' proposal of including the Greek men in the food distribution issue, a robust discussion ensued. After a while, Thomas suggested we take a break and sleep on it, and perhaps wait on more clarity from the Spirit. During the night, I tossed and turned in a struggle with my ego, feeling the conviction of the Spirit over my pride but not wanting to admit it. Finally, I surrendered, confessed my fault, and slipped into sleep.

THE HOLY SPIRIT KNOWS THE BEST WAY

The next morning, John walked up to our group and said, "The Holy Spirit made it absolutely clear to me we should let our family of believers decide who would best serve."

At that moment, I knew he was speaking God's words. Later that morning, we made the announcement to all those gathered with us at Solomon's Porch. Our proposal pleased the whole group. They chose Stephen, a man full of faith and of the Holy Spirit; also Philip, Procorus, Nicanor, Timon, Parmenas, and Nicolas from Antioch, a convert to Judaism. They became known as the Seven. When they presented these men to us, we prayed with them and laid hands on them.

I hope you can see this was the perfect solution. The issue originally arose from the Greek Jews. If I'd had my way, choosing only our Israelite Jews, we likely would have alienated them. The Holy Spirit knew this was the best way, and he made it clear to us, just as Jesus had said he would.

Saying Yes Means Saying No

As I said before, and in my first letter to the believers: Your enemy the devil is constantly looking for ways to distract and discourage you. His number one weapon is busyness.

If you can learn this one thing, you will be on the road to conquering busyness: Whenever you say yes to something, you will have to say no to something else.[3] The problem is we all say yes to many things, but we do not take into account the more important things to which we will ultimately be forced to say no.

We say yes to groups and activities, even church activities, and we end up saying no to time with our family, time with the Lord, time to recuperate and rejuvenate, or time just being still.

We can all see pride; it is so obvious, at least in others. But busyness is much more subtle. Busyness does not look like sin. But do you think Satan cares what it looks like to us? All he cares about is separating you from your Father. If he can do this with obvious sin, the Ten Commandments type sin, it is fine with him.

But all he really cares about is hurting your Father. If he can distract you enough to miss salvation, he is deliriously happy because he knows your Father painfully mourns your loss. But if he must settle for causing you to live a lukewarm, average life, and therefore to miss the riches of God's kingdom, he will certainly settle for that.

It is a smaller victory for him, but a victory nonetheless. It saddens your Father. Do not give Satan that victory. Satan hates God. He knows how much God loves you. He also knows he cannot fight directly against God. He tried that and was thrown out of God's presence. His only alternative is to try to hurt God by hurting his children.

He knows your Father wants you to have the riches of his kingdom. Jesus talked about the kingdom of God all the time. He said he came so we could live in the kingdom, here, now. Not sometime later. Kingdom living begins now. "If you want to go to heaven, go now"[4] captures Jesus' message perfectly.

Start living with the riches of the kingdom now. Learn to say no to the good things so you can say yes to the best.

THAT ONE THING

Jesus had pointed out to Martha the one thing she was missing was her heart devoted to him. Jesus said, "If anyone would come after me, he must deny himself and take up his cross and follow me." Please notice he did not say, "He must deny himself *things*." He said we must deny Self, which raises a deeper issue: What exactly does "deny Self" mean? What does it look like in my day-to-day life?

God our Father is always and foremost interested in our hearts. Even though we all have multiple issues (I know I do), each of you knows there is that one thing, one area, one heart issue, about which the Spirit is convicting you right now, even as you read my words.

It is that one thing you must surrender and deny to your Self. Perhaps you are thinking even now about some habit or some issue of your heart that you know would not stand the light of day.

We can all list multiple areas that could be improved, but the Holy Spirit is typically pressing in on one thing we know is not pleasing to him. We know it is not beneficial for us either. It has actually become your master; you know it and God knows it. The question is, "What will you do about that one thing?"

One day not too long ago, I was sitting with some of the Twelve, and we were discussing this. It was a warm day, and I was about to drift off when Phillip issued this challenge: "Let's each write it down—that one thing—and commit to freeing ourselves from it. If we are serious about this, if we know something has mastery over us, let's step up and defeat it."

I wish you could have seen the various expressions on the men's faces as we struggled with writing down that one thing. You see, we all knew if we wrote it down, we were committed.

Thomas said, "I have too many things; I need time to think about it." Two minutes later he said, "No, I do not need any more time; I know exactly what it is."

I know some of us, me for sure, were thinking, "I do not know if I can really do this." Or, "I really don't want to even try to do this. It is easier to just let it slide. I can get to it later. Oh sure, I know it is not beneficial, but I will deal with it later."

Remember Jesus' words, "Whoever wants to save their life will lose it, but whoever loses their life for me will find it?" I know, I know, I keep repeating it to you, but it is such a defining statement.

When we attempt to save our life, we are trying to keep our life exactly like we think it must be for us to be happy. Whatever that one thing is for you—be it a bad habit, a dark heart, lust, a secret only you know about—if you are trying to save it, to hold on to it, then Jesus is speaking directly to you, right now, in this moment.

Your one thing may not be a bad habit. It is always more about our hearts. Perhaps you just cannot forgive someone, you are resentful or envious, or perhaps it is pride? Perhaps someone or something has become a god for you.

That one thing is indeed retarding your growth. That one thing is blocking the Light. That one thing is holding you in bondage. It might even be blocking your salvation. Jesus told the rich young ruler his one thing was the security his money gave him. He helped the Samaritan woman at the well to see one thing: she thought the right man would make her happy. What do you think you must have to be happy? Is that your one thing?

Trust and surrender are the keys to the life that is truly life. Trust. Surrender. Obey out of love. We were about to find out just how much we did or did not trust Jesus, and just how much we were willing to surrender our will to his.

---

[1] Statement attributed to Oswald Chambers.

[2] Statements attributed to C. S. Lewis.

[3] Statement attributed to Melissa Walker.

[4] Quote attributed to Dallas Willard.

24

STEPHEN STONED

HAVING SETTLED THE CONFLICT WITH THE GRECIAN AND Hebrew widows, and the Seven now attending to the day-to-day operations of our new family of believers, we were able to put our entire focus on teaching and witnessing for Jesus. I loved every minute of the time I spent with our growing family, and I truly enjoyed meeting the men and women who were visiting us for the first time.

Often, whole families would show up at our morning gatherings at Solomon's Porch. We would then invite them to join us for the Lord's Supper evening meal, which was hosted at one of the many home gatherings. This was joyous, but I must admit I sometimes found myself becoming a bit frustrated with the children who came with their parents. They could be noisy and interrupting, which began to get on my nerves.

EFFICIENCY AND INTERRUPTIONS

As you can see, even though I was growing with the power of the Spirit, I could still quickly revert to the old Peter. I tend to forget that ministry so often happens in the interruptions[1] and that efficiency is the enemy of relationships.[2] Please do not forget that.

With children around, efficiency goes out the window and interruptions come crowding in. My irritation was nothing more than Self rearing its ugly head and King Peter getting back on the throne. Oh, how quickly it can happen.

But the Spirit is quick to convict me and remind me what a calm, relaxed pace Jesus always had. Once, when people were bringing little children to Jesus for him to place his hands on them, I rebuked them and told them the Master had more important things to do than to be interrupted by these children.

I do not recall exactly where we were headed that day, but we were walking somewhere. In my mind, this meant we had a goal, and we needed to get there. I—I mean Jesus—did not need to dally with children. I was only looking out for him. *Let's keep moving*! I was thinking.

But when Jesus heard me, he was indignant. With a frown on his face, he said to me, "Let the little children come to me, Simon, and do not hinder them, for the kingdom of God belongs to such as these. You were a child once," and I could sense him perhaps thinking, "and you seem to revert a little too often to your childish ways."

His rebuke stung, but he was right. He knew my heart. He knew my tendency was to place efficiency over relationships. He then spread his arms out to the children and said, "Truly I tell you, anyone who will not receive the kingdom of God like a little child will never enter it." He took the children in his arms, placed his hands on them, and blessed them.

We continued to gather every morning at Solomon's Porch and again for our evening meals in various homes.

We were a close-knit family. We did, however, have some men who would venture out into the synagogues around Jerusalem to try to take the gospel message of Jesus directly to the Jews.

There were over 300 synagogues in Jerusalem. Can you imagine that many? At least 10 men were necessary to form a synagogue, and because people just cannot seem to get along, there were synagogues set up throughout Jerusalem, including synagogues for freedmen, who were ex-slaves.

In the synagogues, women sat in a separate section and were not expected to take part. Our new gathering certainly departed from that practice. We encouraged women to participate. Jesus had actively engaged women and included them, and they had traveled with us during his earthly ministry.

UNITY

We wanted to keep unity in our family, as Jesus had so often impressed upon us. On his last night with us, he had talked about unity with so much emotion: "A new command I give you: Love one another. As I have loved you, so you must love one another. By this everyone will know that you are my disciples, if you show them you love one another."

He paused and then said, "I want this for you so that you may be one, as the Father and I are one. If you have this complete unity, then the world will know you are my disciples."

I could sense his heart already despairing as he said this because he must have known what a sorry mess Christians would ultimately make of any semblance of unity. He knew the heart of man—good gracious, over 300 synagogues in Jerusalem alone? I fear as our family of believers grows, and the heart of man takes over in the churches, there may one day be hundreds of different churches in any given city.

What a sorry witness this will be to those watching us. "By this everyone will know that you are my disciples, if you love one another." Jesus was saying if we nourished his unity among our new family, the unity of the trinity, then the world will know that we are his disciples. Three hundred synagogues in Jerusalem alone certainly spoke to man's tendency toward disunity.

I do not think Jesus would be very pleased if Christians separate into a multitude of different church families. It would be the antithesis of what he wanted. Even though our larger family met in individual homes at night, no one ever thought of these as separate groups—and certainly not separate churches.

But I have wandered yet again and must get back to my story. Stephen, as you recall, was one of the Seven and was full of God's grace and Holy Spirit power. He performed great wonders and signs among the people. I encouraged him to take more of a lead role in our morning gatherings, but he insisted instead on going out into the synagogues around the city. As I feared, he ran into a hornet's nest at the Synagogue of the Freedmen.

Here, Jews of Cyrene and Alexandria, as well as the provinces of Cilicia and Asia, met. They did not like Stephen's message about Jesus being the Messiah and would argue vehemently with him. But they could not stand up against the wisdom the Spirit gave him as he spoke.

STIRRING UP TROUBLE AGAINST STEPHEN

Saul of Tarsus attended this synagogue because he was from Cilicia, and he was especially aggressive with Stephen. He was called Saul in Jerusalem because this was his Hebrew name. Paul was his Greek name, which he used extensively as he later traveled among the Gentiles. I tried to warn Stephen he was wasting his time and casting his pearls before those who had no ears to hear, but he was young, stubborn, and hard-headed, like I used to be.

I could sense this Pharisee, Saul, was going to be trouble. He was a real stickler for the law, extraordinarily bright and intellectual, with a tenacious personality. He viewed our Way, quite frankly, as the way to hell. Apparently, a group of the Jews at his synagogues decided they'd had enough of Stephen, so they secretly persuaded some men to say, "We have heard Stephen speak blasphemous words against Moses and against God."

They stirred up the people and the elders and the teachers of the law. They seized Stephen and brought him before the Sanhedrin. They produced false witnesses who testified, "This fellow never stops speaking against this holy place and against the law. For we have heard him say that this Jesus of Nazareth will destroy this place and change the customs Moses handed down to us."

You might recall the Jewish leaders tried to bring witnesses against Jesus saying the same thing. You see, with Rome in charge, the Jews could not exact a death sentence for insurrection; only Rome could do that. But they could and would order stoning for blasphemy against the temple.

You may recall this is the charge they were trying to make stick against Jesus but could not.

They were trying to do the same to Stephen, but, as with Jesus, they could not get their witnesses to support their claim. Later, after Saul's conversion, he told me that all who were sitting in the Sanhedrin looked intently at Stephen, and they saw that his face was like the face of an angel.

RESISTING THE HOLY SPIRIT

At that moment, the high priest asked Stephen, "Are these charges true?"

Instead of answering the high priest directly, Stephen, as he was wont to do, went into a long retelling of the story of our nation, beginning with Abraham. The men of the Sanhedrin were already angry, and they sure did not like being lectured to. They exploded with anger when Stephen suddenly stopped his long story and pointed at the men and said, "You stiff-necked people! Your hearts and ears are still uncircumcised. You are just like your ancestors: You always resist the Holy Spirit!"

Before I go on with the story, may I take a moment to comment on what Stephen said at the end of his "defense" to the Sanhedrin? "You stiff-necked people! Your hearts and ears are still uncircumcised. You are just like your ancestors: You always resist the Holy Spirit!"

Isn't this always the case? Those who reject Jesus, or even just ignore him, are in fact resisting the Holy Spirit. The Holy Spirit is always reaching out, wooing us, and convicting us; we can resist him to our peril, or we can open our hearts to him.

You may think you are resisting organized religion, or hypocritical Christians, or whatever other excuse you have, but, in fact, you are resisting the Holy Spirit. That is the one unforgivable sin to which Jesus referred when he said,

> Every kind of sin and slander can be forgiven, but blasphemy against the Spirit will not be forgiven. Anyone who speaks a word against the Son of Man will be forgiven, but anyone who speaks against the Holy Spirit will not be forgiven, either in this age or in the age to come.

All the men of the Sanhedrin stood up and hurled threats at Stephen as their anger turned to rage, but Stephen was undaunted. "Was there ever a prophet your ancestors did not persecute?" he continued, pointing his finger around the room. "They even killed those who predicted the coming of the Righteous One. Now you," and with this, he stopped and looked slowly, directly at each man, "you have betrayed and murdered him—Jesus, the Messiah— you who have received the law that was given through angels but have not obeyed it."

If I had been there, I would have grabbed Stephen and taken off running, but there was no one from our family there to defend him. But Stephen knew he was not alone. He knew Jesus' assurance that he would never leave him or forsake him was real.

STEPHEN'S DEATH

At this point, the men of the Sanhedrin were furious and gnashed their teeth at him. But Saul later told me Stephen was full of the Holy Spirit. He looked up to heaven and saw the glory of God, and Jesus standing at the right hand of God. "Look," he said, "I see heaven open and the Son of Man standing at the right hand of God."

As Saul and I discussed this years later, he asked me, "Simon, did you notice he said Jesus was standing up, not sitting down at the right hand of God? It is almost as if Jesus was standing up and stepping forward to greet Stephen as he joined him in heaven. I have to tell you, Cephas, this shook me up at the time, and I have wrestled with this image ever since." Saul looked down and shook his head as he said this.

The Sanhedrin covered their ears and, yelling at the top of their voices, they all rushed at him, dragging him out of the city, and began to stone him. While they were stoning him, Stephen prayed, "Lord Jesus, receive my spirit." Then he fell on his knees and cried out, "Lord, do not hold this sin against them." When he had said this, he died.

Saul approved of their killing Stephen; he was actually proud of the murder and that day became the leader of those who began to persecute us. It was as though Stephen's blood incited in them an almost primordial animal instinct to kill, and great persecution broke out against the church in Jerusalem. All except the apostles were scattered throughout Judea and Samaria.

We were heartbroken, dismayed, and discouraged by this evil exacted upon Stephen, such a sweet and innocent man. Many believers left Jerusalem to avoid this dangerous persecution. We would later see how the Father brought so much good out of this scattering, as he used it to expand his kingdom. New families of believers would spring up across our region because of this dispersion, even as far as

Damascus and Antioch, Syria. But at the time, I could not possibly see any good coming out of this catastrophe.

The Seven asked for the privilege of burying Stephen. It took great courage on their part to step out and be publicly aligned with Stephen, but they were determined to honor his body. We all mourned deeply for him. That night I cried out to Jesus, "Why? Why would you allow this? Stephen was a good man, a holy man. He did not deserve this. Why would you stand by and let these evil, religious monsters murder one of your most devoted disciples?"

Tears were flowing down my face. I felt so much anger and despair. I was angry with Jesus. I was scared. If I am honest and transparent, my fear fueled my anger. I knew this could happen to me, or to any of us, at any time. We had no protection from the hatred and evil of these powerful men. Or at least none that we could see.

They had all the power.

POWER?

We had no power against them. Saul was out to destroy the church. Going from house to house, he dragged off both men and women and put them in prison. But that night as I was on my hands and knees, sweating and almost nauseated with pain and fear, I could sense Jesus saying to me, "Peter, I am here, and I am with you. I am with you all. None of this is happening apart from the Father's will. He could have stopped this, and he can at any moment. In due time, he will."

I knew if Jesus were sitting next to me, he would say to me, "Do not despair, my son. Satan is not in control. This power you think the Sanhedrin has, and the powerless feeling you have, indicates your feelings are getting in the way, my dear friend." I then remembered what Jesus said to Pilate when it looked to all the world like he had absolute power over his life. Jesus looked him square in the eyes and said, "You would have no power over me, Pilate, if it were not given to you from above."

Pilate had no true power over Jesus nor did the guards who came to arrest him the night before. You may recall that I was swinging my sword around trying so pitifully to exert my own power. Jesus said to me, "Put your sword back in its place, for all who draw the sword will die by the sword. Do you think I cannot call on my Father, and he will at once put at my disposal more than 12 legions of angels? But how then would the Scriptures be fulfilled that say it must happen in this way?"

AN ETERNAL PERSPECTIVE

I then reminded myself that what had happened to Stephen did not sadden just me. This is not all about me; there is a much bigger battle going on in the spiritual realms. Battles, yes, but the war was won on the cross. Jesus disarmed the powers and authorities, and made a public spectacle of them, triumphing over them by the cross.

Yes, these appear to be fierce battles we are now in, but they are, in fact, mere skirmishes from an eternal perspective. The war is won. The Scriptures are being fulfilled. You and I can trust that the Father has a plan, and he has the power to exert his control to accomplish his plan.

And he will.

You and I can trust his plan is immeasurably, abundantly more than anything you could ask or even imagine asking for.

I began to regain my perspective as I fought off my feelings and let the facts take precedence. Stephen was with Jesus now, and I knew he would not come back for anything: not for me, not for the Seven, not even for his family. His reward has just begun and will last for eternity. I believe Stephen's absolute trust in Jesus, in the face of such danger, compelled Jesus to stand up from his seat at the right hand of the Father and step out to greet him, even as they were stoning him.

What an entrance to heaven that would be.

STILL IN DUE TIME

Here is what I learned that night after Stephen's death, as I was on my knees crying out to Jesus, and now what I teach everyone I encounter: "Humble yourselves under God's mighty hand, that he may lift you up in due time. Cast all your anxiety on him because he cares for you."

I have mentioned this to you before, but I repeat it because you still might not believe me. Oh, you might say you do; you may have even memorized my words by now, but do you live it? The "in due time" part of this does not sit well with you because you still have not learned to totally trust the Holy Spirit and wait on him to move ahead of you.

Instead of casting your anxieties off on Jesus, you hold on to them. In doing so, you continue to give Satan a victory over the Father.

Do you believe the Spirit's words to you through the Psalmist?

> You have searched me, LORD,
> and you know me.
> You know when I sit and when I rise;
> you perceive my thoughts from afar.
> You discern my going out and my lying down;
> you are familiar with all my ways.
> Before a word is on my tongue
> you, LORD, know it completely.
> You hem me in behind and before,
> and you lay your hand upon me.
> Such knowledge is too wonderful for me,
> too lofty for me to attain.

The "in due time" part causes uncertainty in your life, yet the Spirit moved Isaiah to express the Father's assurance that you can humble yourself under God's mighty hand:

> So do not fear, for I am with you;
> do not be dismayed, for I am your God.
> I will strengthen you and help you;
> I will uphold you with my righteous right hand.

I say this because I know that the God of all grace, who called us to his eternal glory in Christ, after we have suffered a little while, will himself restore us and make us even stronger, firm, and steadfast. To him be the power forever and ever. Amen.

---

[1] Statement attributed to Clark Bynum.

[2] Statement attributed to Clark Bynum.

25

SIMON THE SORCERER

DURING PAUL'S REIGN OF TERROR, THOSE WHO HAD BEEN scattered preached the Word wherever they went. Philip went down to a city in Samaria and proclaimed the Messiah there. When the crowds heard Philip and saw the signs he performed, they all paid close attention to what he said. For with shrieks, impure spirits came out of many, and many who were paralyzed or lame were healed. There was great joy in that city.

Now for some time, a man named Simon had practiced sorcery in the city and amazed all the people of Samaria. He boasted that he was someone great, and all the people, both high and low, gave him their attention and exclaimed, "This man is rightly called the Great Power of God." They followed him because he had amazed them for a long time with his sorcery.

Let me add a reminder and a warning here: when you are called anything like, "The Great Power of God," and especially if you allow people to keep saying this about you — and even worse if you believe it — you are grossly out of favor with the God Almighty, El Shaddai. Look out!

But when Philip arrived, the people believed him as he proclaimed the good news of the kingdom of God and the name of Jesus Christ. They were baptized, both men and women. Simon himself believed and was baptized. He followed Philip everywhere, astonished by the great signs and miracles he saw.

As I said earlier, the Twelve had stayed in Jerusalem because the Spirit told us to stay until he gave us further instructions. I was waiting to hear his direction before making any moves. Are you tired of me repeating "wait on the Spirit" repeatedly? I am undaunted. You must hear it many times because you are like me: for an idea to take root, we have to hear it often. We must then put it into practice, often.

But when we heard that Samaria had accepted the Word of God, the Spirit made it clear to John and to me to travel over to see Philip.

VISITING SAMARIA

When we arrived, we were so surprised to see these hated Samaritans full of the joy of Jesus. I say hated, but I mean hated by Jews in general, not by us. We had learned our lesson about ethnic bigotry toward the Samaritans when Jesus encountered the Samaritan woman at Jacob's well. Believe it or not, this was the very same city.

Her name was Naomi, and the day she encountered Jesus by the well was such a surprising day for all of us. Because of Jesus' interaction with Naomi, and her declaration to her fellow villagers that she had met the Messiah, the Samaritans of her city received Jesus with joy. Jesus' encounter with her is now being called, 'The Samaritan Woman at the Well.' But that was before Pentecost, so even in their joy at meeting Jesus back then, they had not yet received the Holy Spirit.

We prayed for these new believers, that they might receive the Holy Spirit. We then placed our hands on them, and they did receive him. What a sight! A city full of what Jews called half-breeds rejoicing with the Holy Spirit. I know Jesus was beaming and smiling with the Father.

THE TRANSFORMATION OF THE WOMAN AT THE WELL

Naomi rushed up to John and hugged him, almost causing them both to fall down. Had she not introduced herself to us, I would not have recognized her. When we had first met her back on that day with Jesus at the well, she was so down and defeated—her very soul was shriveled up.

The hole inside her soul had collapsed in on her and she was just a shadow of what the Father intended for her to be. An encounter with Jesus, as it so often did, changed all that. Her previously insatiable need for a man who would fulfill her was now replaced by the fullness of Jesus.

The woman now before us was vibrant and full of life. She exclaimed, "I am so glad to see you! I never imagined I would see any of you ever again. After I met Jesus at the well, my whole life changed. No, not changed, *transformed.* I had such a hole in my heart until I met Jesus. I had been trying to fill it with men, over and over. But no man, no one, and no thing could ever fill that hole—only Jesus. I will never forget him saying to me that day, 'The water I can give you will become in you a spring of water welling up to eternal life.'

"Well," she continued, almost bursting with pride and joy, "I now drink the Living Water! I am now filled to the measure of all the fullness of God the Father. I have no need for a man to complete me, to make me whole, as I used to think. I am complete and whole in Jesus."

Naomi was standing between John and me, and she kept smiling and nodding her head as she swept her eyes back and forth between us. I knew this woman had the Spirit. There could be no question about this.

"I no longer concern myself with questions like where to worship, or how to worship, or if you Jews have it right or we Samaritans?" she continued. "I know now that true worshipers worship the Father in the Spirit and in truth, for they are the kind of worshipers the Father seeks. But until today, before the Spirit arrived in my heart, I did not really understand what Jesus meant by, 'God is spirit, and his worshipers must worship in the Spirit and in truth.' But now I do!"

She grabbed me and hugged me so hard we did indeed both fall to the ground. John thought this was hilarious and doubled over laughing. I was joyful too, but my dignity was a little bruised. Yet looking into her eyes, seeing the joy and exhilaration that can only come from the Holy Spirit lighting someone up, I gave up all pretense of personal dignity, and as we stood up, I lifted her up in my arms and swung her around.

WHEN THE SPIRIT MOVES

Everyone was watching us now, and everyone started clapping and laughing as the Spirit moved so mightily among us.

Over these many years of witnessing the Spirit's arrival, and even with the variety of different ways he shows up, one thing is always true: there is no mistaking when he does arrive. When he comes, it is obvious. Is this true in your life? Do you know when he arrived to indwell you? If not, please do not ignore the Holy Spirit's conviction that you may not have been born again. Perhaps you are sensing a conviction in your heart right now, even as you are reading this?

When the Holy Spirit indwells you, you know it. If you are not sure, you are likely not saved. I say this with grace and no judgment, but with the salt of truth. I must say it and I must challenge you because the stakes are so high. When Jesus indicated only a few would be saved, he meant it. Too many well-intentioned followers have missed the new birth but do not know it.

THE SALVATION OF SIMON THE SORCERER

As we rejoiced with Naomi, Simon the Sorcerer was standing near us. Naomi and I laughed and carried on with John. Simon saw that the Spirit was given at the laying on of our hands, so he offered us money, saying, "Give me also this ability so that everyone on whom I lay my hands may receive the Holy Spirit."

In the midst of our joy with Naomi, his offer of money caught me so off guard it took me a moment to process his request. When I realized the vulgarity of his offer, I was taken aback and blurted out, "May your money perish with you because you thought you could buy the gift of God with money!"

John and Naomi stopped and stared at me, as did everyone gathered around us. Poor Simon was mortified. The look on his face was one of total collapse and confusion. Perhaps the Spirit understood that Simon's misunderstanding needed to be addressed quickly and decisively, but whatever was going on, I was moved to continue sternly with poor Simon: "You have no part or share in this ministry," I stated boldly, "because your heart is not right before God. Repent of this wickedness and pray to the Lord in the hope that he may forgive you for having such a thought in your heart, for I see that you are full of bitterness and captive to sin."

Simon wanted to crawl under a rock, and I have to admit I felt bad for being so blunt and demonstrative with him. He stepped toward me and fell on his knees and answered, "Pray to the Lord for me so that nothing you have said may happen to me."

I did pray for him right then and there, motioning to those nearby to gather around and lay hands on Simon. This was this new Samaritan branch of our family of believers' first prayer meeting, and the Lord was clearly present. The Holy Spirit came on Simon and he began to sing and praise Jesus.

As Brother Paul likes to say, "No one can say, 'Jesus is Lord,' except by the Holy Spirit." It was obvious Simon had been born again, and the whole village celebrated as he made a pile of his various potions and little trinket gods and proceeded to burn them. We stayed with the people two days, just as Jesus had done. It felt good to be there. I think John and I both felt closer to Jesus, being where he previously had so boldly knocked down the barrier between Samaritans and Jews.

To the Ends of the Earth

After we further proclaimed the word of the Lord and testified about Jesus, John and I returned to Jerusalem, but we stopped in several Samaritan villages along the way, preaching the gospel—the good news of the kingdom of God.

Philip left Samaria when we did, but he took the desert road that goes down from Jerusalem to Gaza. Years later, I visited him in Caesarea where he ended up living, raising four daughters, all of whom were prophetesses. He told me about a fascinating encounter with an Ethiopian eunuch, an important official in charge of all the treasury of Kandake, the queen of the Ethiopians.

Philip recounted that after we left Samaria, the Holy Spirit told him, "Go to that chariot and stay near it." After discussing the Book of Isaiah with the eunuch, the Ethiopian said he wanted to surrender to Jesus as his Savior. He did, and Philip baptized him in a river nearby.

The gospel, the good news of the kingdom's presence with and within us, was spreading. Now on to Ethiopia. Just as Jesus said, "You will be my witnesses in Jerusalem, and in all Judea and Samaria, and to the ends of the earth." Ethiopia was the end of the earth in my little world!

I loved Philip and missed having him with us in Jerusalem. But the Spirit was moving through him and I thanked the Father many times for Philip's ministry. Imagine that! The Holy Spirit was now moving out from our little family in Jerusalem, into Samaria, and now even Ethiopia, just as Jesus had said he would.

But what was to soon follow would practically eclipse anything we had witnessed the Holy Spirit do. The buildings would indeed rumble and tumble, but these buildings would be in the form of one Saul of Tarsus, the feared and loathed enemy of our Way.

Blinded by the Light!

PART THREE

BLINDED BY THE LIGHT—
15 DAYS IN JERUSALEM

26

LIKE LITTLE CHILDREN

BEFORE I TELL YOU THE STORY OF SAUL'S CONVERSION, when he was blinded by the Light, may I share a few thoughts on what Saul experienced?

I remember so well the day Jesus said, "The greatest among you will be your servant. For those who exalt themselves will be humbled, and those who humble themselves will be exalted. I praise you, Father, Lord of heaven and earth because you have hidden these things from the wise and learned and revealed them to little children. Yes, Father, for this is what you were pleased to do."

"WHO IS THE GREATEST?"

Before I was born again, I would have taken great offense at Jesus referring to us as little children. In fact, I remember the day we were arguing among ourselves about which of us would be the greatest when Jesus set up his kingdom on earth. Can you imagine? The great Peter and John, the "pillars of the church," actually arguing about who would be the greatest?

I must admit I started it. Well, to be specific Andrew started it, but only because he was defending his prideful big brother. He had heard me quietly debating it with James, John's big brother, so the two little brothers, Andrew and John started discussing it. Matthew overheard it and called them out in front of Thomas and Nathaniel, and the next thing you know, there we were, all listing our resumes and puffing out our chests.

Well, except for Matthew. You see, he had been a tax collector, hated by all Jews for doing business with Rome—and what a crooked business it was. Matthew had no trouble remembering his spiritual poverty apart from Jesus. Can you see how fortunate he was? His gratitude to Jesus for saving him—for "salvaging him," he liked to say—never waned. Therefore, his humility was deep and true.

But the rest of us obviously forgot from time to time who we were before Jesus saved us. Now I want you to understand this display of ignorant pride on our part, talking about who would be the greatest, was not long after I had made my Spirit-filled declaration to Jesus, "You are the Messiah, the Son of the living God." Keep in mind this was after we had seen Jesus transfigured on the mountain. This was even after he had sent the 12 of us out with the power to heal and perform miracles.

Please let this be a stark reminder to you of just how pathetic it is to live without the power of the Holy Spirit. One minute I am declaring Jesus to be the Messiah, the next I am arguing about being the greatest. One minute we see Jesus transfigured with a blinding light, the next we are blindly debating in the darkness of our hearts our place in the hierarchy of Jesus' kingdom.

EMOTIONAL EXPERIENCES

Do not ever be deceived into thinking that since you might have had an incredible "spiritual" experience, you are therefore surely saved and filled with the Holy Spirit. I have seen this far too often: men and women telling me about an extremely emotion-filled spiritual experience they have had, and, therefore, convinced they are saved and right with God—when it is so clear they have not yet been born again.

Emotion is not salvation. Emotional experiences do not equate to being born again. We were so earthly back then, so small-minded, so lost. We did not know what we did not know because we were not yet born again. We did not yet have the Holy Spirit permanently living within us.

LITTLE CHILDREN ENTER THE KINGDOM

Tired of the ignorance of my fellow disciples, and sure of how Jesus would answer, I called out to Jesus, who was walking ahead of us, "Master, who, then, is the greatest in the kingdom of heaven?"

Jesus knew I expected him to say something like, "Why you, Peter. Did I not call you the rock?" Instead, he took a little child, had him stand beside him, and said, "Listen to me all of you, and you too, Peter, little *pebble*: unless you change and become like little children, you will never enter the kingdom of heaven. Therefore, whoever humbles himself like this child is the greatest in the kingdom of heaven."

Do I need to tell you this was not the answer I was looking for? "Change and become like little children?" Humble myself like a little child? All 12 of us were both embarrassed and offended, some more embarrassed than offended, some more offended than embarrassed. I was equal parts big ego, little mind, no Spirit.

What is it about a child, what are the characteristics of a child to which Jesus is referring? Well, it is surely not that a child is pure and innocent. One has only to be around a group of two-year-olds to know that! No, children are dependent—totally dependent on their parents. A child trusts in his parent's love. A child looks solely to his parents to provide for him or her.

Children know they are totally helpless without the love and care of their parents, so they are totally reliant on them. No, a child is not innocent; a child is dependent.

When Jesus told Nicodemus, "Whoever believes in me will have eternal life," the word he used for "believe" carried with it a much deeper meaning than most people realize. "Believe" to Jesus meant to trust, but not just to trust, but to trust to the point of action … to the point of change. Jesus' 'believe' means to thrust one's entire dependence on the object of your trust: Jesus.

Today, I meet men and women who think because they believe Jesus was real, and they believe the facts about Jesus, and they like what he taught, that they have eternal life with him. But how could it be that simple? There is no transformation in this. They believe with their minds, but not their hearts.

Cast Your Dependence on Him

I remember once when John and I were traveling together in Syria, we came upon a sorcerer named Agabai. This man was very talented. Even though both John and I knew he was a fake, we were certainly impressed with his show-manship.

One of his tricks was to balance on a rope he had stretched across a steep ravine. He would walk out on the rope, sing songs, and even do a little dance. The people were awed by him and applauded and shouted out praises for him.

We watched him that day walk back to the crowd from the rope, and ask them, "Do you believe I could put one of you on my back and walk safely across the rope? The crowd enthusiastically cried out, "Yes, we believe in you. We believe you could do that! We believe you can do anything!"

Agabai then said, "Okay, who will volunteer to get on my back and go out with me?"

Silence. The crowd shuffled a bit and looked down, but no one said a word. No one stepped forward. Do you see my point? They believed Agabai in their minds, but not enough to trust him with their lives. They believed intellectually, but not with their hearts. There was no action, no response, associated with their belief.

This sounds a lot like the Twelve before the Holy Spirit indwelled us. Does it sound like you?

This is what Jesus is saying about becoming like a child. We trust Jesus so deeply that we cast our entire dependence on him. We surrender to him, and to his love and his power. By this surrender, we are saved.

Now do you see the reference to being born again within Jesus' statement: "Unless you change and become like little children, you will never enter the kingdom of heaven?" Do you see how close this is to what Jesus said to Nicodemus: "No one can see the kingdom of God unless you are born again?"

In our Aramaic language, Jesus was saying the same thing in both statements. When Matthew wrote his recollection of this same event, he wrote in the Greek language. These two statements by Jesus are almost identical in the Greek language as well.

Matthew understood—we all understand now—that, after Pentecost, Jesus was saying, "An improvement in your lifestyle will not get you into the kingdom of God; a little polishing up will not do it; more learning will not do it; even repenting will not do it.

RADICAL SHIFTING

No, you must change so radically it is as though you are born again: "a new creation." As Brother Paul says, "Therefore, if anyone is in Christ, he is a new creation. The old has gone, the new has come!"

Born again means there is a radical change, a radical shift inside you.

There is a shift inside that is so significant you know you will never be the same again. You know equally well you will never turn your back on this change. You simply could not. To be sure, you may backslide and you may, *will*, do sinful and stupid things—you are human, after all. But the shift inside you is so real and so deep and so penetrating to your core, you know it is permanent, and you know it is not going to be just an emotional phase.

Many religious types—those who make it a weekly habit of attending our worship services, mistake this change for maturity. They are getting older, more settled, and not as blatantly sinful, or as anxious, or as competitive, or as whatever they once were. Our worship services feel good to them too. It is nice to be there on Sundays; the children like it; the family is involved. It's all warm and fuzzy.

I had a conversation with such a man once. He was telling me about his life and lamenting that he had been divorced and had made some bad mistakes. He had lost sight of God and lived life for himself. But then his face brightened, and he said, "But I was lucky enough to marry again to a wonderful follower of Jesus. In fact, she brought me back to God. I changed my bad behavior and life is so much better now."

I smiled and asked, "Did she bring you back to God or just back to our worship services?"

That caught him off guard, but it did not take long for him to nod his head slightly, understanding exactly what I was hoping he would see. He whispered, "Back to the worship services."

He had repented; he had changed his behavior. He had become more involved with us, but he had not been born again. His change was mere window dressing.

He then asked me how he could know if he had been born again, and what it felt like to be born again? I simply said, "You will know, my friend. You will know because it will be a shift inside you. Perhaps no one will even see this shift happen, but you will. You will see it with the eyes of your heart.

"At that point, you will never again wonder if you have been born again. You will absolutely know it."

RELIGIOUS EXPERIENCES OR TRULY KNOWING JESUS?

In another conversation with yet another man, I listened to him tell me about his lifelong commitment to God. He had joined our group and was dutifully attending our gatherings, but I could see he was not yet saved. The Holy Spirit had not yet entered him.

As he told me his story, he said, "I have been a follower of God all my life. My mother, God rest her soul, took me to synagogue every time the doors opened. After that day at the feast of Pentecost, when everything changed for her, she started taking me to the dinners and gatherings of the new Way.

"I have been an even more committed follower of God ever since," he said with firm conviction.

I said, "Jacob, I can see you are sincere about God, and I can see the Lord is moving all around you. But I have to tell you, I do not think you know Jesus."

He gaped at me and stammered, "Why, why would you say that?"

I replied, "You have been telling me about all your religious experiences and talking about God for an hour now. But you have not once mentioned Jesus. People who know Jesus personally say his name, and often."

His eyes widened, and his lips started to quiver—I thought perhaps he was going to strike me—but then he started to cry, and amidst his tears, he said, "You are right. You are so right. I have been sitting under your teaching and listening to the stories of the others who have been so radically changed—like my dear mother—and all the while wondering to myself, *"Who is this Jesus? Why have I not experienced this radical shift inside?"*

He went on, "I have changed my behavior and cleaned up my act, but inside, I am still the same old me—still wanting to be in charge of my life; still wanting to be king of my castle; still being ruled by Self. What can I do, Simon? Help me!"

I simply said, "You must surrender all that, Jacob. You must surrender your pride. You must surrender your performance. You must surrender your Self.

"You must recognize your spiritual poverty apart from Jesus. You must be born again."

27

BAPTISM OF REPENTANCE: FROM CHANGE TO TRANSFORMATION

THE COMMON THEME I SEE IN ALL THESE MEN AND women is: "The way I was living my life was not working, so I changed direction. I quit—or cut back on– the things that created problems in my life."

These folks—and you maybe?—effected what God calls a "baptism of repentance." Repent means, "To change direction," and that is exactly what they did. They did it well. They got involved in church life. They got better. They behaved better. Life got better. Can you relate to this? Is this perhaps striking a familiar chord?

But change will only get you a better life. Transformation is the key to the *best life*—the Holy Spirit's best.

You can do change in your own power, but you cannot *do* transformation at all. True transformation is what the Holy Spirit does to you, in you. Living with the power of the Holy Spirit is transformational: the average life becomes the extraordinary life; the empty life becomes the full life.

EVERYTHING JESUS WANTS FOR US

Let me share with you a story Doctor Luke shared with me about one of his many journeys with Paul.

Paul and Luke were on their way to Ephesus, and as they entered Ephesus, they met 12 men who looked like disciples of Jesus. They were dressed nicely and were just leaving a Lord's Supper gathering of the Way. Paul greeted them and asked if they were believers. They responded with a resounding, "Of course!"

He then asked them, "Did you receive the Holy Spirit when you believed? Did you sense a cosmic shift inside?" They looked confused, so he said, "Did you take God into your mind only, or did you also embrace him with your heart? Did the Holy Spirit get *inside* you?"

Now they were really confused, and exclaimed, "We have never even heard of this—a Holy Spirit *inside* us? We were baptized in John's baptism. Since then, we have really changed a lot. It has been so good. Our lives are so much better."

"That explains it," said Paul, with a sympathetic smile on his face. "John preached a baptism of repentance, a way of life change. I can see you have all had a change, but not a radical one. You will need the Holy Spirit to be transformed into a new person, not just a changed person."

On hearing this, they looked at each other, confused, and then at Paul, and then at Luke. But soon their confused look started to change, and a smile arose on each of their faces. Almost in unison, they said, "Oh, now I see what you mean!" They had sudden clarity. "Please, sir, if we have missed something as important as this Holy Spirit, we did not mean to. Will you help us? We want everything Jesus wants for us!"

Paul stepped up to the men and hugged each one. He said, "Holy Father, in the name of Jesus, I ask you to send your Holy Spirit into these men. They know all about you, but now we want them to know you!"

There was a creek near the road, and although it was not deep enough for the men to be fully immersed, they did not care. Dr. Luke said it was quite a sight, each of the men being lowered into the shallow water by Paul. They were laughing and hugging each other as they were baptized in the name of the Lord Jesus. Then Paul placed his hands on them, the Holy Spirit came on them, and they spoke in tongues and prophesied.

One man said, "It's like scales have fallen from my eyes." The others agreed, nodding their heads as they smiled. "Yes, I know what you mean," said another man. "I can sense a new clarity and new energy. I want more!"

They had previously repented, they had changed, and they had improved, but now they were new men. Before that day, they had been sincere, but sincerely wrong. Now they were sincerely saved.

CHANGED OR TRANSFORMED?

I know now change will only take me so far. I need more. I need help. I need the Holy Spirit. Can you see you do too? The baptism of repentance is, "God, I want things to change, so I will change as best I can." The baptism of the Holy Spirit is, "Father, I want to be more than just changed; I want to be transformed into a different person … a new creation! My old Self is bankrupt. I want out; I want you in."

My friend, if you are not as wild or as stupid or as loud-mouthed or as argumentative or drunk or as whatever as you used to be (sounds a lot like me!), you are no doubt living a better life. But if you want the best, ask for the Holy Spirit, and then start asking him to transform you into the new creation you were created to be.

The best question is not, "Have I changed?" but "Am I being transformed?"

My journey with my Lord and Savior has been a fascinating shift from the darkness into the Light. I have encountered many ups and downs, with the ups always coming from Jesus and the downs always, and I do mean always, coming from me—my Self.

One thing is for sure: I have changed, but even more so, he has transformed me—from the inside out, not from my outside behavior, but from my inside Holy Spirit. It began with Jesus becoming my Savior. But over the years, he has become more and more my Lord, as in Lord over my life— Lord over the details of my life.

He is Lord of my life, but he is not *lording* it over my life. Instead, life with Jesus—and the Holy Spirit within me—is a steady flow of his goodness and grace, peace and love, washing over me and flowing through me, like living water.

INTIMACY THROUGH NOURISHMENT

Intimacy develops through nourishing a relationship, not just maintaining one.

To me as a child, Yahweh was a vague notion of some goodness and some badness: as in bad punishment. In my early years, my interaction with God was at first just that: an interaction with God ... El Shaddai ... this overwhelming cosmic power in the sky. Our teachers and leaders of the synagogue may have thought they were teaching about a loving God, but that is not what I heard. All I heard was this talk about "the fear of the LORD," which to me meant I should be afraid of this big, all-powerful God. And I was.

I mostly maintained an interaction—not a relationship—with much fear and trembling. I did not want to disobey this huge God because I did not want him mad at me, nor did I want the bad consequences that would surely follow.

Consequently, there was no "Life to the Full."

But as I grew in my relationship with Jesus, I started to see God in a different Light: more goodness and grace than punishment. My perspective changed from not wanting to disobey God to avoid consequences, to wanting to obey him—but still mainly because I thought it would mean good things for me.

Looking back, I was still stuck in a maintenance relationship and not a nourishing one. My intimacy was a shallow intimacy, if any at all. After Pentecost, I had the Holy Spirit inside me, but I was not living with the power of the Holy Spirit.

TRANSPARENCY LEADS TO INTIMACY

But then came another shift: slight at first, hardly noticeable to the outside world, but gathering momentum toward transformation. I was becoming a new person. I was changing from the inside out, and my interaction with this huge, impersonal God was shifting to a relationship with my intimate friend: my Savior, Jesus.

For intimacy to thrive, there must be transparency. I remembered Jesus' words of encouragement to us on our last night with him, "Whoever has my commands and obeys them, he is the one who loves me. He who loves me will be loved by my Father, and I, too, will love him and show myself to him."

That night, I could sense my soul shifting. A pinhole of light was shining through. I suddenly realized how truly important his words were: Jesus promised to "show himself to me."

Really? Could this be true? God himself, in the nature of the Son, Jesus, would become so intimate with me that I could see him—with the eyes of my heart, actually see him, even after he left to be in heaven? Would Jesus, the Son of the living God, who rose from the dead and ascended to heaven, show himself to me—sinful, selfish, self-absorbed me?

Well, he wouldn't show himself to the sinful, selfish, self-absorbed me, but to the seeking, searching, surrendering me—still flawed, but now seeing Jesus with more and more clarity. I saw Jesus as someone with whom I could be even more intimate through the Holy Spirit than when he was with me those four years.

People often ask me, "Is there a catch to Jesus' promise, 'Whoever has my commands and obeys them, he is the one who loves me?'" I know they are asking, "Do I have to obey perfectly or be extra holy to share this intimacy?"

This may surprise you, but no. Notice Jesus's words: "… he is the one who loves me." He did not say, "When you obey me, you prove that you love me," although this is certainly true. But he was saying, "You will obey me out of love for me. You will more and more naturally obey because of our growing intimacy."

Can you see this is much more like a personal relationship than like personal performance? There is nourishment in this type of relationship, not just maintenance. There is a sweet and honest transparency here. Intimacy thrives with nourishment and transparency.

Okay, but there is a catch: You and I can only change so much. Change is good, but this obedience that comes from and through love must involve transformation. Remember, change is what I can do; transformation is what the Holy Spirit does in me.

How do we move from change to transformation? Let's start, as we always should, with our relationship with Jesus.

PLEASING GOD

As mentioned, in my journey of learning to live in the power of the Spirit and not in the power of Peter, I could see I was progressing. I went from seeking not to disobey God to avoid punishment, to then wanting to obey him to gain favor and rewards, but then on to something much deeper—pleasing God. I was still trying to change, often with gritted teeth and self-discipline.

Then came another shift, my transformation was deepening *because* my interaction with this huge God was shifting to a relationship with an intimate friend—my Savior, Jesus. I knew Jesus had modeled for us that obedience that leads to intimacy is through love, not fear.

LOVE, NOT FEAR

Previously, I was seeking to change out of fear, but now the Spirit was showing me –and he will show you—transformation comes through love, not fear, never the other way around. So the next shift came—love, not fear. The Light was getting brighter.

Consider your closest relationships. Perhaps your spouse (or child, parent, or best friend). If it is a maintenance interaction and not an intimate relationship, you act and react from fear. You seek to get along with them and to try to keep them happy more out of fear than love.

In other words, you seek *not* to do what will anger them to avoid the unpleasantness sure to follow. Or perhaps you obey them—you do what they want—to get the good results that come from them being happy. This was my former relationship—no, not a relationship, my interaction—with Yahweh.

But intimacy develops as you seek to please Jesus because you love him. Fear is being replaced by love. Dutiful obedience is being replaced with intimacy. Change is being replaced with transformation. Life to the Full is evolving.

Now you want to please Jesus, and you sure do not want to disappoint him—not because he might get mad, but because you love him. You live and act from love, not fear.

I remember two girls in our group in Caesarea who connived to slip out one day and attend a heathen idol temple. They lied to their parents, but someone saw them as they were leaving the temple and told their parents.

One of the girls was upset, but only because she got caught and knew her dad would be furious and would punish her. She was operating out of fear, not love. The other was upset because, and I will never forget her anguish when she cried, "I have disappointed my abba!" She loved her papa and wanted to please him, out of love for him, not out of fear of him.

Love, not fear.

So it is for us. Seeking to please the Lord out of love opens the gates deeper into the kingdom. This is a whole new frontier to discover. It is rich pasture and you will find yourself wanting to linger here, as you should.

HONOR THE FATHER

The Promised Land is one step further as we seek to *honor* our Father. As we are being transformed through the power of the Spirit toward Life to the Full, we shift from pleasing to honoring. I have seen this in marriages that developed over decades. The husband or the wife lives to honor their spouse out of love and affection developed over their years together.

Sadly, I rarely see it in anyone's relationship with Jesus. Do you want to honor your heavenly Father out of gratitude, out of reverent awe, and perhaps because of a sense of his sheer magnificence?

Are you seeking to please Jesus because he deserves it? Are you seeking to honor him because he is worthy of it: worthy of your worship; worthy of your obedience? As we pursue this pleasing and honoring out of love, not fear, our intimacy grows; the Light is getting brighter; transformation is in full swing.

The journey from not disobeying, to obeying, to pleasing, and then to honoring, evolves as we are being

transformed through intimacy—intimacy through transformation and transformation through intimacy.

How could this not be Life to the Full?

Thank you for allowing me to teach a little. It has become my habit to interrupt the flow of my stories with a
theme or message.

28

BLINDED BY THE LIGHT

JOHN AND I RETURNED TO JERUSALEM FROM OUR TIME IN Samaria with Philip, but we were staying away from the temple due to the Pharisee Saul's savage campaign against us. Saul was still breathing out murderous threats against all the Lord's disciples. He went to the high priest and asked him for letters to the synagogues in Damascus, so that if he found any there who belonged to our Way, whether men or women, he might take them as prisoners to Jerusalem.

It was a very difficult time for our family. No, to say it more accurately, it was a horrible time for us. Saul and his temple guards might kick down our door at any time. We had beloved women dragged out of their homes and publicly humiliated. Men were beaten. It was scary and discouraging, and there was no end in sight.

Do you see the viciousness of Saul? He was hunting down men and women and was so full of hatred. It was obvious to us Satan controlled him. We could not help but worry Satan might even be winning. Could our Way survive this onslaught? I cried out to Jesus, "Why are you allowing this hateful man to persecute us? Why won't you stop him? We are doing your will. We are obeying you. Are you going to allow Satan to defeat us?"

Everything was so out of control. My faith, my trust, was wavering and wobbling, and my feelings of fear were taking over. But we soon learned Satan, and Saul for that matter, was under the Spirit's control the whole time.

ON THE ROAD TO DAMASCUS

We were relieved when Saul left Jerusalem for a while because he was the heart and soul of the persecution. With him gone, no one was likely to break down doors and arrest us. I remember thinking during this time, *If only the Lord would capture Saul's heart and make him his own, what a force he could be for the Way.* I knew it was ludicrous to think this, but then again, he captured and saved a wretch like me. If he could save me, King Peter, as blind and as lost as I was, no one was beyond his power.

To our dismay, reports started to reach us that this enemy of the gospel had been born again! Could this be true? My heart would not yet let me hope for such. The story went something like this: As Saul neared Damascus on his journey, suddenly a light from heaven flashed around him. He fell to the ground and heard a voice say to him, "Saul, Saul, why do you persecute me?"

"Who are you, Lord?" Saul asked.

"I am Jesus, whom you are persecuting. Now get up and go into the city, and you will be told what you must do."

The men traveling with Saul stood there speechless; they heard the sound but did not see anyone. Saul got up from the ground, but when he opened his eyes, he could see nothing. They led him by the hand into Damascus. For three days, he was blind and did not eat or drink anything.

I must admit as I heard the story, I secretly hoped he would remain blind and suffer more than three days. I am not proud of this, but I must be transparent with you. The old Peter wanted this enemy to suffer, as he had caused so much suffering for us. Jesus' admonition to love one's enemy was echoing in the back of my mind, but I was not yet ready to listen.

Ananias' Obedience

In Damascus, there was a disciple named Ananias. He had been with us during Pentecost but had returned home to Damascus. The Lord called to him in a vision, "Ananias! Go to the house of Judas on Straight Street and ask for a man from Tarsus named Saul, for he is praying. In a vision, he has seen a man named Ananias come and place his hands on him to restore his sight."

Ananias was naturally hesitant to go anywhere near Saul, but the Lord said, "Go! This man is my chosen instrument to proclaim my name to the Gentiles and their kings and to the people of Israel. I will show him how much he must suffer for my name."

Here is yet another example of the Holy Spirit telling someone to "Go." (I will soon explain in more detail what I mean by the Spirit's directing us with what I call his "Go's and No's and Waits.") He told Ananias to go, so he went to the house and, placing his hands on Saul, he said, "Brother Saul, the Lord Jesus, who appeared to you on the road as you were coming here, has sent me so that you may see again and be filled with the Holy Spirit."

That took some guts, didn't it? Ananias' first response to the Father was just as mine would have been, "Lord, are you sure? I have heard many reports about this man and all the harm he has done to your holy people in Jerusalem. he has come here with authority from the chief priests to arrest all who call on your name."

I cannot blame Ananias for hesitating. I certainly would not have wanted to be the first to encounter Saul. His hatred for us made the Sanhedrin look like choir boys. Immediately, something like scales fell from Saul's eyes, and he could see again. He got up and was baptized, and after taking some food, he regained his strength.

A Transformed Saul

Saul spent several days with the disciples in Damascus. At once, he began to preach in the synagogues, "Jesus is the Son of God." All those who heard him were astonished and asked, "Isn't he the man who raised havoc in Jerusalem among those who call on this name? Hasn't he come here to take them as prisoners to the chief priests?"

Yet Saul grew more and more powerful—as I knew he would—and baffled the Jews living in Damascus by proving that Jesus is the Messiah. What a God we serve! He humbled the powerful and hated Saul. He knocked him down, turned him around, and then, beyond anything we could hope for, or even think to ask for, he put him to use in the expansion of his kingdom. As the Master once said, "With man this is impossible, but with God all things are possible."

Yes, all things.

Saul stayed there awhile but had to leave because a conspiracy arose among the Jews to kill him. Warned by the Holy Spirit, our brothers took him by night and lowered him in a basket through an opening in the wall. Three years passed before we heard any more about Saul, and during this time, our family of believers throughout Judea, Galilee, and Samaria enjoyed a time of peace and was strengthened. Living in the fear of the Lord and encouraged by the Holy Spirit, our family increased in great numbers, and we were so encouraged.

SAUL'S RETURN

During this time, we dug our roots down deep within our community of believers. We never ceased talking about the new life that was now available to all because of Jesus' perfect sacrifice. We had priests, leaders of the local synagogues, wives of important officials, and whole families joining our Family.

The wives of the important officials joined us and helped support us financially. This was a big help and encouragement to us. Their husbands did not join us because, well, they were too important. Surrender was out of the question for them.

Several wives told us similar stories: She would try to talk to her husband about the gospel, but he would rebuff her, saying something like, "Why are you bothering me with all this odd talk about a risen Messiah? I'm okay. I'm doing just fine, thank you. I may not be perfect, but I'm not all that bad, either. You go ahead and enjoy your newfound spirituality. I'm religious. I'm a spiritual man too. I just prefer the intellectual approach."

You already know how I would respond to such a common refrain—there are going to be a lot of intellectuals in hell.

After about three years had gone by, we got word from our Brothers in Damascus that Saul was coming to Jerusalem. He wanted to meet us. I can tell you none of us were eager to meet him. We were suspicious of his motives for sure, but truthfully, I was having a hard time forgetting what he had done to Stephen as well as all our brothers and sisters he had thrown into jail.

I know, I know, we are supposed to forgive. With the Spirit's help—I should say *only* with the Spirit's help—I was trying to forgive him. But forgetting? Well, that is another issue. I can still see the hatred in his face as he kicked in doors and dragged our people to jail. Forgive? Maybe. Forget? Not likely.

FORGIVING—RELEASING

Later, I will share with you what the Spirit has shown me about forgiving. For now, please know forgiving is first about releasing—as in releasing your offender in your heart. You must release your anger, your hurt, and your resentment. Forgiving what happened to you is part of your work and a lot of the Spirit's work. You cannot do this on your own.

I was trying to release my anger and resentment toward Saul, but, sadly, I was far from forgetting. Reconciling was going to be a real challenge.

When he came to Jerusalem, he tried to join us, but we were all afraid of him, not believing he really was a true disciple. But Barnabas, always the encourager, took him in and spent time with him, listening to his story. He then told us we should hear him out. Barnabas viewed everyone in a favorable light—a gift I had not yet received or had yet to cultivate.

SEVEN TIMES SEVENTY

The Twelve gathered to consider meeting with Saul. Barnabas stood up and told us how Saul had seen the Lord on his way into Damascus, and that the Lord had spoken to him. He told us he had preached fearlessly in the name of Jesus while in Damascus. I noticed Thomas swore under his breath, and Matthew shifted uncomfortably in his seat.

John looked at me and said, "Do you remember, Peter, when you asked Jesus how many times we should forgive someone?" I remembered. At the time, I had tried to show off a bit by upping the number from the usual rabbinic teaching of three times to seven times, but the Master saw right through me. He raised the bar even higher, saying there should be no limit to our forgiveness.

As the Spirit has exposed my sinful heart to me, I am now so glad there is indeed no limit because I need forgiveness every day—many more than even 7 times 70. Don't you?

As the Twelve discussed the idea of meeting with Saul, the Spirit told me in no uncertain terms I was indeed to meet with him, no matter how much we debated it among ourselves. I heard him clearly, even as I attempted to quench him, so I quickly acquiesced. I interrupted Barnabas and said simply, "I will meet with him alone. I want the rest of you to stay away for this first encounter. In fact, this would be a good time for you to visit around Judea."

Barnabas started to object, as did John and Matthew, but I knew it was what the Spirit wanted, and I said so. This quieted their objections. "Bring him tomorrow to John Mark's home after our morning meeting at Solomon's Porch," I instructed Barnabas.

THE BEGINNING OF A FRIENDSHIP

I will never forget when Saul first walked in. He was cautious and a bit timid, but I could see the fire burning in his eyes. Great goodness, this little man was intense! Barnabas started to formally introduce us, but before he got two words out, Saul rushed over and hugged me. It caught me by surprise. I did not know what to make of it.

He quickly stepped back and gathered himself and said, "I want to first beg for your forgiveness, Simon. My heart and soul are tormented because of my previous way of life. I hear the screams of those families I arrested in my dreams at night. I anguish over my rage and blindness." Saul hesitated, looking at me with deep pain in his eyes. I could see tears forming.

"There are times when I am walking from one place to another, and I literally bend over in pain, viscerally reliving my hateful actions," he gasped. "I know our Savior has forgiven me, and I know this should be enough. But I am here to beg forgiveness from you and the Brothers," he cried out and fell to the floor in tears.

My heart ached for this man, so visibly in agony. But my head argued, saying, "Watch out. It's just a front. Do not trust this man." My heart quickly won out, and I wanted to hug him and reassure him of my love and forgiveness. I motioned for Barnabas to leave. James, Jesus' brother, was with me too. He had insisted on joining us. He had become the leader of the Jerusalem family, and he was not going to miss this meeting.

"Brother Saul, please stand up. I am just a man, like you. No better, likely worse. You do not have to beg forgiveness from me, or from anybody. We are all beggars before the Lord. Although your actions were in the public eye for everyone to see, your sins are no more than mine. We both denied the Master. The difference between us is that I denied him while knowing him; you did not."

I pulled Saul toward me and embraced him. "I am perhaps guilty of the greater sin, but that is immaterial. We are all sinners here, saved by grace. Now come, sit, we have much to discuss." This seemed to calm his nerves, and he sat down next to me, still shaking a bit.

Little did I know this was the beginning of a friendship—a brotherhood—one that would encourage me and instruct me and bring great joy to my heart. For the next two decades, we fought the good fight alongside each other for Jesus. Through thick or thin, Saul never wavered in his commitment to Jesus and his joy for having been rescued from both a life of hell and an eternal life in hell.

GOD *LIKES* US

Saul stayed with us 15 days and moved about freely in Jerusalem, speaking boldly in the name of the Lord. Each day, he would join us at the morning gathering, after which the two of us would sit down and talk about a variety of things. He wanted to know all about Jesus: what he was like in person; what it was like to walk with him each day for three-plus years. He wanted to know every detail of his teachings. He almost wore me out! In his subsequent visits over the years, I would try to get John, Matthew, James, or anyone else to spend time with him. He was too smart for me. He was just so intense.

The one thing I kept emphasizing to Saul, and I continue to emphasize to you as well, is the overwhelming sense that Jesus liked us. He liked being around us. He enjoyed our company. He was our friend. Saul would not have expected this. God Almighty, Creator of the universe, actually liked us?

Saul said in response to this revelation, "Simon, I thought perhaps it was his job to love us; he is God after all. But *like* me? Enjoy my company? I could not have ever anticipated something as wonderful as this!"

If you hear nothing else, hear this again. Over the three-plus years I spent with the Master, the overwhelming gift I carry forward is his companionship, his friendship. He was my friend, and I was his. He is my Savior and my Lord, and he is God Almighty, but when I cut through all the doctrine, the teachings, and his parables, the bottom line is he is my friend. He wants to be yours too.

I shared one more thing with Saul about my time with the Master: he was fun to be around. I don't think Saul could relate to what I was saying—Saul is not a particularly fun person. He tries to be cordial and casual, but the man is just too intense. I shared with Saul that everyone who met Jesus liked him. There were so many times walking out on the dusty roads of Galilee or sitting around a fire at night that we belly-laughed together. He was and is a fun companion. Even now, when I am talking with him throughout the course of the day, I sense his humor and joy.

What a gift!

29

IN ME?

IN ONE OF OUR MORNING CONVERSATIONS, SAUL SAID,
"If I may, I would like to talk about something that has been
on my mind ever since the Holy Spirit indwelled me that
day in Damascus."

I nodded and motioned for Saul to continue.

"You see, I read about the Spirit throughout our Hebrew Scriptures. I read how the Spirit was hovering over
the waters at the beginning of creation. I read how God sent
the Spirit to King Saul to accomplish his purposes, but then
the Spirit was taken back from Saul."

He waved his hands and continued, " I have read
Isaiah's words from God as he spoke about the Messiah, 'I
will put my Spirit on him,' and when he wrote, 'My Spirit,
who is on you, will not depart from you.'

"I guess what I am trying to say is my understanding
about the Holy Spirit was that he could be placed *on* someone, or maybe *around* someone when the Father wanted to
accomplish something through that person." Saul hesitated, and then said, "But I missed the fact that the Spirit
would be *in* us, Simon. *In* us?"

I smiled and said, "Now that is the great surprise, isn't
it, my Brother? In the same way, for all these hundreds of

years, we anticipated a warrior Messiah—a man from God who would be for us and with us, leading us like King David. A king who would conquer Rome and reestablish Israel as a great nation. We certainly did not anticipate an itinerant rabbi like Jesus.

"But," and I smiled, suddenly sensing clarity and creativity coming from the Holy Spirit, "Remember the words of the prophet Ezekiel:

"'I will give you a new heart and put a new spirit in you; I will remove from you your heart of stone and give you a heart of flesh. I will put my Spirit in you and move you to follow my decrees and be careful to keep my laws.'"

SAUL'S REVELATION

Saul's eyes lit up. He sat back and pondered this for a moment, then burst out laughing. He could tell I was confused by his laughter, so he said, "Don't you see the humor here, Simon? I am the scholar. You are the fisherman. I have been schooled by the great Gamaliel. You are a mere fisherman. You are not supposed to be able to teach me anything about our Hebrew Scriptures!"

I smiled, and said, "Brother, I hope you can see that was the Spirit teaching you, not me."

Saul laughed again, slapping his knee and exclaiming, "How did I miss this—the Spirit *in* me!" Saul's eyes were blazing with excitement. "So this is the great mystery now revealed, isn't it, Simon?" Saul continued. "This is the mystery that has been kept hidden for ages and generations but is now disclosed to the Lord's people. To them, God has chosen to make known among the Jews and the Gentiles the glorious riches of this mystery, which is Christ *in* you, the hope of glory."

Saul then launched into a litany of praise, in what would become a consistent theme in his writings: "Praise be to the God and Father of our Lord Jesus Christ, who has blessed us in the heavenly realms with every spiritual blessing in Christ. For he chose us in him before the creation of the world to be holy and blameless in his sight. In him—*in* him, Simon!—we have redemption through his blood, the forgiveness of sins, in accordance with the riches of God's grace that he lavished on us."

Saul stood up and walked around the room. He was really animated now. "With all wisdom and understanding, he made known to us this mystery, which he purposed in Christ, to be put into effect when the times reach their fulfillment, which they now have, my Brother.

"In him—*in* him, Simon!" Saul kept repeating. "We were also chosen, in order that we, who were the first to put our hope in Christ, might be for the praise of his glory. All future believers will also be included in Christ."

I was just sitting there taking all this in. This scholar, this perfect Pharisee, this Hebrew of Hebrews, Saul paced around the room. How did I find myself sitting in the same room with this former blasphemer, this persecutor, this violent man? Only the Holy Spirit.

"With man this is impossible, but with God all things are possible."

Yes, all things.

He then concluded with, "When we believe, when we place our trust in Jesus, we are marked in him with a seal, the promised Holy Spirit, who is a deposit, *in us*, Simon, in us!—guaranteeing our inheritance until the redemption of those who are God's possession, to the praise of his glory. Amen."

Wow. This Saul could articulate the Lord's purposes like no other among us. As I thought about Saul's eloquent words, I had to admire his depth of understanding. He was far beyond me intellectually. In fact, he was an intellectual giant—a giant humbled to be a servant. Yet I had the same Spirit indwelling me, and even though my examples were less eloquent, I felt the creativity of the Spirit coming.

WITH GOD—WITH US—IN US

As Saul sat down, I said, "Think of it like this, Brother Saul. Before Jesus, in the days of old, our people had to go to the Tent of Meeting in the desert, or later to the Temple, in order to be with God. They went to be with God in God's presence. When Jesus came, it was as though God was coming out of the temple to be with man.

"But," and I hesitated for the full effect, "After the resurrection and the coming of the Spirit, God now dwells *in* us, not just *with* us. This is our hope of glory—our confident expectation of eternal life: Jesus, through the Holy Spirit, in us—the guarantee of eternal life with and within the Trinity."

Saul motioned for me to continue.

"Originally, man went to be with God, and then Jesus came from God to be with man. Now God and Jesus are not just with us, they are in us."

Saul was listening intently, so I continued, "Before Jesus, and even during Jesus' earthly ministry, it was God in human form with us. Now, with the Holy Spirit's presence, it is God in us."

Saul smiled, "That is a beautiful way of saying it, Simon. With God in us, our hope—our confident expectation—is guaranteed. It's not just wishful or hopeful thinking but a guarantee, which I realize now my education and piety could never guarantee."

First, there was the presence of God in the temple of God. Then Jesus became the presence of God among us. Now we have the presence of God Almighty, creator of the heavens and the earth, in us.

"With man this is impossible, but with God all things are possible."

Yes, all things.

No's and Go's and Waits

On another morning, Saul sat down and said, "Okay, I heard you talk about how the Spirit directs us with what you called "No's and Go's and Waits." I want to understand this better."

"Well," I began, "You have already seen it in your own life, Saul of Tarsus."

Saul winced when I addressed him like this, but he soon came to see I was lovingly teasing him. "The Spirit told Ananias to go to you. The Spirit told John and me to go to Samaria where Philip was evangelizing. Before all this, just before Jesus ascended, Jesus told us to go back to Jerusalem and wait on the Holy Spirit.

"He wanted us to wait before we tried to do anything because without the Spirit leading and directing us, without his Go's and No's, how could we know the way? This has been a long, hard growing pain for me, Brother Saul, because I am not the type who likes to wait."

Saul nodded and said, "Neither am I, Simon. But please continue. I want to know more."

I began, "Jesus said the Spirit would guide us into all truth. I have experienced this promised guidance when he tells me to 'go,' and I have sensed him telling me 'no.' I know you remember hearing about the time John and I were walking to the temple for the afternoon prayer time. As we approached the Gate, I noticed this lame man sitting by the side of the road begging."

Saul smiled and nodded.

"I would have walked right by that lame beggar. I had, in fact, walked by him many times before, but the Spirit nudged me to stop and engage the man. I had no intention of talking to him or engaging with him, and I certainly did not anticipate healing him, but the Spirit told me plainly to go over to the man.

"I had no idea what or why—I just knew the Spirit was directing me."

Saul interrupted me and asked, "When you say the Holy Spirit told you, did you hear an audible voice as I did on my way into Damascus?"

I smiled and said, "No, and thank goodness I was not struck down with blindness!"

Saul smiled and lowered his eyes and said, "Well, I deserved much worse than that."

I continued, "The voice I hear from the Holy Spirit is clear and distinct, but more like a whisper or a gentle nudge, not an audible voice. There is no mistaking his voice, though. But since he whispers and nudges instead of bullying us, we can easily ignore him. I have done this at times, refusing to listen because I did not want to wait; I wanted action." I frowned and shook my head in disgust.

Quenching—Grieving

"So that is what you mean when you taught about quenching the Holy Spirit?" Saul asked.

"Yes, we quench the Spirit when we do not do what he asks us to do. It's like we are throwing water on the flame he wants to power up in us—quenching the Holy Spirit power. At these times, he is convicting and directing me. I feel it, but I choose to ignore him."

I shook my head and continued, "For instance, he might ask me to go see someone who is hurting or needs an encouraging word. He might direct me to help someone financially. More recently, I have heard him prompting me to start writing down what I have learned from Jesus."

Saul interrupted me and asked, "How do you feel about that, Simon? I know you do not consider yourself a learned man, but, good gracious, we would all benefit greatly if you would."

"Well, John Mark is writing down just about everything I say and teach, and Matthew has already begun to write out our journey with the Master, so I am satisfied an appropriate history is in the works. There is nothing new I could add."

"But," Saul said, "those in the future may not get to hear it in your voice. Think about it and I will be praying about it." Saul smiled and added, "The great Simon Peter certainly does not want to quench the Spirit now, does he?"

We both chuckled at this, then Saul asked, "But what about grieving the Spirit? I have heard John talk about this. How do we grieve the Spirit?"

"John has such a sensitive heart, you know, and he does include in his teaching this idea of grieving the Holy Spirit.

You see, we quench the Spirit when we do not do what he directs us to do. We grieve the Spirit when we do something he is convicting us not to do."

"Oh, I think I see what you mean," Saul replied, closing his eyes for a moment in thought. He continued, "The Spirit tells us to 'go' do something, and if we do not, we are quenching him, dousing out the flame he is igniting in us. But when he directs us *not* to do something, and we do it anyway, we are grieving him."

I nodded and said, "Yes, that's it, Saul. For instance, if I sense myself getting frustrated with Ruth, I hear the Spirit saying, 'Do not say what is on your mind, Simon.'"

"Do you often ignore his direction in that area?" Saul asked with a sly smile.

"Sadly, at times I do, but thankfully not nearly as often as in my early days. In fact, learning not to say the first thing on my mind has been a real transformation, and a key to living with more harmony in my relationships, thank the Lord," I said, shaking my head.

"I have also talked with many men, and some women too, about their struggle with lust."

Saul's eyes perked up.

"They know the Spirit is telling them not to look and lust, but they often ignore him, and, thus, they are grieving the Holy Spirit."

THE WAR INSIDE

Saul shook his head and looked down at the floor and said, "I can be so unspiritual, Simon, practically sold as a slave to sin. At times, I do not understand what I do. For what I want to do, I do not do—but what I hate, I do."

"I know, Brother!" I exclaimed.

Saul continued, shaking his head: "I have the desire to do what is good, but I cannot carry it out. For I do not do the good I want to do, but the evil I do not want to do—this I keep on doing." Saul hesitated, then continued, "Now I will say the evil I do is nothing compared to the evil heart I used to have. I have made every effort to add to my life the fruit of the Spirit, such as love, joy, peace, and patience. Thankfully, the Spirit has joined with me in this transformation of my heart.

"But," Saul stopped and looked at me, "I have so far to go. Does this discourage you, Simon, even though you have grown in the power of the Holy Spirit so much, that you still have so far to go?"

"Actually, no," I replied. "It is different with the Spirit. Yes, I see how far there is to go, but I also see how far he has taken me. I know the richness that awaits me as I surrender more and more my claim to my personal rights and dig deeper in my relationship with Jesus through the ever-present power of the Holy Spirit.

"So I find this law at work," I concluded, "although I want to do good, evil is right there with me. For in my inner being I delight in God's law; but I see another law at work in me, waging war against the law of my mind and making me a prisoner of the law of sin at work within me." I paused, looking at Saul and said, "What a wretched man I am!"

Saul nodded and exclaimed, "Who will rescue us from this body that is subject to death? Thanks be to God, who delivers us through Jesus Christ our Lord!"

We stopped for a moment, each in deep thought about what we had just shared, knowing the Spirit was moving in us to give us this clarity. "Amen!" we said in unison.

I put my hand on Saul's shoulder and said, "For this reason, I remind you to fan into flame the gift of God, which is in you through the laying on of Ananias' hands. For the Spirit God gave us is not a spirit of timidity, but a Spirit of power, of love, and self-discipline.

Saul smiled mischievously and said, "Simon, do not be surprised if I repeat your words often. I am going to write down these things we are discussing so I may use them later." I smiled, having no idea how much writing Saul actually would do.

SATAN RUSHES—GOD GUIDES

I paused, and then said, "One last thing about these 'go's and no's' from the Holy Spirit, Saul. The Spirit may also say, 'Wait. Go slowly here. Do not rush into this.' You know so often we feel we have to make a decision or take some action. But, more often than not, we actually do not, at least not right away. We just want to rush ahead so we can get our way."

Saul nodded, then shook his head.

"But always remember, my Brother, Satan rushes, but God guides."

"Satan rushes; God guides," Saul repeated, musing over this truth. "That is so true, isn't it? There are so many times I wish I had just waited, either to speak or to act. I could have avoided so much disharmony if I had just waited."

James, Jesus' brother, joined in and said, "My dear brothers, take note of this: Everyone should be quick to listen, slow to speak, and slow to become angry because human anger does not produce the righteousness that God desires."

Saul and I nodded in agreement, and James continued, "Think about the mighty horse. When we put bits into the mouths of horses to make them obey us, we can turn the whole animal. Or take ships as an example. Although they are so large and are driven by strong winds, they are steered by a very small rudder wherever the pilot wants to go." James was up and walking around the room now.

"Likewise," he continued, "The tongue is a small part of the body, but it says such stupid things and makes such great boasts. Consider what a great forest is set on fire by a small spark. The tongue also is a fire, a world of evil among the parts of the body. It corrupts the whole body, sets the whole course of one's life on fire, and is itself set on fire by hell," he concluded.

Saul shook his head and added, "All kinds of animals, birds, reptiles, and sea creatures are being tamed and have been tamed by mankind, but no human being seems to be able to tame the tongue, that is for sure."

I smiled and said to them, "The old Peter might have added, 'especially the tongues of women!' But I know now the fault actually lies in me. I know we men tend to say the first thing that pops into our minds rather than just waiting and listening for guidance and insight."

James smiled and said, "Do not be quick to speak and to act; be quick to … wait!"

We finished our discussion at this point, but I would like to remind you one more time about life with the Spirit.

The Spirit guides us. He nudges us with go's and no's, and even 'waits'—especially the waits. When we ignore him, we miss the life that is truly life. The closer we are to him the more we will feel his conviction.

Always remember, the Spirit is about convicting us, not condemning us. There is now no condemnation for those of us in Christ. Only Satan, the accuser, condemns. Please, my Brothers and Sisters, listen for the Spirit. When he says 'go,' go. when he says 'no,' stop. when he says 'wait,' take a deep breath, slow down, and ask him to lead you.

30

FRUIT OF THE SPIRIT

THE LAST MORNING SAUL WAS WITH US, HE SAID TO ME,
"Simon, in one of our earlier discussions, you used a
phrase, 'fruit of the Spirit.' I would like to know more about
what you mean by this phrase."

We were sitting across from the temple. The busyness
of the temple business was on full display. It saddened me
and wearied me to see so much energy directed toward
busy religious activities. I hope one day this ceases and all
the energy is toward true worship in the Spirit. Sitting with
my brother Saul, I could not help but fear that one day the
Way would be more about people in motion than the
Spirit's movement.

I turned to Saul and said, "My dear Brother, it is so vital
that you learn to live with the power of the Holy Spirit. Do
you realize the Holy Spirit is the only God left on earth?[1] I
know this sounds odd, startling actually, but in some ways,
it is absolutely true. The Holy Spirit is the only God—he is
the God on earth."

Saul raised his eyebrows. I continued, "It seemed so important to Jesus that we understand the Spirit and the
Spirit's immense power. The Master put such an emphasis
on the coming Spirit on our last night with him, I could

almost conclude he felt one of his primary reasons for coming into our world was to pave the way for the Holy Spirit to come live in us."

Saul turned to look at me, a quizzical expression growing. I smiled and continued. "In fact, Jesus said, 'It is for your good that I am going away. Unless I go away, the Advocate will not come to you, but if I go, I will send him to you.'"

Saul looked at me with confusion. I put my hand on his shoulder and said, "Think about it this way, Saul. God the Father told Joseph he was sending Jesus to save his children from sin. John the Baptizer said he was the Lamb of God to take away the sins of the world. Brother John likes to say Jesus came to destroy the work of the devil. But Jesus said, 'I have come so that you may have life, life to the full.'

"It's like Jesus is saying, 'The reason I have come, what energizes and compels me, is to show you what life is really like, the full life, the abundant life. I want you to know the heavenly Father as I know him, so you can share in our life to the full. To have this, you must have the Holy Spirit. I have come to fulfill the law and the prophets so you can understand what this full life looks like. Right now, you have completely missed who the Father is, what he cares about, and how much he loves you. Because of this, you are living average lives. I want so much more for you.'"

"On our last night together, I could sense Jesus emphasizing, 'I am leaving, and please understand this is the best thing for you. Because when I leave, the Holy Spirit can then come.' Saul, it was like he was saying, 'You just wait. If you think I have done great things, you are going to be amazed at what the Spirit can do, and will do, in you! In fact, you will do even greater things than I because the one who is in you is greater than the one who is in the world.'"

WHEN THE HOLY SPIRIT COMES

Saul was mesmerized by all this, so I continued, clearly feeling the Holy Spirit's energy, clarity, and creativity. "Now you know in the Hebrew Scriptures, the Holy Spirit was given by God and taken back by God. As you mentioned, King Saul is a good example. The Holy Spirit was sent to execute and empower the things God the Father had ordained—his plan and his will. But he was not a permanent resident in anyone before Jesus.

"King Saul would not wait for Samuel to arrive at Gilgal. He waited seven days, but after that, he took control. This greatly displeased God. Sarah would not wait on God's timing to fulfill his promise of a son, so she persuaded Abraham to help God out, and Hagar and Ismael were the result."

Saul interjected, "Throughout our Hebrew Scriptures, the Spirit was given and the Spirit was taken away as God orchestrated his plan."

I nodded and said, "This is why Jesus said, 'Now I am leaving, but I am not leaving you as orphans. I am telling you that when the Holy Spirit comes, He will live in you forever!' Those were his words, Saul: 'He will live *in* you *forever.*'"

THE FRUIT TEST

I motioned for Saul to sit down and I continued. "Now to your question about the fruit of the Spirit. Here is an exercise I do from time to time with men. I ask them to grade themselves on the fruit of the Spirit in their lives—on the degree of love, joy, peace, patience, kindness, goodness, faithfulness, gentleness, and self-control evident in their day-to-day living."

Saul interrupted and asked, "Simon, do you think our heavenly Father is constantly grading us?"

He seemed anxious about this, so I said, "No, Brother, I do not. We are holy in his sight, without blemish and free from accusation. Please never forget this. There is now no condemnation for those of us who are in Christ. But the Holy Spirit convicts us, and that is what my little test is all about: conviction."

Saul seemed to relax, and he motioned for me to continue.

"No, I do not think he is grading us. But," I looked at Saul, his eyes boring a hole in me with curiosity, "John shared with me something the Holy Spirit told him: 'Examine yourselves to see whether you are in the faith. Test yourselves. Do you not realize that Christ Jesus is in you, unless, you fail the test?'"

Saul smiled and said, "I like that. Do not be surprised if I use that again!"

I laughed and continued, "I think it is helpful to examine in ourselves the Holy Spirit's fruit of love, joy, peace, patience, kindness, goodness, faithfulness, gentleness, and self-control in our lives, and to give ourselves a grade on each. The Holy Spirit will then convict us where our grades are low. But remember Saul ..."

Saul interrupted me and said, "There is now no condemnation for those in Christ Jesus."

I laughed, patted him on the back, and continued. "Each time I do this exercise, the lowest grades for the men are … can you guess, Saul?"

Saul nodded and answered, "Patience and self-control. They would be the lowest for me too, no doubt. I might add, not once has my lack of patience or self-control done anything but cause problems."

NO SELF-HELP PROGRAM

I nodded and smiled and said, "Anyone who knows me knows this was true of me as well, my friend. Now, my first point to the men and my first point to you, Saul, is, 'Do you think you can isolate these two and improve them on your own? Do you think to yourself, 'I am going to be more patient this year? I am going to have more self-control?' Because I can tell you right now, you will not be able to do that, and certainly not on your own.

"This is no self-help program, my friend. This is only by and through the power of the Holy Spirit—and his fruit."

I paused as Saul shifted in his chair, leaning in, his brow furrowed. I continued, "Oh, you may be able to grind out a bit of improvement—perhaps some change, but certainly no real transformation. My guess is if we went back three years, your low grades would be in this same area, wouldn't they? The challenge is, if you do learn to live with the power of the Holy Spirit, you will receive the same grade three years from now as well."

Saul shook his head and said, "No doubt."

"Saul, I can guarantee you that in your own power, trying to separate any one of these fruit of the Spirit will

perhaps get you only a little change. But we are after transformation, my Brother. This fruit, these aspects of the
Spirit's fruit, were given to me by the Spirit in the exact order I gave them to you—love, joy, peace, patience, kindness,
goodness, faithfulness, gentleness, and self-control. I am
absolutely convinced they are in this order for a reason."

Saul looked confused and motioned for me to continue.

LOVE

"You will notice love is listed first. We are simply won't be
able to make headway with patience and self-control, gentleness, goodness, kindness, joy, or peace until we understand and absorb this idea of love. As you well know, my
Brother, the top two commandments are to love God and
love others. Jesus said this takes the whole law and the
prophets into account. He said these two cover everything—learning to love God and to love others.

"In fact, he stated plainly, 'All the Law and the Prophets hinge on these two commandments.' Jesus pointed to a
door as he said this to us, wanting us to see that these two
commandments are like door hinges: without them, the
door does not operate properly."

Saul motioned for me to pause and said, "If you place
'Love God' as the top hinge and 'Love your neighbor' as the
lower hinge, it gives us a clear picture of what Jesus is saying."

Saul was thinking ahead of me, as he usually is, so I
looked at him quizzically, motioning him to continue.

"Don't you see, Brother Simon, a door will operate, although poorly, with just the top hinge in place? We can love
God but not our neighbor and still get along through life,

although not very well. The door's swing will be awkward and troublesome, as will be our lives. But no door will work at all with the top hinge off. If I do not love the Father first with all my heart, my life will be totally unhinged. It will not work properly; in fact, it will not work at all." Saul hesitated, thinking through the implications of what the Spirit had just given him.

LOVING WITH ALL OUR HEARTS

I studied Saul's face for a moment and then challenged him, "How are you going to do this, Saul? How are any of us going to love God and love others with all our hearts?"

Saul shook his head and replied, "Not on my own, that is for sure. You are saying we have to first understand and appropriate this first fruit of love into our lives before we can progress on toward more fruit, more holiness? But where, how do we start?"

"Well," I replied, "Yes, we have to learn to love God — through the Spirit's power—before we can learn to love others. But before we can learn to love God, we must understand his love for us—his perfect, unconditional love for you, Saul. You must absorb this love and live each moment with the knowledge and awareness he loves you perfectly. He is proud of you, Saul. You are his beloved child."

Saul closed his eyes and shook his head. "He loved me even while I was persecuting Jesus. He loved me even while I was persecuting all of you." Saul's eyes filled with tears and he looked at me with sadness. "I have to say it again, Simon. I am so sorry for my evil behavior. I live with that anguish every day. Please forgive me," his eyes pleaded with despair.

"Stop that, my dear Brother. You are already forgiven. Do not let Satan have that victory; do not let him discourage you. Although your actions were in the public eye for all to see, your sins were no worse than mine. I feel your pain, but let it go. Cast your anxieties off on Jesus because he so cares for you."

Saul smiled, dried his tears, and motioned for me to continue.

LIVING WATER OVERFLOWING

I smiled at Saul, raised my arms to the air and said, "As I have learned to absorb and live with his love, loving others has become more natural. His love for me is like Living Water, spilling forth into my love for others—spilling forth like a fountain overflowing, brother. Streams of living water will overflow from within you."

Saul smiled at my reference to Jesus' words.

"As you learn to live with this overflowing love, Saul, you will then start to have joy in your life—true joy, not giddy happiness. Happiness depends on happenings. Joy is that deep down in your heart sense of shalom, a thorough and pervasive sense of wholeness and well-being. You won't have true joy without first being saturated through and through by his love."

FLOWING NATURALLY IN THE FRUITS OF THE SPIRIT

Saul said, "You are talking about Shalom: wholeness and well-being and joy. Okay, the love of the Father saturates us, filling our hearts so we start to overflow with his love for others. With this love, true joy becomes a reality. Peace then naturally flows from this joy, right, Simon? No joy, no peace?"

"Absolutely Saul," I said. "Without joy, you can forget peace, and with no peace, you can forget patience."

Saul responded, "True joy, like true peace, is not contingent on our circumstances. I want to learn to be content whatever the circumstances. I know what it is to be in need, and I know what it is to have plenty. I want to learn the secret of being content in any and every situation, whether well fed or hungry, whether living in plenty or in want." Saul hesitated, then said, "I know the secret, Brother Simon: I can do all this through him who gives me strength."

I nodded enthusiastically and said, "Amen! Without the Spirit, I have no strength. But now, as I learn to look to the Spirit, I get this sense of quiet confidence—of hope: confident expectation—and it gives me peace. With this peace, I am going to have more patience. Peace engenders patience.

"Then the rest of the fruit naturally grows and flows and thrives in my heart," I continued. "Kindness flows naturally. I think of kindness like this: an affection toward others, wanting to help them, truly desiring to serve them. Goodness: viewing others in a light most favorable, as you see Brother Barnabas does so well—being generous in the way we view others as well as the way we deal with others. Faithfulness: being trustworthy, being someone who can be depended on."

I finished with this, "Gentleness and self-control then become real in my life. I do not have to affect a pose in front of others. I no longer have to pretend I have this fruit. Pretending only works in public, if at all. We cannot fake any of these aspects of the fruit of the Spirit, and we sure cannot fake gentleness and self-control, especially around our family."

Saul stood up and began to walk around the room. He stopped and looked at me and said, "Gentleness. Hmm. I have observed men with their wives and families, Simon, and I do not think these men understand the force they carry, the weight their wives and children feel when they walk in the front door of their homes. When a man is in the house, the wife and children either feel safe, or they feel shaky with a sense of anxiety, sometimes even fear."

Saul paused, then continued, "They don't fear that he is going to beat them, necessarily, but that they have to walk on eggshells: 'What is father's mood going to be like? Is he happy or agitated?'" He looked at me and said, "I know the Jews have this saying, 'If momma ain't happy, ain't nobody happy.'"

I laughed and motioned for Saul to continue.

"But the truth is, if the father is not happy, no one is going to be happy. If abba does not have a gentle spirit, his wife and his children will always feel some degree of anxiety when he is around. Men simply do not realize that they are a strong force in their families, a force for good or for bad," Saul concluded.

No Roots—No Fruit

After a moment, Saul asked, "Simon, how am I going to improve these low grades?"

I pondered his question for a moment and replied, "Well, let me ask you this, Brother. What is the number one responsibility of a fruit tree?"

Saul looked confused and replied, "To grow fruit, what else?"

I said, "Actually it is not to grow fruit, but to grow roots—to dig its roots deeper into the ground. No roots, no fruit.[2] A fruit tree with healthy, deep roots will naturally produce much fruit."

Saul said, "Okay, I see what you are saying. As we dig our roots into the ground—yes, the deeper the roots, the fuller the fruit. Our outward fruit depends on our inward roots. No roots, no fruits. I see this so clearly now. We are typically trying to produce fruit through our activities. But this is true inward fruit of the Spirit: love, joy, peace, and patience. As this Holy Spirit fruit grows inwardly, our outward activities are transformed. They are in fact energized by the Spirit's fruit inside our heart."

I nodded and said, "To dig your roots down deeply, we start with a quiet time in the mornings: spending time with your heavenly Father in prayer and Scripture. Then we start bringing him into the details of our lives, more and more throughout the day. Even when doing ordinary things such as lacing our sandals or helping Ruth, I am learning to practice the presence of the Spirit, and with this, my roots are going deeper."

Saul contemplated this for a moment, then his eyes lit up and I could sense another oratorical masterpiece coming. "So then," he began, "Just as you received Christ Jesus as Lord, continue to live your lives in him, rooted and established in him, strengthened in your faith and overflowing with thankfulness."

Saul lifted his arms up, saying, " I pray that we, Brother Simon, through the power of the Spirit within us, being rooted and established in love, may have power, together with all the saints, to grasp how wide and long and high and deep is the love of Christ, and to know this love that we may be filled to the measure of all the fullness of God. Amen."

"Amen!" I exclaimed.

---

[1] Idea attributed to Jack Taylor.

[2] Dialogue attributed to Perry Bowers.

31

SPIRIT FRUIT—OUR FRUIT

JAMES HAD REJOINED US, SO I SAID, "JAMES, YOU KNOW
we have often talked about the fruit of the Spirit: love, joy,
peace, patience, kindness, goodness, faithfulness, and so
on, right?"

James is not given to banalities, so he nodded his head,
smiling somewhat impatiently.

I continued, "But do you see what we are *not* saying?
We are not saying, 'the fruit of James is love, joy, peace,
etc.,' are we?"

He smiled and simply said, "No, of course not."

"Let me ask it yet another way," I said. "Are we even
saying, 'The fruit of James *with* the Spirit'?"

James replied, "No, we are not saying that, either. But
what is your point? It seems you are just splitting hairs."

Saul jumped in and said, "I think I see what Simon is
getting at, Brother James. It is not *our* fruit. It is the Spirit's
fruit. It is his fruit growing within us. We cannot grow this
fruit ourselves. Our role is to dig our roots in. As we do this,
by abiding with Jesus, our lives will be overflowing with
these fruits—his fruits."

I nodded and said, "This is so important because if I
think in terms of the 'Fruit of Peter' it becomes about my

performance again. I am back to measuring outcomes. I am getting the cart before the horse." I smiled and said, "I am getting the fruit before the roots."

James and Saul rolled their eyes at my play on words.

But I was on a roll. "You see, what the Spirit does inside me, inside my heart, is to produce these fruits of love, joy, peace, patience, kindness, and goodness. If that is not happening inside me, I will be producing no crop on the outside. The fruit of the Spirit is inward because it is all about our inward growth. Our inward fruit informs and directs our outward activities."

NO ROOTS, NO FRUIT

Saul said, "From the overflow of the Spirit's fruit in our hearts, our mouths speak and our bodies act."

James nodded and said, "In big brother's parable of the four soils, he said the seed that fell on good soil is like someone who hears the Word and understands it and absorbs it and lives it. This is the one who produces a crop, yielding 30, 60, even 100 times what was sown. Those would be deep roots, right?"

We nodded in agreement. James continued, "But remember the seed falling on rocky ground refers to someone who hears the Word and at once receives it with joy. But since they have no root—the Master said *no root*, mind you—they last only a short time. When trouble or persecution comes because of the Word, they quickly fall away. Again, no roots, no fruit."

Saul chimed in, "In our Hebrew book of Numbers, the LORD says, 'If part of the dough offered as first fruits is holy, then the whole batch is holy, and if the root is holy so are the branches.'"

I joined in, "Our role is to abide with Jesus, seeking the Holy Spirit in everything we do. The work he does inside us is always far more important than any work we do on the outside. The Master said if we abide in him, he will abide in us, and we will then bear much fruit. But without him, he said, we can do nothing."

"With him, abiding with him, we will bear fruit—but fruit that will last, mind you," James added.

NURTURING THE SOIL

I continued, "It may seem obvious, but after a farmer plants his seeds, he cannot reach down into the earth and force the fruit to grow in his own power, can he? This growth must happen inside the seed, then the fruit grows as the vines and roots thrive and spread. Yet the farmer can and must nurture the soil. He must spend much time cultivating the soil, enriching the soil."

Saul interjected, "The soil is our heart, obviously. Our role is to cultivate our hearts, preparing our 'soil' for his seed. As Solomon said, 'Above all else, guard your heart, for it is the wellspring of life.'"

James and I nodded, and I continued, "As I see it, our role is to nurture our relationship with Jesus, and as we do this, his Fruit, through the Spirit within us, will grow and fill our lives as well as our activities."

James jumped in, "But what if the farmer plants his seed, then does nothing else? Is he going to get robust fruit? Of course not. Or what if he plants the seeds, nurtures and cultivates the soil for a couple of weeks, but then loses interest or gets distracted with other things? Any fruit?"

Saul and I shook our heads. "Plenty of weeds, that is for sure. Weeds of distraction and trouble." Saul said.

"Or, what if, after the first couple of weeks, he just visits the crops once a week?" James continued.

"You mean like just going to worship once a week, right?" Saul asked.

James nodded and continued, "Now each of us knows we have to provide food for our families. Many of our friends are farmers. If they do not nurture their crops, putting time into their care, cultivating the crops so the roots grow strong and produce fruit, are they not in fact failing their families?"

We nodded in agreement, not sure where he was heading with this line of thought.

"It is the same with our relationship with our Lord," James said. "We are to be the spiritual leaders of our families. If our roots are shallow and weak, and our fruit small and marginal because we fail to invest our time abiding with Jesus, are we not, in fact, failing our families?"

Saul chimed in, "Yet those weeds keep coming in. We must keep nurturing the soil by diligently pulling out those weeds. This must always be a primary part of our focus—pulling those weeds out constantly. Remember Jesus said the third soil was the seed falling among the thorns. He said this refers to someone who hears the Word, but the worries of this life and the deceitfulness of wealth choke the Word, making it unfruitful."

James nodded and said, "I see this all around me. Busyness and distractions, chasing after the things of this world instead of seeking first the kingdom of the Father.

These are the weeds that attack the soil and choke out the fruit of the Spirit: busyness, activities, and distractions."

"I see what you are saying, James," I said. "We fail our families when we do not cultivate and nurture our inward soil—and we do not continue to attack the weeds of busyness and activities and distractions. If I do not help the roots grow deep, then I am, in fact, failing my family."

FOUNTAINS OVERFLOWING

I say to you who are reading my words today, men and women, if you are not digging your roots deep into the soil of the kingdom, you are indeed failing your family. You will not be the man or the woman Jesus wants you to be, and sadly, you will model this for your children.

I know you want to be the kind of person about whom others would say, "That person is filled with the Spirit." Think about it this way, when we encounter someone who is filled with the Holy Spirit, we do not have to see them doing things for us to see the fruit of the Spirit within them. We just sense it, do we not?

The overwhelming sense of the fruit of the Spirit inside this person is overflowing like a fountain cascading down, entirely apart from anything they are doing. It is who they are.

When you become someone in whom the fruit of the Spirit is strong, it overflows all around you. People will see your love, joy, peace, and patience, and they will want what you have.

We spoke earlier about love being the first fruit, so let us apply this image of a cascading fountain to the fruit of the Spirit. Picture love at the top of the fountain, then joy, then peace, then patience, and so on. As love fills up inside us, it overflows out and onto each of these.

Love is first overflowing and engendering our joy. As our joy fills us up, it then overflows into our peace, which then overflows, filling us with patience.

LIVING WATER

My friends, when Jesus was at the great Feast of Tabernacles, he stood up on the last day and declared, "If anyone is thirsty, let him come to me and drink. Whoever believes in me streams of living water will flow from within."

Our Jewish Feast of Tabernacles was often called the Feast of Living Water because each day during the seven-day feast, the priests would draw water from a spring called Shiloach, near the temple at the foot of Mount Moriah.

Each day of the festival, the priests descended to the Shiloach accompanied by all the congregation assembled in the temple. They filled a golden flask with the Living Water. The whole assembly then ascended back to the temple, the priests carrying the flask with great song and praise. The assembly then entered through the Water Gate, one of the gates on the southern side of the temple. As they entered, they were greeted by the incredible sound of trumpet blasts. Once in the temple, the priest carried the golden flask up the altar ramp, pouring the Living Water over the altar.

On the last and final day of the feast, the shouting and singing and praising, together with the trumpets blasting, mounted up to an overwhelming crescendo. At this precise time, Jesus chose to stand up and proclaim he was the

Living Water. He declared loudly and passionately that from him streams of living water would flow into and through his followers.

By this, he meant the Spirit, whom those who believed in him were later to receive. "Streams of living water will *overflow* from the Spirit within." Isn't this a beautiful picture? I want to become the kind of person who has those strong roots—the Holy Spirit fruit growing within me and then overflowing around me.

Don't you?

BE, FIRST—THEN DO

The more I open my heart to the Spirit, the more his fruit grows inside me. I start to be more Christ-like. As I become more like Jesus, with these powerful fruits growing inside, then, and only then, will I *do* more like Jesus.

As I become more holy, I will naturally *do* more holy.

Most of us want a checklist. We want to say to Jesus, "Give me something to do to gain your approval. Give me a list and I will work hard to accomplish everything on that list!" Isn't this what the rich young ruler was all about? He approached Jesus and said, in essence, "I have done everything right. I am a high performer. I am squeaky clean. I have done it all—but something just does not feel right. There has got to be more.

"Give me something else to do, Jesus, so I can feel better about my performance and, therefore, better about my Self. Give me something else to add to my list of accomplishments. I feel good, but I cannot help but wonder how good is good enough?"[1]

Jesus made it clear to us—it is not about doing but about being. It is who you are, first, before what you do.

In his great teaching on the Mount, Jesus said, "You might think because you have not 'done' murder, you are holy in your heart. But you are not 'being' holy when you are angry with someone. It is always about who you are, first and foremost—before it is about what you are doing."

To 'be' we must slow down. We must learn to be still. I have seen people in various groups where I have preached who will just not be still. They are so busy doing things they miss the Spirit's message. They will just not stop and be and slow down enough to just be in Jesus' presence, to be quiet and to be still.

---

[1] Question attributed to Andy Stanley.

32

GENTILE MIRACLES

IT WAS NOW ABOUT EIGHT YEARS SINCE JESUS RETURNED
to the Father. Have you noticed we rarely speak in terms of
Jesus' death, but instead of his resurrection? His resurrection is the defining moment in the story of God—his story,
our history, your story—the only story that matters. Jesus'
death was a means to a new beginning. Death did not happen to Jesus; Jesus happened to death. He was certainly no
martyr.

The cross did not happen to Jesus; Jesus happened to
the cross. Jesus conquered death. Hosea prophesied this:

> I will deliver this people from the power of the
> grave; I will redeem them from death. Where, O
> death, are your plagues? Where, O grave, is your
> destruction?

I have heard Brother Saul say:

> When you were dead in your sins and in the un-
> circumcision of your flesh, God made you alive
> with Christ. He forgave us all our sins, having
> canceled the charge of our legal indebtedness,
> which stood against us and condemned us; he

has taken it away, nailing it to the cross. having disarmed the powers and authorities, he made a public spectacle of them, triumphing over them by the cross.

No, the cross did not happen to Jesus. His resurrection is everything. Saul and I discussed this, and I remember him concluding, with astonishing insight,

> If Christ has not been raised, our preaching is useless and so is your faith. More than that, we are then found to be false witnesses about God, for we have testified about God that he raised Christ from the dead. But he did not raise him if in fact the dead are not raised.
>
> For if the dead are not raised, then Christ has not been raised either. And if Christ has not been raised, your faith is futile; you are still in your sins. Then those also who have fallen asleep in Christ are lost. If only for this life we have hope in Christ, we are of all people most to be pitied.

TOURING OUR COMMUNITIES

I still missed Jesus—his physical presence, but with the Spirit so real within me, it was as if Jesus was right beside me. As he had predicted, it was, in many ways, better than his physical presence. It felt like he was right beside me because he was now inside me. The Spirit was growing in me and filling me to overflowing with his energy, clarity, and creativity.

I would need all three as I set out to tour some of our communities of believers around Western Judea. I headed out toward the coast with a couple of brothers. Ruth stayed behind, but I did not intend to be gone for more than a couple of weeks or so.

I was going to first visit the Lord's people who lived in Joppa, but on the way, the Holy Spirit told me to detour about three miles over to Lydda. We had already walked about 20 miles from Jerusalem, so it was early evening when we arrived. Although we were tired from the trip, we met with some of the brothers and sisters who had been with us at Pentecost and spent the night talking about all that had been happening with the Way.

AENEAS

A man named Aeneas was paralyzed with palsy and had been bedridden for eight years. I was moved by his condition and felt so much compassion for him. As he lay there, his body would have these uncontrollable tremors.

He looked at me with sad, defeated eyes. My heart welled up and I felt Jesus saying, "This is my child. I love him and I want you to help him." With the Spirit pushing me, I stepped closer and said, "Aeneas, Jesus Christ heals you. Get up and roll up your mat."

Immediately, Aeneas got up and stood, feeling his legs and turning around in circles, his eyes as big as saucers. "I can walk," he shouted, and then grabbed me with a hug that almost knocked the breath out of me. He exclaimed, "I had heard about your Jesus, but who can believe such fantastic stories, especially lying here in my condition with no hope." He looked around the room and laughed and exclaimed, "But now I know God Almighty, El Shaddai, is real! He is personal. He cares about the least of us. He cares; can you believe this—he cares about me?"

I looked him in the eye and said, "He is not just my Jesus, Aeneas. He is now *your* Jesus too. He can be anyone's Jesus! Now I want you to follow him. I want you to know him. He is your Savior, and as you surrender your life more and more each day, he will become your Lord. But please never forget this, my new Brother—Jesus can be your best friend as well as your Savior if you will let him."

Aeneas dropped to his knees in tears of gratitude. All those who lived in Lydda and Sharon saw him healed and they turned to Jesus. Our fledgling family of believers in that area began to grow as a result—a growing community of followers of Christ, a new family in Lydda.

What a Savior we serve!

TABITHA

About 10 miles away in Joppa lived a disciple named Tabitha (in Greek her name is Dorcas); she was always doing good and helping the poor. While I was in Lydda, she became sick and died, and her body was washed and placed in an upstairs room. When the disciples heard I was in Lydda, which was near Joppa, they sent two men and urged me to please come at once.

Joppa was the seaport for Judea, and you know how much I love the sea. But even more so, the Spirit was giving me a clear "Go," so I went with them. We arrived late in the day, as 10 miles is about a half day's walk. When I arrived, I was taken upstairs to the room where Tabitha was lying dead. All the widows stood around me crying and showing me the robes and other clothing Tabitha had made while she was still with them.

She was obviously dearly loved by many, and as I listened to their stories, I could sense the Holy Spirit's power welling up inside me. I knew I was there for a purpose, which I assumed was to encourage the bereaved and point them to our eternal hope in Jesus. But I was not prepared for what would happen next.

Tabitha was dead. Yes, I had been with Jesus the three times he raised the dead, but that was Jesus. I had healed before, yes, but healing is not raising someone from the dead. Why was the Spirit telling me to move toward this dead body? I wanted to move away from her and start preaching, or something, anything but engage a dead corpse. I felt a trickle of sweat start down my back and turned to the ladies and asked them to leave the room.

When Jesus had raised Jairus' daughter, he asked everyone to leave the room and then immediately healed her with just a word. Again, that was Jesus. I got down on my knees and prayed. I do not remember exactly what I said because it is somewhat of a blur.

I said something like, "Jesus, I will do whatever you ask of me. I do not think I have the power to raise the dead, and I must confess I am afraid of failure. I am unsure I have the faith to heal the dead." Sweat was now dripping down my back. Does it surprise you to hear my anxiety? Remember, I am just a human like you. Man or woman, we are all fragile and full of doubt—on our own, that is, in our own human power.

But I am not just a human, and neither are you—not if you have the Holy Spirit. You can do anything with the Spirit. Yes, *you*. You can. I am no greater than you; perhaps

I am even more unworthy. Your worthiness or my worthiness is not the issue—it is the Spirit and what he chooses to do.

As John the Baptizer said, "A man can receive only what is given him from heaven."

In that moment, I heard Jesus say, "My Brother, you have the same Spirit in you who raised me from the dead. Resurrection power! I told all of you that you would do greater things than I. Now kick the devil out of your mind, and his pathetic attempt to distract and discourage you, and tell my Sister Tabitha to get up and get going."

Okay. I heard that loud and clear.

Turning toward the dead woman, I said, "Tabitha, get up."

She opened her eyes and, seeing me, she sat up. I think I was as surprised as she was. I took her by the hand and helped her to her feet. Then I called for the believers, especially the widows, and presented her to them alive. Oh, the celebration that kicked off! If you think those women can grieve, you should see them celebrate!

MY FISHING BUSINESS

This became known all over Joppa, and many people believed in the Lord. Therefore, I felt the Spirit directing me to stay in Joppa to minister to this new family of believers. I stayed with a tanner named Simon who had a home by the sea. It might come as no surprise to you I stayed in a home near the sea. My love for Jesus was overwhelming, but that did not cancel my love for the sea.

In fact, I continued to fish for many years after Jesus left. We had fished during our three years with him, just as he had spent time working his family construction business with his brothers. We would work during the week most weeks, then travel together two to three days or sometimes four days. Other times, we traveled together for days and weeks at a time.

I felt completely in the Master's will continuing my fishing business for a while after he returned to heaven. I know you remember me talking about that time on the beach back in Galilee, a few weeks after his resurrection, when he took me aside for a walk down the beach. He asked me three times that day if I loved him. The first time, he was looking down at my fishing gear when he asked, "Simon, do you unconditionally love me more than these?"

He knew my identity and self-worth was tied up in my work back then. But after I surrendered that work to *the* Master, I was freed from work's mastery over me. From that time on, I knew I was free to pursue and enjoy my fishing business. This is an important lesson for all believers. To be a disciple of Jesus does not mean we sit in a closet and pray, expecting Jesus to work out all our problems or to run our business for us.

A follower of Jesus should rarely feel compelled to give up their business to follow Jesus. If the Holy Spirit directs you to give it up, you will know it and, in that case, you should. Yet so often, we can be even more effective staying in our businesses and being a witness right where we are planted.

AVODAH

I have met businessmen who hesitated to surrender to Jesus with all their heart because they mistakenly thought they would have to quit working—or quit working hard. Somehow, they got the idea a follower of Jesus should not make money—and certainly not enjoy making money.

These men liked to work hard at their businesses. They enjoyed the success of their efforts more than the money, but certainly, they enjoyed making money as well. I love to see the look on men's faces when I tell them there is nothing wrong with being successful and making money. Money is not the problem; greed and the mastery of money is the problem.

It is the *love of* money, the mastery of money, that is the root of so much evil.

We have a word in our Hebrew language for this working and worshiping synergism: *Avodah*. This captures the essence of our work and worship balance and combines our work with our worship. Yes, your work is a part of your worship and your service for the Father. Imagine that!

In Genesis at the beginning, *avodah* is the Spirit's word for work: "The LORD God took man and put him in the Garden of Eden to work (*avodah*) it and take care of it."

Yet in our book of Exodus, we see Moses saying to Pharaoh, "This is what the Lord says: Let my people go, so that they may worship (*avodah*) me." One of our Psalms reads, "Worship (*avodah*) the Lord with gladness."

By using this word *avodah* for both work and worship, the Holy Spirit is incorporating our work with our worship as an integral part of our service for him and with him. With the Holy Spirit guiding us with energy, clarity, and creativity, we work God's way, for his glory, not ours. We are worshipping and serving him with all our hearts!

As a man or woman surrenders to Jesus, and Jesus more and more becomes Lord of their lives, he will show them the contrast between working hard at their business and being *hard worked* by their business.

If Jesus is your Master, then money, success, greed, or any of the snares with which Satan seeks to enslave you will simply lose their grip on you. If you like to work and you are good at it, then enjoy it. Be active, be competitive, you can even be proactive and aggressive as long as his love overwhelms your old love. Then be enormously generous with the rewards the Lord helps you earn.

Forgive me for yet again wandering from my story, but this is so important to understand. I am a man who loves to fish, and I enjoy the fruits of my efforts. But I have come to know I am not responsible for the outcome. I work hard, I do my best, I use the brain and the experience the Lord has given me, but then I abandon the outcome to him. It was a blessed day when I finally realized once and for all, King Peter does not, has not, and never did control the outcome of anything.

SETTLING IN JOPPA

From Joppa, I sent word for Ruth to join me because it was now obvious the Spirit wanted me to stay in this area for some time. I knew the circumcision group back in Jerusalem would not approve of me staying with a tanner because anyone who handled dead animals like my host Simon was considered unclean. But that was immaterial to me because I could now see it was immaterial to Jesus.

At this point, it was becoming clear there was to be no distinction between Jew and Gentile, free or slave, even priest or tanner. We would all be of the royal priesthood if we followed Jesus.

I also knew Ruth would not mind. In many ways, she knew the Master better than I, and she knew he was not put off by a man's occupation, clean or unclean. In fact, there was nothing unclean to Jesus, only the lost and the saved. I missed my dear Ruth, and I would need her wisdom and perspective for the next episode the Spirit would introduce into my life.

33

CORNELIUS—A GENTILE PENTECOST

CAESAREA WAS AN IMPORTANT CITY UP THE COAST FROM
Joppa. It was named for Augustus Caesar and was the
headquarters for the entire Roman occupation forces. As I
mentioned earlier, Philip ended up living and raising his
family in Caesarea, but I had not yet visited him there.

King Herod, who was a pig but also a master builder,
took this seaside resort from an unimpressive town to an
important Roman seaport. Caesarea's port was incredible
indeed.

The sea palace of Pontius Pilate, another pig (forgive
me) was located along its beautiful beach as well. Herod
built a large hippodrome where the Romans held magnificent horse races. In a few years, as the Roman persecution
of Christians grew savage under Nero, this hippodrome
was also used as an amphitheater, where both Christians
and Jews were fed to the lions.

It was from this port that Paul set sail to preach in communities all over the Mediterranean, and where he was
later imprisoned for two years and made his appeal to

Caesar before Felix, Festus, and King Agrippa. Caesarea was obviously an important city to Jesus.

CORNELIUS' ENCOUNTER

There was a man there named Cornelius, a Roman centurion in what was known as the Italian Regiment. He and all his family were devout and God-fearing; he gave generously to those in need and prayed to God regularly. A God-fearer is an uncircumcised Gentile who worships the God of Israel.

One day at about 3 p.m., as he was praying, he had a vision. He distinctly saw an angel of God, who came to him and said, "Cornelius!"

Cornelius stared at him in fear. "What is it, Lord?" he asked.

The angel answered, "Your prayers and gifts to the poor have come up as a memorial offering before God. Now send men to Joppa to bring back a man named Simon, who is called Peter. He is staying with Simon the tanner, whose house is by the sea."

When the angel who spoke to him had gone, Cornelius called two of his servants and a devout soldier who was one of his attendants. He told them everything that had happened and sent them to Joppa to find me.

MY VISION

Now about noon the following day, as they were on their journey and approaching Joppa, I felt a strong urge from the Spirit to go up on the roof to pray. I felt uneasy inside for some reason, and because I have learned in those times to be still and spend time with my Master, I wanted to get away to be alone with Jesus.

I had already asked Simon's cook to prepare something to eat, as I was getting hungry. Not everything has changed about the old me; I was feeling the Spirit, but I was feeling the hunger too!

As soon as I started to talk with Jesus, I fell into a trance. I saw the sky open and something like a large sheet being let down to earth by its four corners. It contained all kinds of four-footed animals as well as reptiles and birds. Then a voice told me, "Get up, Peter. Kill and eat."

"Surely not, Lord!" I replied. "I have never eaten anything impure or unclean." The voice spoke to me a second time, "Do not call anything impure that God has made clean." This happened three times, as you by now can see was the pattern Jesus employed with me, and immediately the sheet was taken back to heaven. Although I was confused by this vision, I know now the Holy Spirit was preparing me to be a part of the Father's reconciliation of the Gentiles.

At that moment, the men sent by Cornelius arrived at Simon's gate. They called out, asking if I was staying there. I was still pondering the meaning of the vision, when the Spirit said, "Simon, three men are looking for you. Get up and go downstairs. Do not hesitate to go with them, for I have sent them."

Do you see yet more examples of the Holy Spirit's 'go' in this story?

I went down and said to the men, "I am the one you're looking for. Why have you come?"

They told me Cornelius' story and his instructions to come get me. By this time, the trip back to Caesarea would take us deep into the night, so I invited the men into the house to be our guests overnight.

GOD DOES NOT SHOW FAVORITISM

The next day, I started out with them and some believers from Joppa went along. We had to go inland a bit through Antipatris, which made the trip about 40 miles—a two-day journey. When we arrived in Caesarea, Cornelius was expecting us and had called together his relatives and close friends.

As I entered the front courtyard inside the house, Cornelius met me and fell at my feet in reverence. As you know, this type of well-intended, but misguided, worship had happened before to me, and each time it made me wince. I immediately lifted him up by his arms and said, "Stand up, Centurion, I am only a man myself and certainly no one to be worshipped."

Cornelius gathered himself as he stood, and we went inside and saw his family and friends, all of them Gentiles. After my vision of the sheet with the animals, my hesitancy to enter a Gentile's home was mitigated. I knew I would have to see this through. I asked Cornelius to explain why he had sent for me.

After Cornelius explained his vision, I looked around the room and smiled and said, "I now realize how true it is that God does not show favoritism but accepts from every nation the one who fears him and does what is right. You know the message God sent to the people of Israel, announcing the good news of peace through Jesus Christ, who is Lord of all."

THE SPIRIT ARRIVES

I paused as I looked around the room at the eager faces of Cornelius' family and friends. I was pondering how far we had come—from a disparate group of 12 ordinary men—to be in this Roman centurion's home in a Roman city stronghold. Was anything impossible—or even improbable—for the Spirit?

"With man this is impossible, but with God all things are possible."

All things.

Peter, a fisherman, selfish and self-absorbed, small-minded, and spiritually myopic, was now representing the Savior of the world. Trust me; the irony was not lost on me. I must continue to remind you—I am no super-Christian. A man can receive only what is given to him from heaven. You may one day find yourself in such a place as this. If the Lord wants it for you, you indeed will.

I regarded each person in the room. Their eyes were as wide as saucers. They were riveted to my every word.

"Jesus wanted us to know—and now it is obvious he wanted you Gentiles to know as well—the kingdom is here, now, and we can step into it and start kingdom-living now. He taught us so many truths and performed so many miracles, winning the hearts of so many. He was a great man—the Son of Man—as he so often called himself."

The group was mesmerized by my words. I continued, "Jesus is our Savior, and now he can be yours too. Yet he was also a great friend, and he can be your friend too. Cornelius, I know you are a God-fearing, devout man—a good man with a good heart. But I also know you are not yet born again, which you must be in order to be saved and start living in Jesus' kingdom."

While I was still speaking, the Holy Spirit came on all who heard the message. The circumcised believers who had come with me were astonished that the gift of the Holy Spirit had been poured out even on Gentiles. We all heard them speaking in the tongues of other languages, just as we had done ourselves on Pentecost. We all started praising God and thanking him for his generous love.

Moved by the Spirit, I said, "Surely no one can stand in the way of their being baptized with water. They have received the Holy Spirit just as we have."

We walked over to Cornelius' mikveh ritual bath, and I baptized each one of them in the name of Jesus Christ. What a joyful occasion it was. Cornelius hugged his family, his military men, and his slaves. Grown men, hard military men, were crying just as the women were. Tears of joy were streaming down their faces. I could not hold back my own tears—tears of gratitude. Jesus had redeemed me from the scrap heap of Gehenna and allowed me to be his messenger to these people.

EVEN TO GENTILES

In that room, no one was superior to anyone else. The Holy Spirit neutralizes superiority and draws us all together as one family.

Can you believe it? A Gentile family of Jesus followers in Caesarea, the bastion of the heathen Romans and their gods—their powerfully pitiful gods—now a community of the redeemed. This was the first of many such encounters, and through each of these, I have observed how we are to reach the lost.

We just show up and share, with no pressure to convert, just a desire for them to know Jesus. We just plant seeds, abandoning the outcome to the Holy Spirit. He does the work. He moves in the hearts of men and women. He calls.

Cornelius and his family spread the word about Jesus throughout the Caesarean region. Many men and women became followers of Jesus. It was such a joy to see these Gentiles realizing that in him we live and breathe and have our being. To me, they were living, breathing miracles.

After this time in the coastal areas, Ruth and I returned to Jerusalem. We had been gone quite a while, and during this time, the family of believers had continued to grow, with many of the priests becoming followers of Jesus. This was good news and bad news. These priests now loved Jesus, but they still loved the Jewish rituals and did not love the Gentiles. To them, the Gentile believers were interlopers. They still lived with the idea it was Jesus plus—Jesus plus circumcision, Jesus plus the keeping of the Law.

The apostles and the believers throughout Judea heard that the Gentiles also had received the Word of God. When we returned home, the circumcision believers criticized me and said, "You went into the house of uncircumcised men and ate with them."

Starting from the beginning, I told them the whole story about the vision from God and how God had told me not to call anything unclean that he had made. I told them about when the Holy Spirit came on Cornelius and his entire family, just as he had come on us at the Pentecost. I called it the Gentile Pentecost, which I must admit was intended to needle them a bit.

I reminded our entire gathering that the Lord had said to us, "John baptized with water, but you will be baptized with the Holy Spirit." I concluded my comments with, "If God gave them the same gift he gave us who believed in the Lord Jesus Christ, who was I to think that I could stand in God's way?"

This seemed to carry the day with them. They had no further objections and praised God, saying, "So then, even to Gentiles, God has granted repentance that leads to life."

34

My Escape

ABOUT THIS TIME, KING HEROD ARRESTED SOME OF OUR
Brothers, intending to persecute them. This was Herod
Agrippa, grandson of "The Great King Herod." All these
Herods were pigs—forgive my bluntness. The grandfather
was ruling Judea when the Master was born and was responsible for the murder of all the boys in Nazareth two
years and under, in his effort to eradicate the baby Jesus.

This first King Herod was truly possessed. He had one
of his wives killed, plus three sons, his mother-in-law and
brother-in-law, his uncle, and scores others. His nephew,
Herod Antipas, beheaded John the Baptizer and was the
one to whom Pilate sent Jesus. He was later exiled by Rome,
and Herod Agrippa had replaced him.

He had Brother John's big brother James put to death
with the sword—beheaded, just like the Baptizer. What a
monstrous pig. The Jewish leaders were thrilled by this, although they acted mournfully in public. They were pigs too.
I am sorry; I know Jesus is not smiling at me right now, but
there are times when my anger toward such hypocrisy and
injustice and evil overwhelms me.

Remember, I am just a man like you. The Master became angry too, but he could get angry and not sin. I doubt

you and I can pull that off. I hear some say, "But what about righteous anger over an injustice?" Yes, it is natural to be angry about such things, but I have experienced very little righteous anger without sinning. You?

MOURNING JAMES

John was devastated by the death of his older brother James. I felt so much compassion for him. Someone once told me compassion means "your pain in my heart."[1] Trust me, I felt his pain deep in my heart. James was a quiet man and kept to himself. But he was rock-solid and loved the Lord deeply. We would miss him dearly.

Jesus had included James on several occasions when he took John and me off alone, such as when he was transfigured on the mountain. I believe his intention was for John and me to experience these important, intimate times together as a way of preparing us for our future ministry. Since James was the older brother, I think Jesus did not feel right leaving him out. I understood, and as it would always be with the Master, it turned out to be a good thing. James, being so steady, was able to reign in my bombastic, reactive nature as well as light a fire under John's sweet, timid soul.

My guess is it was James who suggested to Jesus that they call down thunder on that village that rejected them. John simply would not have thought in those terms. We all had a good laugh with James and John each time Jesus would bellow out, "Here come the Sons of Thunder!"

I took John aside and suggested we take a walk out to the Mount of Olives. This was a place of comfort for us, as I have told you before. We were sitting together, just the two of us, close to the olive garden of Gethsemane, when he said, "Simon, do you remember back when my mother approached Jesus and said, 'Grant that one of these two sons of mine may sit at your right and the other at your left in your kingdom?'

I smiled. "Yes, I remember it well, my friend. I remember what nitwits the rest of us were when we became angry."

"Well, looking back, you should have been indignant," John said. "What was my mother thinking? I remember Jesus calling us together and saying, 'You know the rulers of the Gentiles lord it over them, and their high officials exercise authority over them. Not so with you. Instead, whoever wants to become great among you must be your servant, and whoever wants to be first must be your slave— just as the Son of Man did not come to be served, but to serve, and to give his life as a ransom for many.'"

TO SERVE OR BE SERVED?

John became silent, lost in his musings. I pondered the Master's words, recalling what a lesson that was for me. The old Peter—King Peter!—loved to be in charge. I was afflicted with the need to be great among any group, including the Twelve. Now, as the Spirit has grown in me, I see it is indeed so much better to serve than to be served. A heart of service creates harmony for any group. A heart of service creates and engenders harmony within the individual as well. If I take my eyes off being first, and important, I can then relax and relish serving.

John furred his brow and then said, "Jesus looked us right in the eyes, ignoring my mother, and said with such seriousness, 'You don't know what you are asking. Can you drink the cup I am going to drink?'

"'We can,' we answered. Because, Simon, as you well know, we did not have a clue what he had meant by 'you will indeed drink from my cup.' I was not prepared for James to die, and certainly not in this manner. Beheaded! This cup is too bitter. I have been prepared for quite some time now to die if it served the Lord, but not James. My heart aches for him and I want to exact revenge."

"I know, my Brother, I know. But the Master is in charge, and this is not happening out of his control or knowledge. He will bring good out of this. I do not know how, or when, but we both know he will. Think about it from James' perspective. He is with Jesus now. He is in glory—surrounded by the riches and majesty of our King! My guess is he would not come back if he could. Would you?"

John smiled weakly and shook his head.

"You may be bitter, my dear brother, and rightfully so. I am angry too, but James is far better off."

John smiled, shook his head, and said, "I guess the reality is my big brother would be saying to us, 'Do not be sad for me. I felt the sting of that blade but for a moment, and now I have eternity with Jesus in paradise. We will be together soon. No more mourning!'"

THROWN IN PRISON

We smiled together at this image and sat for a while longer, reminiscing about James, and some of our times with Jesus and just the three of us. I know now in my old age John will outlive me. The Master has made this clear to me. It is fitting. He is such a dear soul, and Jesus loved his sweet spirit so. I hope he lives a long, full life, and I hope he gets around to writing about our experiences with Jesus in his own voice.

John's perspective is one of encounters. He is constantly talking about the men and women who had such defining encounters with the Master. I hear him often referring to the Samaritan woman at the well and Nicodemus. With John's sweet nature, he processes events through the prism of relationships. He reminds me often that relationships are the currency of life.[2]

Oh my, I have wandered again in my thoughts.

When Agrippa saw that his murder of James met with approval among the Jewish leaders, he seized me as well. This happened during the Festival of Unleavened Bread. I was teaching at Solomon's Porch when the guards swept in and seized me. It happened so fast no one had time to react. Afterward, I was put in prison. Herod was determined to exterminate me, thinking, I suppose, he could exterminate the Way with my murder. He had me guarded by four squads of four soldiers each. Herod intended to bring me out for public trial after the Passover.

I knew as I sat in prison the believers were earnestly praying to the Father for me. I knew Jesus was right there with me, but I still experienced those waves of fear and anxiety. I sat there, my hands and feet in shackles, hungry, hurting, and harried. One moment I would be so confident in the Lord, and not long after, a feeling of dread came over me.

THANK YOU NOW, JESUS

Do you recall my earlier words about how Satan uses feelings to overwhelm our faith? With each wave of fear and anxiety, I would steady myself and say, "Master, I am choosing to capture these fearful thoughts and make them obedient to the facts. You promised you would always be with me. You promised that not even two sparrows fall from the sky apart from the Father's will. You promised you love me perfectly. Those are the facts, and I choose this moment to focus my faith and my trust on these facts, not on my feelings."

I repeated several times, with my trust and confidence growing, "I am going to thank you now, Jesus, before I see how you work this out. I know I will be thanking you later, as I always have."

I always have. No matter what the situation or challenge, I have always thanked Jesus afterward because he is always, and I do mean always, true to his promise to bring good out of every situation. As I thanked him, I sensed his overwhelming presence, his power and his perfect love, and his peace that passes all understanding enveloped me.

ANGELIC RELEASE

The night before Herod was to bring me to trial, I was sleeping between two soldiers, bound with two chains, with sentries standing guard at the entrance. Suddenly, an angel of the Lord appeared, and a light shone in the cell. He struck me on the side and woke me up. "Quick, get up!" he said, and the chains fell off my wrists.

I do not know how to describe it any other way. This is exactly how it happened. I was not sure at the time if this was a dream or if it was real, but then the angel said to me, "Put on your clothes and sandals. Wrap your cloak around you and follow me."

I hurriedly did as he said and, stumbling a bit, followed him out of the prison.

We passed the first and second guards as they slept and came to the locked iron gate leading into the city. It opened for us by itself and we walked through it. I felt like I was dreaming. The gate opened by itself? When we had walked the length of one street, suddenly, the angel left me. I then realized without a doubt the Lord has sent his angel and rescued me from Herod's clutches, and from everything the Jewish leaders were hoping would happen.

I was so joyful! Yes, I had prepared myself for the worst, doing my best to abandon the outcome to the Father. But that does not mean I cannot rejoice when the Father delivers me from a wretch like Herod. I was confident in the Lord's perfect love, but I was sure happy his perfect plan did not include my death at the hands of this monster.

Rhoda

It was before dawn and no one was out on the streets yet, but I knew the Brothers and Sisters would be gathered together praying, so I made my way to the house of Mary, the mother of John Mark. I knocked at the outer entrance and a servant named Rhoda came to answer the door. When she recognized my voice, she was so overjoyed she ran back inside without opening the door. She exclaimed to the crowd, "Peter is at the door!"

Rhoda was a sweet girl and would do anything for you, but she was young, and a tad flighty. There I was, just standing there outside, waiting for someone to let me in. I had just miraculously escaped the clutches of Herod but could not get into a simple house. What a comical scene. I had just escaped sure death, and yet I could not get past a simple handmaiden!

I could hear the crowd inside saying to Rhoda, "You must be out of your mind. Peter is locked up and there is no way he could be at the door." When she kept insisting that it was so, they said, "It must be his angel."

I kept on knocking, and when they opened the door and saw me, they were astonished. I knew time was of the essence—the Lord provided a miracle, but that did not exclude some common sense on my part. I motioned with my hand for them to be quiet and described how the Lord had brought me out of prison.

"Tell James and the other brothers and sisters about this," I said, and then I left.

HEROD'S DEMISE

In the morning, there was no small commotion among the soldiers as to what had become of me. After Herod had a thorough search made for me and did not find me, he cross-examined the guards and ordered that they be executed.

Still a pig.

I later heard that Herod went from Judea to Caesarea and stayed there. He had been quarreling with the people of Tyre and Sidon; they now joined together and sought an audience with him. On the appointed day, Herod, wearing his royal robes, sat on his throne and delivered a public address to the people. They shouted, "This is the voice of a god, not of a man." Immediately, because Herod did not give praise to God, an angel of the Lord struck him down. He was eaten by worms and died.

He deserved it. Jesus may not be pleased with me saying such a thing, but it is how I feel. I know John took at least some solace in Herod's disgraceful demise, although John was further along in his forgiveness and surrender to the Lord than I. Herod had tried to extinguish our Way, but God extinguished him instead. The Word of God continued to spread and flourish.

BARNABAS GOES TO ANTIOCH

You recall that many of our family of believers had been scattered by the persecution that broke out when Stephen was killed. They traveled as far as Phoenicia, Cyprus, and Antioch, spreading the Word only among Jews. Some of them, however, men from Cyprus and Cyrene, went to Antioch and began to speak to Greeks also, telling them the good news about the Lord Jesus. The Lord's hand was with them, and a great number of people believed and turned to the Lord.

When news of this reached us, we sent Barnabas to Antioch. Who else would we send but our chief 'encourager'? Barnabas was perfect for such an assignment, and he was eager to visit this new Gentile family of believers. Imagine that—the fellowship of the Trinity now spreading to Syria.

When Barnabas arrived and saw what the grace of God had done, he was glad and encouraged them all to remain true to the Lord with all their hearts. Barnabas was a good man, full of the Holy Spirit and faith, and a great number of people were brought to the Lord.

Barnabas later told us he could see this family of believers was truly filled with the Spirit. They were bright and highly intelligent and in tune with the movement of the Spirit. He realized Saul, being the intellectual he was—and a Jew raised in a Hellenistic environment—would be a perfect match for this Antioch family. He was fluent in Greek and familiar with the Greco-Roman world, with all its idiosyncrasies.

KNOWLEDGEABLE TEACHERS

Barnabas went to Tarsus to look for Saul, and when he found him, he brought him to Antioch. For a whole year, Barnabas and Saul met with the church and taught great numbers of people. Can you imagine how the Spirit moved through this new family of believers with Saul and Barnabas teaching them? I wish I could have been there with them—as their pupil. No doubt I would have learned much sitting under their teaching.

I have seen many times that I can still learn more, and I can always go deeper if I am seeking to do so. If I allow the Holy Spirit to illuminate my heart and spirit. He can do so even if the teacher is not particularly gifted: it is the Word through the Spirit that penetrates, even to dividing soul and spirit, joint and marrow.

These two men were no ordinary teachers.

Barnabas later explained to me why he went for Saul—who was now going by his Greco-Roman name, Paul. Remember, Saul was his Jewish name, but Paul was his Greek name, given to him at birth. Jews born in the Greco-Roman world were given two names at birth: their Jewish name and their Greek name. This is why John Mark was named such. His father was Greek, but his mother was Jewish. My Jewish name was Simon; my Greek name, given to me by Jesus, was Peter.

Saul's extensive knowledge of our Hebrew Scriptures, combined with his Roman citizenship—not to mention his extraordinary passion for Jesus—made him the perfect teacher for these new Greek-speaking Gentile converts.

THE FIRST "CHRISTIANS"

The church at Antioch became the most important church in evangelizing the Roman Empire. When that crowd got together to pray, the Holy Spirit showed up and showed out! The disciples were called Christians first at Antioch, but it was not meant as a compliment. Their obvious passion for the Messiah made them very conspicuous, and the city dwellers took to calling them "Christus-men."

Many of the citizens of Antioch thought this new Way was crazy, and I can hardly blame them. I mean this family of believers could make the roof rattle and rumble when they started praying.

LIFE IN ANTIOCH

I decided it was a good time to stay out of Jerusalem for a while. I was not so much afraid for myself, although, to be honest, I was a bit—I am human, you know. It was more that my presence posed a hazard for our community of believers. The Jewish leaders in Jerusalem associated me with the success of the Way, so anyone associated with me could be in danger.

I made my way to Antioch alone. It took a few days to get there, and I stayed at night with various believers along the way. When I arrived, Saul was not there, but Barnabas greeted me warmly. It was so good to see him and hear of the growth of this new community of fellowship in this most Roman of cities.

Antioch was the third-largest city in the Empire, behind Rome and Alexandria. it was full of Gentiles of all nationalities. It was a prosperous city—commerce and trade everywhere. The hustle and bustle was a bit overwhelming at first, but the new family was strong with the Spirit and welcomed me with open arms.

Barnabas and I would teach in the mornings, just as we did in Jerusalem. But instead of dividing into individual homes for dinner, this group was still small enough to share dinner together. One of the converts was a successful businessman and had made his large house available. Each night we would all dine together, Jews and Gentiles alike. I had no problem dining with Gentiles—these were my Brothers and Sisters. After my experience with Cornelius, I knew there was no difference between any of us in the Lord's eyes.

But after a while, some priests and converted Pharisees showed up from Jerusalem. Remember, this was the group we called the circumcision group. They loved Jesus, but they still dogmatically clung to the belief that since Jesus was a Jew, and since he adhered to the Jewish customs and worship, so should all followers of the Way.

They insisted all new believers should be circumcised and adhere to the various Jewish rituals and sacrifices. I cannot explain exactly why, but I felt a growing anxiety around this group after they arrived. In Jerusalem, I tolerated them and co-existed with them, even with our different outlooks. But here in Antioch, for some reason, the fear of man started to creep into my heart, and I lost my focus.

---

[1] Quote attributed to Search Ministries.

[2] Statement attributed to Andy Stanley.

35

ANTIOCH DRIFTING

NOW HERE IS A LESSON IN THE DARK SIDE OF THE HUMAN
heart. Do you think I am a super-Christian? Well, sadly, I
can still allow Satan to bluff me and intimidate me. You see,
these men who had just arrived from Jerusalem made it
clear they did not approve of my eating and socializing
with the Gentiles. They said it with their whispers to be
sure, but their condemning eyes spoke even louder. Why
should I care what they think? I am human and can still lose
my focus. When I do this, I inevitably drift.

I started to slip away from the tables with the Antioch
Gentiles and slowly eased my way over to the Jewish tables.
Can you believe that? After so many years of walking with
the Spirit, I could still drift so easily. It reminds me of the
Spirit's words through Apollos in his letter to the Hebrews
when he wrote, "We must pay more careful attention,
therefore, to what we have seen and heard, so that we do
not drift away."

I was drifting from what I knew to be right, but I did
not notice it. My other Jewish Brothers in Antioch followed
my example, so that by my hypocrisy, even Barnabas was
led astray. Oh my, what a mess.

HOW DRIFTING HAPPENS

You see, I did not wake up one day and say, "Today I am going to ignore everything the Lord has shown me and stop associating with those Gentiles." Neither would you. Am I right? Do we not just sort of drift away, slowly, from the truth?

I have experienced this drifting often when fishing. There have been times when the water seemed so still, we would not bother to set the anchor. Perhaps I would set a landmark on the shore in my mind as I start to concentrate on casting and retrieving the nets. But with no anchor set in a short time, we would have drifted well away from our starting point and the landmark is no longer visible.

It is like this with our lives. We are focused and thriving with the Master, sensing his presence and his power, but then we get distracted. Remember Satan's Three D's: destroy, distract, and discourage?

I doubt you would make a conscious decision to move away from the Father. No, instead you drift, a little at a time. One day you realize, usually through some dumb mistake or sin, you have missed the mark. "How did this happen?" we ask ourselves.

We drift away from the facts of our faith, and before we know it, feelings have distracted us, and our faith—our trust—fades. This doesn't happen all at once; it is a slow process. We do not notice it at first, but the movement away from the Father leads us to make dumb decisions. At times, they are just that—dumb decisions. Other times they are out and out sin. Then we say, "How could I have done such a stupid thing?"

The answer: you drifted.

OPPOSED AND EXPOSED

When Paul returned to Antioch, he opposed me to my face, and he was right to do so. When he saw I was not acting in line with the truth of the gospel, he said in front of everyone, "You are a Jew, Cephas, yet you live like a Gentile and not like a Jew. How is it, then, that you force Gentiles to follow Jewish customs?"

He was glaring at me, and I felt the sting of his words.

He continued, "What is this? You are eating only with these Jews from Jerusalem? You, Cephas, who shared with all of us your experience with the centurion Cornelius?"

He was using my village Aramaic name, Cephas, I think on purpose, to sting me even more. I was so ashamed. I know my face was turning red, but he was right, so there was nothing for me to say. To try to vindicate myself would have been ridiculous. But my silence did not deter Paul, and he continued his tongue lashing. One of my Gentile Brothers started to defend me, but I shook my head. I knew I had it coming.

THE NEED TO VINDICATE OURSELVES

As I was sitting there, wilting under Paul's rebuke, I could not help but think about our human tendency to try to vindicate ourselves. I do not like to be exposed in my sin—no one does. We think up excuses for our behavior when we would be much better served to just accept the rebuke and learn from it.

I can only imagine how many times I have missed the opportunity to grow because I was sidetracked by my need to defend myself. Is one of your strongholds a controlling need to vindicate yourself? If so, release it. Humble yourself under the Father's mighty hand, that he may lift you up in due time. Let the Spirit expose you and then grow you.

SAVED BY GRACE

Paul continued, "We who are Jews by birth know that a person is not justified by the works of the law, but by trust in Jesus Christ. For through the law, I died to the law so that I might live for God." He paused for a moment, looked around the room and then said, "I have been crucified with Christ and I no longer live, but Christ lives in me. The life I now live in the body, I live by faith in the Son of God, who loved me and gave himself for me."

How beautiful is that? "I no longer live but it is Christ who lives in me, through the Holy Spirit."

I stood up and cleared my throat, turning around the room as I spoke so everyone could hear me. "Brother Paul is right," I said. "I am sorry for my weakness and my sinful nature. I ask your forgiveness. I will not set aside the grace of God, for if righteousness could be gained through the law, Christ died for nothing!"

You could have heard a feather drop. Everyone was riveted on me. I concluded with, "I want to be certain you all know that by grace we have been saved, through faith, through trust in Jesus. Not by works, certainly not by circumcision, so that no one can boast."

I had drifted because of fear, but if I could go back and relive those days, my guess is I would see I had drifted first from spending time with my Master. To be sure, I would not have made a decision to avoid Jesus. Instead, busyness and distractions seeped in. I was traveling and meeting new people. Ruth was not with me to hold me accountable, nor John. Without their accountability, I lost my perspective and I could not see my own hypocrisy.

Let this be a valuable lesson to you, my friend. Without accountability, without someone in your life to hold you accountable, you will drift too—and the results are never pretty.

FEAR IS A FENCE—LOVE IS A FUEL

After this, I felt the need to stay a week or so longer so Paul and I could reconnect, catch up with each other, and talk more about leading our new believers to become disciples, as the Master had commanded. We would meet privately in the mornings and then share our thoughts with the group the next day.

I began the first morning by saying, "Brother Saul, what I did with the circumcised group was unacceptable, and I am so sorry."

Paul waved it off and said, "I was perhaps a little harsh with you, so I apologize and ask your forgiveness."

"Thank you for that, but I needed to be held accountable. I fear this sort of accountability will fade as the years go by. We all need to be held accountable—everyone. We drift, or we become enamored with someone or something, and we lose perspective. In these times, we simply cannot see the issue with any sense of clarity, so we need someone to speak truth to us in love. "You did just that. Thank you!"

Paul nodded with a smile.

I continued, "I want to share with you a thought I had about this incident. The Holy Spirit gave me a word on this, Saul: Fear is a fence; love is a fuel."

Paul looked at me puzzled, so I continued. "You see, if we try to obey Jesus out of fear of punishment, it is like trying to erect a fence between us and the object of our sin. This fence of fear will help protect us for a while, but as the temptation grows in intensity, we will eventually find a way over or around that fence.

"But when are motivated—*compelled* even—by his love for us, our gratitude and our love become fuel for our obedience—a fire burning within us to please Jesus, not to avoid punishment. Fear is a fence, but love is a fuel."

OBEDIENCE OUT OF LOVE

Paul interrupted me and said, "We fan into flame the power of the Spirit within us, fueled by love, not by fear. I remember you telling the Gentile Brothers and Sisters that the Father is about protecting us, not prohibiting us, right?"

"Yes, you understand exactly what I am saying," I answered with a smile. He wants to protect us from stupid mistakes, like the one I just fell into with the circumcision group, not prohibit us from having our way. Obedience from love, and from the desire to please the Father, is the life to the full the Master talked so much about. It is a positive and energizing way to live. With it comes love, joy, peace, and a power to really live the life Jesus wants for us."

Paul thought for a moment and then said, "I remember you telling me that the Master said his burden was light and his yoke was easy—his "yoke" being his teaching and his way of life. To follow Jesus, to love Jesus, to obey Jesus out of love instead of fear is lighter and easier than the oppressive burden of obeying out of fear."

Paul thought for a moment and continued, "I can see what you are saying fits with this perfectly. If we live in fear of punishment, the heart of the Father is not in us. If anyone acknowledges that Jesus is the Son of God, God lives in them and they in God. So we know and rely on the love God has for us."

I joined in, "God is love. Whoever lives in love lives in God, and God in them. This is how love is made complete among us so that we will have confidence on the Day of Judgment."

Paul concluded, "I see now your idea of fear as a fence but love as a fuel. There is no fear in love, but perfect love drives out fear because fear has to do with punishment. The one who fears is not made complete in love."

We both said a quiet "Amen" to this revealed truth from the Spirit.

THE PRIESTHOOD OF ALL BELIEVERS

As my time drew to a close in Antioch, I gathered the family of believers together and exhorted them to continue to seek a closer relationship with Jesus, and to continue to see— seek—want—and wait to learn to live with the power of the Holy Spirit.

I embraced many of them as I was leaving and said, "Praise be to the God and Father of our Lord Jesus Christ! In his great mercy, he has given us new birth into a living hope through the resurrection of Jesus Christ from the dead, and into an inheritance that can never perish, spoil, or fade.

"Now that you have purified yourselves by obeying the truth so that you have sincere love for each other, love one another deeply, from the heart. For you have been born again, not of perishable seed, but of imperishable, through the living and enduring Word of God, and the enduring power of the Spirit of God."

I continued hugging various friends as I spoke: "Therefore, with minds that are alert and fully sober, set your hope on the grace to be brought to you when Jesus Christ is revealed at his coming. As obedient children, powered not by your efforts alone, but by the power of the Holy Spirit, do not conform to the evil desires you had when you lived in ignorance."

I continued, "But just as he who called you is holy, so be holy in all you do; for it is written: 'Be holy because I am holy.'

"But you are a chosen people, a royal priesthood, a holy nation, God's special possession, that you may declare the praises of him who called you out of darkness into his wonderful light."

I concluded, "Be alert and of sober mind. Your enemy the devil prowls around like a roaring lion looking for someone to devour. Resist him, standing firm in the faith because you know that the family of believers throughout the world is undergoing the same kind of sufferings."

With my voice rising, I said, "The God of all grace, who called you to his eternal glory in Christ, after you have suffered a little while, will himself restore you and make you strong, firm, and steadfast with the Spirit's power within you. To him be the power forever and ever. Amen."

36

LISTEN, LEARN, LEAD–THE
JERUSALEM COUNCIL

OVER THE NEXT FIVE YEARS, THE WAY GREW IN NUMBERS
but even more in power. Those who were born again at
Pentecost were now mature believers, and we encouraged
them to take on teaching roles. Some we encouraged to return to their original homes and preach the good news of
the kingdom of God there.

We received news the Holy Spirit had directed the family of believers in Antioch to send Paul and Barnabas out
into Gentile areas where Jesus was totally unknown. Do
you see this is yet another example of the Spirit's "Go" direction and interaction with us? They took Barnabas'
nephew, John Mark, with them, but he returned early from
the trip.

When he arrived back in Jerusalem, Mark confessed the
trip was just too hard. He related to us the many dangers
from both thieves and the weather, and just how scary and
difficult traveling was. He was distraught that Paul was so
upset with him for bailing out on them. There was nothing
for us to say, so we just comforted him and encouraged
him.

Listening to his stories about the three of them sleeping outside with no shelter, avoiding bands of thieves, spending some nights in flea-infested inns surrounded by shady characters, my respect for Paul and Barnabas' courage grew immensely. I was happy to be in Jerusalem, even with our challenges from the Jewish leaders. Paul and Barnabas were out there in the nations, risking their lives daily for Jesus.

THE JERUSALEM COUNCIL

After Paul and Barnabas returned to Antioch from Cyprus and Galatia, certain of our Brothers from the circumcision group left Jerusalem for Antioch. They were well-intentioned, but they were teaching the believers: "Unless you are circumcised, according to the custom taught by Moses, you cannot be saved." This brought Paul and Barnabas into sharp dispute and debate with them.

Brother Paul in sharp debate—does this surprise anyone?

As I had already so vividly experienced, Paul was trigger-quick to push back against this type of teaching. This was a hot topic for Paul and, in his eyes, a non-negotiable. I would guess Paul was so passionate about this precisely because he was imprisoned by this performance mentality before Jesus waylaid him. He was right to defend the freedom we have in Jesus and our salvation by grace alone.

Paul and Barnabas were appointed, along with some other believers in Antioch, to come up to Jerusalem to see us about this question. We welcomed them, as did the entire family of believers, and gathered to hear about their mission trip into Cyprus and Galatia. They reported every-thing God had done through them.

They minimized the beatings and flogging they had en-dured, but, in fact, they were often treated poorly and un-justly. I wonder if future believers will appreciate the sacrifice these two men undertook for Jesus. I praise Jesus for their courage and strength. They were undaunted in the face of such extreme pain and danger. They simply kept their eyes on Jesus, the author and perfecter of their faith.

They are giants.

THE DEBATE OVER CIRCUMCISION

But during our gathering, some of our Brothers who be-longed to the party of the Pharisees stood up and said, "The Gentiles must be circumcised and required to keep the Law of Moses."

This set off a firestorm of discussion and debate. I could see we were on the verge of this turning ugly and conten-tious, so I closed my eyes for a moment and asked the Holy Spirit to give me the energy, clarity, and even creativity to resolve this the way he would want it resolved—not Peter's way, but his. I waited—do I need to remind you again to wait?—for a bit longer to let everyone speak their minds.

After much discussion, in my mind way too much, I felt the Spirit giving me the "go" to address the group. "Broth-ers, you know that some time ago, God made a choice among you that the Gentiles might hear from my lips the message of the gospel and believe. God, who knows the heart, showed that he accepted them by giving the Holy Spirit to them, just as he did to us."

I spread my arms and motioned to the men around me, "He did not discriminate between us and them, for he purified their hearts by faith. Now then, why do you try to test God by putting on the necks of Gentiles a yoke that neither we nor our ancestors have been able to bear? No! Surely you have not forgotten the Master's own words about his yoke: 'Come to me, all you who are weary and burdened, and I will give you rest. Take my yoke upon you and learn from me, for I am gentle and humble in heart, and you will find rest for your souls. For my yoke is easy and my burden is light.'"

"We believe and we have come to know it is through the grace of our Lord Jesus that we are saved, just as they are," I concluded.

HELPFUL FOR HARMONY

I motioned to Paul and Barnabas to continue with their stories, and the whole assembly became silent as they listened to them telling about the signs and wonders God had done among the Gentiles through them. When they finished, James spoke up. "Brothers," he said, "listen to me. Simon has described to us how God first intervened to choose a people for his name from the Gentiles. The words of the prophets are in agreement with this, as it is written:

> After this I will return
> and rebuild David's fallen tent.
> Its ruins I will rebuild,
> and I will restore it,
> that the rest of mankind may seek the Lord,
> even all the Gentiles who bear my name.

"It is my judgment, therefore," James continued, opening his arms wide and looking around the entire group, "that we should not make it difficult for the Gentiles who are turning to God. Instead, we should write to them, telling them to abstain from food polluted by idols, from sexual immorality, from the meat of strangled animals, and from blood."

James later told me the Spirit had clearly directed him to single out these three commands to impress upon the Gentile believers. Can you see these would be most likely to offend the sensibilities of the Jewish Brothers and Sisters among us: the food offered to idols, sexual immorality, and eating the meat of strangled animals? James was in no way claiming these were helpful for salvation but, instead, helpful for harmony.

James had become the leader of the Jerusalem community by this time, so his opinion carried much weight. His thoughtful conclusion satisfied just about everyone. James' approach to this council was in keeping with what he often taught, "My dear brothers and sisters, take note of this: Everyone should be quick to listen, slow to speak, and slow to become angry because human anger does not produce the righteousness that God desires.

"But the wisdom that comes from heaven is first of all pure; then peace-loving, considerate, submissive, full of mercy and good fruit, impartial, and sincere. Peacemakers who sow in peace reap a harvest of righteousness."

KINGDOM LEADERSHIP

There is a valuable lesson to be learned here, and a pattern of leadership I would like to share with you. Spiritual leaders are called to be leaders, not dictators. We are not to be dogmatic and emphatic, at least not in the way most people in a position of power behave. We are to instead listen, learn, and then lead.

Please do not miss this: Listen to the various points of view. Be aware of hot spots. Learn what is important. Then, after waiting for Holy Spirit clarity and guidance, take the lead, if appropriate.

We see in our Scriptures many exhortations "to stand" and "stand firm," but we do not see "to push," as in pushing others around. As leaders, we stand firm in our convictions and knowledge of the holy truth, but we do not push others down or out of the way to get our way.

Surely you can see this style of leadership applies to all leaders—in business, in groups, around the community, and especially, *especially* in the family. I teach all men that they are to be the spiritual leaders of their families, but they are not to be spiritual dictators.

A simple observation the Spirit has given me is this: "What works at work rarely works at home." Being dogmatic and emphatic may help you succeed in the marketplace—at least by the world's standards—but it simply will not work in the home. Gentleness must balance with leadership at home.

LISTENING WITH GENTLENESS AND SURRENDER

I tell the men if they surrender to Jesus and look to the Holy Spirit to lead them day in and day out, their wives and children will see their hearts and *want* them to lead. But they cannot just announce it. They must live surrendered to

Jesus first before they can effectively lead. They must be followers first, of Jesus, before they can be leaders.

Men are to be strong and courageous with respect to their duties and responsibilities, yet sensitive and compassionate in their relationships.[1] This is a balance that does not come naturally to men. It takes much surrender, much practice, and much humility. But this balance, this approach of being strong and courageous, yet sensitive and compassionate, is invaluable.

My own governing principle is to listen, and as I listen, I learn what the various issues are as well as the feelings and pressure points for those involved. Then I wait on the Spirit's guidance before I lead.

Listen, learn, and then lead.

This Jerusalem Council gathering was the perfect example of this. The Pharisees and their circumcision group were dogmatic and emphatic. Trying to view them in the most favorable light, I know they meant well and were sincere, but they were sincerely wrong. They were not just standing on their convictions; they were pushing their convictions down everyone else's throats.

If I immediately reacted to them and stated my case emphatically, without first listening and learning their points of view, do you think they would really hear what I have to say? No. By listening and learning their facts as well as their hearts, I learned their pressure points before I responded.

By listening first, they could see I was interested in learning about their viewpoint, as opposed to just advancing my own. By listening first, I gained common ground with them, demonstrating I care. This is what leaders should convey: "I care enough about you to listen, and to learn what you are thinking."

POWER DOWN—NOT POWER UP

Leaders lead by listening, learning, and then responding in love, not reacting in fear. Leaders also lead by powering down, not powering up. You can see this in this Jerusalem Council. Both James and I could see the potential for discord and perhaps a damaging schism among our family, so rather than powering up—which used to be my way—we were meek and humble, powering down, in order to dissipate the negative energy.

Powering down instead of powering up is especially important in family situations. Men tend to power up when, in most cases, we should trust the Spirit enough to power down and allow the Holy Spirit to power up. You ladies do this too. You know you do. Your tactics are often different, but the unhealthy result is the same.

Powering up can be aggressive, or passive-aggressive. It is our Self wanting to get its way, plain and simple. Jesus taught us this powering down approach, and he modeled it for us day in and day out.

I remember the time a dispute also arose among about which of us was the greatest. Can you believe that? But we were just men. We were still blind. We did not have the Holy Spirit, so we did not know what we did not know.

Jesus pulled us aside, sat us down, and calmly said to us, "The kings of the Gentiles lord it over them; and those who exercise authority over them call themselves Benefactors. But you are not to be like that. Instead, the greatest among you should be like the youngest, and the one who rules like the one who serves. But I am among you as one who serves."

POWERING DOWN THROUGH HUMILITY

As I have mentioned several times already, our last night with the Master left me with memories and images that are burned into my heart and my mind. One of those was when Jesus washed our feet. John tells the story like this:

"Jesus knew that the Father had put all things under his power, and that he had come from God and was returning to God; so he got up from the meal took off his outer clothing, and wrapped a towel around his waist. After that, he poured water into a basin and began to wash his disciples' feet, drying them with the towel that was wrapped around him."

I want you to think about what Jesus knew. He knew he lived in God's kingdom. He knew he was powered by the Holy Spirit. He knew it was safe for him to power down, lowering himself to be a servant, and showing us leaders lead by serving.

He knew he lived in a God-saturated world, and so it was both appropriate and safe for him to become a servant in order to lead us. With this knowledge, this assurance, he had the freedom to humble himself under God's mighty hand, that he may lift him up in due time.

Dear Brothers and Sisters, do you know you can trust in the power and perfect love of your Father? Can you then lead by powering down? Please, all of you, listen, learn, and then lead. As James would say, be quick to listen, learn what the issues are, the feelings and the fears, and then after considering these, lead with clarity and compassion, holding to the Spirit's convictions—not dogmatic and emphatic. Wait, not powering up, but powering down.

Blessed are the peacemakers, for they will be called children of God.

POWERING DOWN THROUGH GRACE AND COMPASSION

May I share just one more instance of Jesus modeling this idea of powering down? Do you remember me talking about Jesus' encounter with the young girl caught in adultery? One day we were all with Jesus as he was teaching with a crowd around him near Solomon's Porch, and the dogmatic Pharisees came storming over with a woman caught in adultery. "Shouldn't we stone her?" they demanded. "She is not perfect, as we are. She showed human weakness, something we never do. She must be condemned!" (They did not say it this way exactly, but it is what they meant, rest assured.)

Do you recall what Jesus did next? He was facing men seething with condemnation, judgment, and human weakness, yet he responded with grace and compassion. If it were me, I would have stepped toward the Pharisees with my chest out, ready to react with strength and control.

But Jesus did not do this, did he? He kneeled down. Instead of powering up, he powered down. In doing so, he sucked all the negative, hostile energy out of the air. The Pharisees were expecting a fight, but they got finesse. They were seeking confrontation; instead, they saw calm. Jesus diffused the strain and stress of the situation, and, ultimately, the Pharisees retreated.

Jesus taught and modeled this in so many ways over the time we were together. Here is just a sampling of his words about powering down versus powering up that are so dear to my heart:

> Blessed are the meek, for they will inherit the earth. Blessed are the merciful, for they will be shown mercy. Blessed are the peacemakers, for they will be called children of God.

> You have heard that it was said, "Eye for eye, and tooth for tooth." But I tell you, do not resist an evil person. If anyone slaps you on the right cheek, turn to them the other cheek also. If anyone wants to sue you and take your shirt, hand over your coat as well. If anyone forces you to go one mile, go with them two miles. Give to the one who asks you, and do not turn away from the one who wants to borrow from you.

Beautiful.

---

[1] Statement attributed to Dr. Harry Reeder.

37

FORGIVENESS
WITH MUSCLE

GRACE IS SWEET; CONDEMNATION IS SOUR. GRACE
engenders affection and gratitude; condemnation aggra-
vates frustration and resentment. We know when we are
being treated with grace, and we know when we are being
judged. We also know when we are neither, when we are a
non-factor. We know when we don't matter.

THE NON-FACTORS

When my father was teaching me the fishing business, he
often corrected my many mistakes. At times he was harsh
with me, even punishing me for repeated mistakes. When
he saw I was feeling condemned by his discipline, he said,
"I'm disciplining you because I love you and I care about
you. I want you to be the best you can be."

Abba would then pause to be sure he had my attention,
and then conclude with, "Because you matter to me."

I have observed many people who feel like they are a
non-factor—that they just don't matter. Jesus' heart went
out to people like this. His entire Beatitudes in his Sermon

on the Mount seemed to me to be directed toward these down-and-out non-factors.

The Samaritan woman at the well knew how it felt to be a non-factor. She didn't matter to anyone—not to her previous five husbands and likely not to her current live-in boyfriend, since he was satisfied to live with her but not marry her.

I certainly know what it feels like to behave so badly as to become a non-factor. I thought my life was over after I denied Jesus so publicly and so vehemently. I wanted to crawl in a hole and cry until I died. But Jesus sought me out to be sure I knew I mattered. He will seek you out too.

Being a non-factor hurts. Being a non-factor injures, but I want you to know you do matter to your heavenly Father. You are never a non-factor to him. The Father's grace goes beyond mere acceptance, and even beyond mere for-giveness.

CHARIZOMAI

Paul and I discussed this idea of a Father who reaches out, who seeks, and who restores. He was fascinated by Jesus' three stories about the Father's passionate restoration: the lost sheep, the lost coin, and the lost son. One day as we were discussing this, he showed me something he had writ-ten the night before:

"Therefore, as God's chosen people, holy and dearly loved, clothe yourselves with compassion, kindness, hu-mility, gentleness, and patience. Bear with each other and forgive whatever grievances you may have against one an-other. Forgive—*charizomai*—as the Lord forgave—*chari-zomai*—you."

I looked at Paul as he awaited my response. "You are using a word from your Greek learning that I am not so familiar with," I said, somewhat confused. "What exactly does *charizomai* mean?"

Paul grinned and said, "Last night, as I pondered Jesus' parable about the lost son, and how the father ran to greet his returning son, the Spirit brought this powerful word to my mind. I have not seen this word *charizomai* used often, but I know the Spirit was intentional with his use of it here.

"You see, Simon, there is a power brewing here," he continued. "We see a glimpse of God's amazing grace with this word *charizomai*. You are probably aware that the word we typically use for forgive is *aphiemi*."

I nodded, even though my Greek is not as advanced as Paul's. I was trying to keep up with his line of reasoning as best I could.

"*Aphiemi* means 'to cancel, pardon, give up, *leave alone*,'" Paul said. "There is a sense of release here. This release, this canceling of debt, this pardoning of an offense, is a wonderful gift. The Father so graciously gives us this gift when we surrender to Jesus as our Savior.

"As Jesus said, we are to give this gift of grace to others. 'Forgive as the Lord forgave you,' the Master said, right?"

I nodded and motioned for Paul to continue.

"The problem arises when we mere humans think forgive means just to 'release and then leave alone.' "Forgive and forget," some of us are fond of saying. But not one of us would want the Father to just leave us alone after he forgave us—as if we did not really matter to him.

THE FATHER'S PASSIONATE RESTORATION

Paul started moving his arms around, becoming animated, "This is where the Spirit explodes with power. Simon, *charizomai* has more muscle than *aphiemi*. It involves repair and restoration. *Charizomai* repairs brokenness, particularly by incurring the cost."

He paused for a moment and then continued, "You see, *aphiemi* prevents conflict. *Charizomai* promotes relationship. *Aphiemi* is about damage control. *Charizomai* is about rebuilding and reconciliation. God's reconciliation is total, as you have taught me so many times Peter."

I nodded with a smile, and Paul continued.

"Was it not you who taught me, 'Once you were alienated from God and were enemies in your minds because of your evil behavior? But now he has reconciled you by Christ's physical body through death to present you holy in his sight, without blemish and free from accusation?'"

I smiled at the memory of Jesus teaching us this profound truth. I knew in my heart this was earth-shattering: "Holy in his sight, without blemish, and free from condemnation." I repeated this again. "You are right, Paul. That is powerful! This is pure grace. God asks us to restore our relationships just as he does with us—not just release and then leave alone. He wants us to restore, reconcile, and rebuild."

I paused as I thought about Jesus and his way with us, and then said, "This is what Jesus did so masterfully with me on the beach a few weeks after I had failed so miserably by denying Jesus. He did not just forgive me, he sought me out to restore me. He brought me back. He *charizomai* me."

Damage from Earthly Fathers

Perhaps you, my friend, feel as though you are a non-factor to God. If so, that is a lie straight from Satan. You are of immense value to him. Never forget this, please. Now, with this in mind, perhaps there is someone you should *chari-zomai* in your life—restore them, reconcile with them, give them value, and give them worth?

Over all these years, I have witnessed a multitude of damaged men and women. They are damaged because their fathers showed them no grace and little love. Instead, they either felt condemnation or their father showed them nothing. For men, it is typically the condemnation of their fathers. For many women, it is the nothing they felt from their fathers—no connection, no engagement.

These wounded men, therefore, have hardened their hearts and are plowing through life, determined to show this often-invisible dad their worth. These wounded women still carry the hurt and feel the emptiness deep down. They have a hard time identifying the cause of their angst, so they cannot seem to find healing. They either work their hurt out with incredibly busy careers, often crippling their relationships with men, without ever knowing why.

Both are stumbling around in darkness, and the fall-out is massive.

A Heavenly Restoration

Jesus offers healing. His point in the parable of the lost son is really about the father and his incredible *charizomai*. The father offers restoration and reconciliation to his wayward child. Your Father does too.

He offers *charizomai*. He offers a way out of the darkness and into the light. The truth is many of us are indeed living in darkness, no matter how clearly we think we see life. The grace of Jesus says, "I am the light of the world. Whoever follows me will never walk in darkness but will have the light of life."

THE RIGHT TIMING

After this conversation with Paul, I began to teach about this *charizomai*. One day a man walked up to me and said, "I want you to know that I went to visit my father as a direct result of this *charizomai* you have been teaching about these last few weeks. I had not talked to my father in almost a year." He looked at me with such sad eyes. "It's a long story, but growing up, I felt the only way to get my father's attention was to perform well. Perform well or face condemnation—those seemed to be my only two options."

The man paused, gathering his emotions. "When I visited my father recently, he did what he always does: he said something stupid, inappropriate, and/or heartless. He just seems to have no sense of warmth. But I just kept repeating 'grace, grace, grace' in my head. I even told him I loved him when I said goodbye, which, believe me, was not easy."

I regarded this man as he told this story, thinking about all the similar sad stories I have heard about fathers who missed this so badly. As I was anticipating yet another sad ending, my friend smiled and said, "That was about two weeks ago. I just heard he collapsed last week. He can no longer talk now, and he probably never will. Do you think the Lord had anything to do with the timing of my *chari-zomai* visit, Peter?"

I will ask you. Do you think the Lord had anything to do with it?

Here is a man who reached out to try to repair and restore his relationship with his lost father. He *charizomaied* his father. He did not just *aphiemi*, he *charizomai*. He restored. This man stepped out to reach out to his father. He did not just forgive and release and forget.

ENDURING HARDSHIP AS DISCIPLINE

Before I conclude my thoughts on the Father's loving forgiveness, I want to point out that you will be disciplined in love by the Father. He loves you just the way you are, but too much to leave you this way.

You will sin and you will fall. My dear Brothers and Sisters, in your struggle against sin, do not forget this word of encouragement from Proverbs that addresses you, just as a father would address his child:

> My son, do not make light of the Lord's
>   discipline, and do not lose heart when he
>   rebukes you,
> because the Lord disciplines the one he loves,
>   and he chastens everyone he accepts as his
>   son.

My friend, I want you to endure hardship as discipline; God is treating you as his children. For what children are not disciplined by their father? If you are not disciplined — and everyone undergoes discipline — then you are not legitimate, not true sons and daughters. Moreover, we have all had human fathers who disciplined us, and we respected them for it.

Discipline comes from the root word *disciple*. Discipline is about teaching us, not punishing us. Just as your Father is about protecting you, not prohibiting you, he is about teaching you, not punishing you. It has been my experience that our sin punishes us effectively all by itself.

How much more should we submit to the Father of the Spirit and live! Our fathers disciplined us for a little while as they thought best, but God disciplines us for our good, in order that we may share in his holiness. No discipline seems pleasant at the time, but painful. Later, however, it produces a harvest of righteousness and peace for those who have been trained by it.

THE GOSPEL CONTINUES TO SPREAD

After Paul and Barnabas had stayed with us a week or so, we decided to choose some of our own men and send them to Antioch with Paul and Barnabas. We chose Judas (called Barsabbas) and Silas, men who were leaders among the believers. We sent with them a letter outlining the conclusions of our Council meeting.

The men were sent off and went down to Antioch, where they gathered the church together and delivered the letter. The people read it and were glad for its encouraging message. Judas and Silas, who themselves were prophets, said much to encourage and strengthen the believers. After spending some time there, they were sent off by the believers with the blessing of peace. But Paul and Barnabas remained in Antioch, where they and many others taught and preached the word of the Lord.

Paul went on to spend many years traveling among the Gentile nations. He has written letters, some of which are indeed hard to understand. He is a brilliant missionary for Jesus, and along with his brilliance is his tenacity. Paul never forgot how lost he was before he was blinded by the Light of the Master. He spent the rest of his life seeking to shine the joy and the love of Jesus into everyone he met.

EPILOGUE:
THE MISSING LINK

WELL, MY FRIENDS, I HAVE SHARED MY STORY AS WELL as my heart with you. Or I should say the Holy Spirit's story and the Holy Spirit's heart. This has been my desire—for you to know the Spirit and to see how the Spirit moved in our lives after the Master's departure, for you to see how he can and will move in yours. There is so much more to share with you, but my time is near, so I must conclude.

Many years have passed since my Savior returned to heaven. I know he is waiting on me, and my heart pounds when I think about seeing him again. I am an old man, but his teachings are still fresh in my mind. The Holy Spirit has carried me all these years, as I learned to live with him and through his power.

MY REMINDERS

I wanted to remind you of all these things, even though you know them and are firmly established in the truth you now have. I think it is right to refresh your memory as long as I live in the tent of this body because I know that I will soon put it aside, as our Lord Jesus Christ has made clear to me. I have made every effort to see that after my departure, you will always be able to remember these things.

We all need reminding, do we not? I sometimes think my role is just to remind you of the things you already know. Please indulge this old man as I remind you of just a few of the things we have discussed.

THE HOLY-SPIRIT, BORN-AGAIN LIFE

First and foremost, unless you are born again, you cannot see the kingdom of God. You cannot see it and you surely will not enter it. You will not have the Holy Spirit.

My utmost desire is for you to learn to live with the power of the Holy Spirit. He is the link between you, and the Father, and the Son—and the link to the power-filled life to the full Jesus wants for you. But, and you must be certain about this, is he your missing link?

The Holy Spirit is real. He is involved. He is powerful. He is personal. But to learn to live with his power, you must See-Seek-Want-Wait. You must learn to see him every-where, and in all the circumstances and details of your life. Because, my friend, he is.

You must then seek him in these circumstances and de-tails. Seeking means to look everywhere for him. Look for his energy, clarity, and creativity. Train yourself to stop and think, "What do *you* want to do here, Spirit?"

As he is woven into the fabric of your life, you will start to see him everywhere and seek him always. You will then begin to want the Holy Spirit to be in control of your life. Perhaps you still just want to want him to be in control? Keep pursuing, keep seeking. As you grow, you will reach the point where you truly do not want your way anymore.

Then and only then will you be willing to wait on the Spirit to move out ahead of you. Then and only then will you want to wait on him to guide you. Why do you not want him to be in charge and, therefore, refuse to wait for him? Because you want to be in charge. You still want to be king or queen of your castle.

How stupid can we be?

Wanting is the key that opens the gates to the depths of the kingdom.

THE BLUFF

Please remember to be alert and of sober mind. Your enemy the devil prowls around like a roaring lion looking for someone to devour. Resist him, standing firm in your trust. He has only one ploy—to bluff you.

Remember his three D's: Destroy, Distract, and Discourage. If he can keep you out of a relationship with Jesus, he will destroy your soul. If he loses that battle, he will seek to distract you and discourage you for the rest of your days.

But he has no real power over you. Jesus saw to this when he defeated him on the cross. He can only bluff you into thinking he does. Call his bluff. Turn the tables on the accuser and accuse *him* instead. Tell him you are not afraid of him and send him on his way. He has no real teeth in his bite. Yes, he is powerful, but a bluffer and a blinder. Never forget he is already defeated.

SET FREE FOR FREEDOM

Remember, it is for freedom that Christ has set you free, my friend. Stand firm, then, and do not let yourself be burdened again by a yoke of slavery.

I say, walk by the Spirit, and you will not gratify the desires of the flesh. For the flesh desires what is contrary to the Spirit, and the Spirit what is contrary to the flesh. But the fruit of the Spirit is love, joy, peace, patience, kindness, goodness, faithfulness, gentleness, and self-control.

Those who belong to Christ Jesus have crucified, and continue to crucify, the flesh, with its passions and desires. Since we live by the Spirit, let us keep in step with the Spirit. Yes, it is as simple as this: keep in step with the Holy Spirit. Step by step, he will lead you and guide you—not mile by mile, but step by step.

Alas, over all these years, as the family and community of believers has grown, and therefore has moved from our intimate gatherings to bigger and more formal settings, I fear we will lose the essence of what Jesus came to show us. You see, the Master did not come to fix our Jewish religion. Jesus did not come to establish a new religion. He came to show us a new life: life in the kingdom—life in his kingdom, powered by the Holy Spirit, who is the link between Jesus and you.

A DIM PROPHECY

Recently, I have seen a vision in my dreams, a vision of the future church, perhaps centuries from now. It breaks my heart.

In my vision, I saw hosts of people gathering on the first day of the week to hear a preacher give a speech, instead of teach—a prepared speech void of any true spiritual connection with the heart of the Master. In my vision, I saw men and women sitting in rows, not circles—formal, not informal, stiff and serious, not relaxed and joyful. I saw what amounts to a show, a performance at these gatherings, instead of a personal, family community gathering.

In my vision, people were singing hymns that had no life in them. They were rotely reciting creeds and liturgies. They stand up and drone on in unison as they lifelessly recite what some now call The Lord's Prayer, as if this was ever Jesus' intention. He said, "Pray like this," not, "Pray this."

In my vision, I saw many programs and activities, all designed to perpetuate the church, not to perpetuate the Christ. In my dream, I heard an angel call these men and women "Churchians," not Christians. They follow their church, not their Christ. Many will be lulled into a false sense of security because they faithfully attend these churches.

I saw men and women in fancy robes, some wearing important-looking hats. They were called Father and Rabbi, Doctor and Reverend, and Teacher and Preacher. This is in direct contradiction to Jesus commanding us, "But you are not to be called 'Rabbi,' for you have one Teacher, and you are all brothers. do not call anyone on earth 'Father,' for you have one Father, and he is in heaven. Nor are you to be called teacher, for you have but one Teacher, the Messiah."

I saw a time when people will not put up with sound doctrine. Instead, to suit their own desires, they will gather around them a great number of teachers to say what their itching ears want to hear. They will turn their ears away from the truth and turn aside to stories and speeches.

I cried out in the midst of this vision, my bedroll soaked in sweat, "Jesus, this cannot be! This is the antithesis of what you wanted!" When I awoke, I lay trembling in my bed until the sun came up. You must all hear me and guard against such a catastrophe.

If this persists, I can only imagine Jesus will be saying to all but a few, a very few: "Not everyone who says to me, 'Lord, Lord,' will enter the kingdom of heaven, but only the one who does the will of my Father who is in heaven. Many will say to me on that day, 'Lord, Lord, did we not prophesy in your name and in your name drive out demons and in your name perform many miracles?' Then I will tell them plainly, 'I never knew you. Away from me, you evildoers!'"

STANDING BY PAUL'S SIDE

Over the past few years, I have spent more and more time in Rome. We call it Babylon. The Holy Spirit gave me a clear and persistent "go" several times, but I resisted. There was just so much to do in Judea and the surrounding areas, but the Spirit eventually won out. Ruth has been here with me on and off, but not as I speak to you today. It has become too dangerous for her here. Against her wishes, I asked her to return to Capernaum.

The emperor Nero has gone mad and is executing our Brothers and Sisters in the most hideous ways. I will spare you the details, as I am sure history will record this madman's horrible deeds. I was arrested and spent nine months wasting away in the Mamertine dungeon prison, awaiting Nero's return from Greece.

Paul had already appeared before Nero before the Emperor left for Greece and was then sent to the same Mamertine dungeon prison. During Nero's absence, Paul's final trial was set, and he was executed just outside of Rome, along the Via Ostiensis. I was there and it broke my heart.

Perhaps Paul's death has hurt me the most. I did not want to witness it, but after all we had been through together, I had to stand by his side, even unto death. He gave me a smile as the executioner lifted his sword, and we exchanged a look I will never forget. We both knew he was the lucky one. He was seconds away from seeing Jesus. "For me to die is gain," Paul said so often.

My dear friend, Paul. Paul and Peter: what a pair. Only the Lord could have used such a pair—an intellectual and a fisherman, the brainy and the bombastic, an apostle to the Gentiles and an apostle to the Jews. We were both simple men, just like you, captured by the Holy Spirit and the compelling love of Jesus.

ONE LAST ENCOUNTER

I know my cup will be Jesus' cup, and my desire is that I be crucified upside down. I am not worthy to be upright on the cross as Jesus was. I pray the Romans will grant me this request, but that is as may be. I must share with you what I know will have been my last earthly experience with the Master.

It has become so incredibly dangerous here in Rome. The elders and apostles gathered around me and pleaded with me to leave. They finally prevailed, and one night under the cover of darkness, they accompanied me to the city gate. From there, I made my way out along the Appian Way. As I was walking in the darkness, troubled in spirit, a lone traveler approached me.

It was black, dark, but as he got nearer, I sensed something unusual about him. Suddenly I saw his face—it was the Master. I fell to my knees and placed my hands on his feet. The wounds were still there, and, to my utter confusion, blood was dripping from his wounds as if they were fresh.

Jesus reached down and pulled me to my feet. He looked me in the eye in such a way I knew he wanted to speak into my heart. The eyes of his heart were in direct communication with the eyes of my heart. This is the way it is in intimate relationships. I was overjoyed to see him, but I could sense the setting was heavy with meaning.

As we looked into each other's eyes, I sensed he wanted to say something to me. I asked Jesus, "Lord, where are you going?"

He answered, "I am going to Rome to be crucified again."

Immediately, my soul connected with his and my heart skipped a beat because I understood his meaning. He was asking me not to flee my coming persecution. I was swept back to that night in the courtyard of the Chief Priest, and my ranting denial of Jesus. My heart dropped, as did my head. But Jesus lifted my chin and smiled his wonderfully warm smile. I had felt that same loving smile on the beach that day he sought me out to reconcile and restore me after his resurrection.

This is what he was doing in this moment.

JESUS' ENCOURAGEMENT

He said, "My dear friend, my Brother, my son, I am so proud of you. You have been a faithful witness to me over all these years. The Father, the Spirit, and I, along with the heavenly host of angels, have marveled and applauded your heart and your life. I want to thank you for faithfully showing the glory of the Father and the power of the Holy Spirit."

I wanted to object to his praise. I wanted to cry out, "I am not worthy! Away from me, Lord, I am a sinful man! I am a failure. I am weak. I am unsteady."

But I knew none of that mattered in this moment. He knew my weaknesses. He had always known my frailty and my flaws. He could see into the depths of my heart, but he had always loved me, despite me. Or maybe he had always loved me because I was me. One thing is for sure, he had always loved me because he was Jesus.

He laid his hand on my shoulder. His touch was so inexpressibly sweet. I have felt his tender touch many times, and each time, I feel his love, his steadiness, and his completeness—the touch of the Everlasting Father, his Son, and the Holy Spirit.

Over these past three decades, I feel as though I have failed him so many times. But I know that is not how Jesus feels. It is not how he feels about you. As I have said already many times, he loves you. You. You, with all your faults and frailties. You, with your doubts. You, with your selfishness. He loves you sweetly and purely.

He likes you too. His friendship is perhaps his sweetest gift of all.

In an instant, he was gone. I sat down in the middle of the dark road and cried, for how long I do not know. I wept with both joy and sadness. I had failed him so long ago, and he had loved me anyway. I would not fail him this time. I would walk right up to cross and thrust my body upon it – for my Master, just as he had done for me—and for you.

As I bid farewell, knowing Nero is closing in on me, I want you to know I am not afraid. He has no power over me except that which the Father allows him, in order to accomplish his perfect purpose. I will soon see my best friend again. I will soon taste the feast of the royal banquet. Do not mourn for me. I am the lucky one. I will soon feel his love, yet again.

ACKNOWLEDGMENTS

As with the previous two Putting Green devotionals, my publisher, Darren Shearer, took my manuscript and turned it into a real book. I am grateful for his and his team's talent and expertise.

Ten-plus years ago, my dear friend Barbara McLees gave me the book *The Fisherman*, by Larry Huntsperger. At that point in my life, I had been born again for 15 years and had grown close to God as my heavenly Father and Jesus as my Lord and Savior. But *The Fisherman* bumped my trajectory in an amazing and even startling way.

After reading *The Fisherman*, Jesus grew to be my best friend. I knew him in a way I had not before: intimate, firsthand, real. Yes, that's it: real. In his most excellent book, Larry brings Jesus to life in a way I had not experienced with any other book—and I have read many outstanding Christian books.

Since then, I have read *The Fisherman* a dozen times or more. Each time, I weep frequently with joy. Each time, I grow closer to Jesus. Each time, my spiritual trajectory bumps to a new and higher plane.

www.ingramcontent.com/pod-product-compliance
Lightning Source LLC
Chambersburg PA
CBHW030817090426
42737CB00009B/758

9 781946 615435